the BENGAL LANCERS INDIAN COOKBOOK

the BENGAL LANCERS INDIAN COOKBOOK

Mohan Chablani and Brahm N. Dixit

HENRY REGNERY COMPANY · CHICAGO

Library of Congress Cataloging in Publication Data

Chablani, Mohan.
　　The Bengal Lancers Indian cookbook.

　　Includes index.
　　1. Cookery, India. I. Dixit, Brahm N., joint
author, II. Title
TX724.5I4C36 1976　　　641.5'954　　　75-38713
ISBN 0-8092-8396-4
ISBN 0-8092-8142-2 pbk.

Copyright © 1976 by Mohan Chablani and Brahm N. Dixit
All rights reserved.
Published by Henry Regnery Company
180 North Michigan Avenue, Chicago, Illinois 60601
Manufactured in the United States of America
Library of Congress Catalog Card Number: 75-38713
International Standard Book Number: 0-8092-8396-4 (cloth)
　　　　　　　　　　　　　　　　　　0-8092-8142-2 (paper)

Published simultaneously in Canada by
Beaverbooks
953 Dillingham Road
Pickering, Ontario　L1W 1Z7
Canada

This book is dedicated to
all the Lancers for their
devotion and loyalty to
Mother India

Contents

Introduction ix
1 Indian Dining 1
2 Spices and Other Basic Ingredients 5
3 Appetizers and Snacks 15
4 Soups and Salads 37
5 Meat Dishes 51
6 Poultry and Egg Dishes 85
7 Fish and Seafood Dishes 109
8 Vegetable and Dahl Dishes 135
9 Rice Dishes 163
10 Breads 193
11 Chutneys and Pickles 207
12 Desserts 223
13 Beverages 245
14 Indian Food and Supply Stores in the United States and Canada 251
Index 257

Introduction

The food of India is as varied as the religions, tongues, and sensuous colorful costumes of her people; as the snow-capped northern Himalayan peaks, the rolling fertile central plains, and the palm-graced beaches of the East, West, and South coasts.

The diverse subcontinental cuisine has been influenced by every invader from the ancient Aryans as early as the sixth century B.C. to the British, who arrived in the sixteenth century. Greeks, Moguls, Portuguese, and French are just a few of the peoples who battled and blended on Indian soil, creating some of the most sublime repasts as well as architecture, philosophies, and religions.

No matter how much the bill of fare differs from Kashmir to Madras, the dishes all entice the palate with the exotic combinations of aromatic spices that are characteristic of Indian foods.

A myriad of spices and herbs are grown all over India: in the cool, deep, silent jungles of the North, on the sweltering tip of Madras and along the East and West coastal line. For centuries India has been the spice supplier to the world. Pungent spices such as cardamom, cinnamon, and turmeric lured traders, conquerors, and visitors to the Indian coasts. As early as 176 A.D., cardamom was included in the list of spices liable to duty in Alexandria. Although the cuisine has traveled for centuries and mingled with many cultures, it has always kept its identity.

One can travel twenty miles from one village to another and find differences in language, religion, and foods. Let us embark upon a journey through some different regions and discover the subcontinental foods, spiced with history and romance.

Entry to India for outsiders is frequently through the Khyber Pass, eleven miles west of Peshawar. For centuries, invaders from Central Asia arrived on the Punjab plain through the pass that is between the subcontinent and Afghanistan. This gateway through the western Himalayas echoes with heroism and bares the bloody shadows of warring armies. The old forts and sentry posts still stand along the boulder-strewn slopes that reach a height of 3,500 feet in some places.

Hollywood film producers have been attracted by the veil of mystery and legend that surrounds the hallowed pass. It has been the dramatic backdrop for film classics such as *Kim*, with Errol Flynn, and *Gunga Din*, with Cary Grant and Douglas Fairbanks, Jr.

Continuing east across the continent, one finally reaches Indian soil in the northern region at Kashmir, as did invading Moguls centuries ago. Kashmir is known for its soft, sensuous wools; plush carpets; walnut wood; silver jewelry; and great variety of fruits, such as apples, strawberries, and mangos.

It was also the resort playground of the romantic Mogul emperors, who were great lovers of beauty. When they saw this land with its many waterways, lotus flowers, and lush forests ringed with mountains, they could not resist it. At Srinagar, in the fabled Vale of Kashmir, Moguls designed romantic flower-splashed gardens, among them the poetic Shalimar Gardens. Today, colorful houseboats line the lovely Dal Lake, nearby.

A visitor's next stop could very well be Delhi. This capital of the Indian Republic is really two cities. New Delhi, the seat of the Union Government, is a beautiful garden city, built by the British in 1931. Old Delhi boasts of great Mogul monuments, such as Shah Jahan's Red Fort and the Jama Mas'jud, the largest mosque in India. It was the seat of the Mogul emperors until the British threw them out in the nineteenth century.

The tomb of the Mogul emperor Akbar at Sikandrabad greets a visitor coming from Delhi to Agra, in the northern state of Uttar Pradesh. Deep in the city, Akbar's Red Fort, with its massive walls, seems to dominate Agra. It was the creation of four successive emperors.

Finally, the visitor comes to the poetic monument to love that is known all over the world—the Taj Mahal. Emperor Shah Jahan, fifth of the Mogul rulers of India, ordered this mausoleum built for his queen, Mumtaz Mahal. It took twenty-two years to complete the majestic marble structure, with jewelers adding semiprecious stones as finishing touches. In the early morning light it is bathed in soft pink, while in the moonlight it is a cool, elegant white.

The ancient Mogul emperors not only had an eye for beauty, but a taste for it as well. On their way to India, the Moguls savored the meat and rice dishes of Persia, which they eventually included on the royal tables they kept in Delhi and Srinagar.

Today, the cuisine of North India still tastes of its Mogul heritage. The cooking medium is *ghee,* clarified butter. There are many typically Moslem meat-based dishes seasoned with saffron, cardamom, and nutmeg. Their sauces are aromatic, rich, and thick, but not hot. *Brown korma* is a braised meat curry with a yogurt-based sauce common to many northern meat curries. *Rogan josh* lamb curry sauce gets its deep red color from the saffron that grows in the hills and valleys of Kashmir. The influence of neighboring Middle Eastern countries is seen in kababs and tandoori cooked dishes. Northerners tenderize their meats with seasoned yogurt and dried crushed mango.

Tenderly spiced, orange-red tandoori chicken is an exquisite North Indian dish, especially in New Delhi and Agra. Meat, fish, and breads also are cooked in the clay tandoori oven throughout North India.

Since India's principal wheatlands are found in the northern states of Punjab and Haryana, it is no wonder that bread, not rice, is the basis of a meal in the North. Unleavened *chapati,* crisp *paratha*, sometimes stuffed with vegetables, and oval-shaped *nan* are some of the common northern breads. The usually disk-shaped whole wheat breads are served with curries to sop up the rich sauces.

Rice, however, does maintain a substantial importance in the northern diet. Persian *pulao*, a pilaf-like rice dish that was loved by Mogul kings, and Persian *biryani*, rice mixed with over three dozen spices, are two of the exotic grain dishes that form the basis of meals enjoyed on special occasions. Saffron and turmeric are often added to northern rice dishes for color. Browned onions, nuts, eggs, and silver leaf serve as garnishes.

North India is the major supplier of vegetables to the subcontinent. It is natural that vegetable curries are a specialty in this region, where they are served with rice and bread. Eggplant, potatoes, cauliflower, and spinach are among the most popular vegetables in this area. Spices and herbs are similar to the ones found in meat dishes. Vegetables are cooked in thick sauces, as are the meat curries in the North. Lentils (*dahl*), in dry or semiliquid form, are eaten with almost every meal in the North and throughout India. *Raita* (seasoned yogurt mixed with fruits or vegetables), mint and mango chutneys, and salads are also taken with meals.

Desserts and sweet dishes are usually milk-based. *Kheer* is made from rice or cream of wheat cooked with milk, then sweetened and garnished with gold or silver leaf and fruits. Carrot *halva*, made with grated carrots, milk, and sweeteners, is a very popular northern sweet dish. *Lassi*, a cooling, milk shake-like yogurt beverage, is taken with breakfast, along with stuffed paratha and chilled fruit.

A visitor might continue south from Agra to the region of Khajuraho, in the state of Madhya Pradesh in central India. It is famous for its medieval temples intricately carved in erotic sculptures, the inspiration for the *Kama Sutra*, an ancient Hindu text on mystical erotics.

After Khajuraho, one moves on to the east to the state of Bihar and the sacred city of Bodh-Gaya. This is where Gautama Buddha, the founder of Buddhism, sought enlightenment while sitting under a pipal tree about 2,700 years ago. For centuries,

Introduction xiii

Buddhists from all over the world have been coming here to worship at the Mahabodhi Temple, where the huge sculpture of Buddha sits peacefully inside. Thus, east India has become known as the land of poetic fantasy and philosophical musing.

From here, a visitor might continue on to the cool, luxuriant jungles of the Northeast, near Darjeeling. Some of the finest teas in the world are grown in the rolling tea gardens of this town located in the northern tip of the eastern state of West Bengal. The exotic aromatic blends are shipped to ports around the globe.

Darjeeling is built on a series of graduated terraces. A visitor winds his way up the different levels and passes by plush villas, exotic bazaars, and local people in colorful silks. Wayside shops beckon one to stop and sip tea and gaze upon the breathtaking view of the snow-capped Kimchenjuna range of the Himalayas.

West Bengal is also the home of a noisy, sprawling metropolis, where jute, rice, teas, and coal are exported around the world.

The cuisine of the East is not as rich as the food of the North, and there are very few meat dishes. Rice, grown in the fertile swamps of Orissa, Bihar and Bengal, is the mainstay of the eastern diet, usually served plain or as pulao.

The eastern coastline also provides an abundance of fish and seafood—lobster, pomfret, shrimp, prawns, and crab, just to name a few. They are caught by deep-tanned fishermen in the Bay of Bengal. Fish dishes of Bengal are considered a major delicacy throughout India. Ginger-and onion-seasoned fantailed prawn cutlets are a favorite in Calcutta. Other regional fish specialties are smoked *bekti* and *nilsa*. Fish dishes are often cooked in hot mustard oil, the cooking medium of the East. Mustard seeds that grow in the area are used as seasoning in many fish recipes. Sometimes fish is cooked with vegetables.

Eggplant, potatoes, and tomatoes are common ingredients for vegetable dishes. One favorite is *alu dum*, in which potatoes are hollowed out and stuffed with almonds, chilies, and onions. *Luchi*, a popular fried white bread, is often eaten with these curries, followed by rice and soupy fish curry.

Bengal is known throughout India for its sweets, made with milk, cheese, and sugar. *Rasgulla* is made from Indian cream cheese (*panir*) and is soaked in rose-water syrup. *Gulab jamon*, another well-known sweet, is made from cheese, condensed milk, and flour.

On to the fiery climate of South India, with its long stretches of sandy beaches, graced with palm trees that yield the coconuts used so much in South Indian cooking. This is the land of magnificent ancient Hindu temples, built between 600 and 1600 A.D., which are still used for worship. There are also a number of old Christian churches here. One of the most famous is St. Thomas, in Madras City. Another attraction is Fort George, built as a trading settlement by the East India Company in 1653 on land leased to them by the Raja of Chandragiri. It eventually became a stronghold of British power in India.

The South also boasts of the Western Ghats, a mountain range whose basalt peaks, the color of elephant hide, are a majestic backdrop to the beaches. In the state of Mysore, some of the richest coffee is grown in the coffee gardens of the Ghats. When the coffee is in bloom during March, the wind carries a heady fragrance throughout the region. Also in the Mysore and Madras region are the Nilgiris, or Blue Mountains, with tea plantations gracing their slopes.

Southern cuisine tends to be simple compared with the rest of the subcontinental foods. Curries are much hotter but not as rich as those prepared in other parts of India. Their fiery character comes from the abundant use of hot chilies and the juices of acidic fruits. The typically watery curries have a cooling effect—they lure the sluggish appetite and make the body perspire. Coconut oil and *gingili* oil are the cooking mediums used to prepare foods. Coconut milk is added to curries rather than yogurt; this accounts for the thinner gravies in meat and vegetable dishes.

Rice, which grows in the vast swamps of Madras and Kerala, is the staple food in the South. It is served throughout meals, usually boiled and plain or with lemon or lime juice added along with nuts. At the end of a meal, rice is mixed with yogurt to cool the palate. This is known as *pachadi*, which is much like the northern raita. *Sambar*, pungently spiced ground lentils and vegetables, and *rasam*, spiced lentil soup, are served with rice at meals.

Popular vegetable curries of this region are *avial*, a mixed vegetable dish, *elan*, a squash dish, and *erishen*, which is a pumpkin and yogurt combination. Pungent asafoetida (*hing*) is fried and used in most lentil and vegetable dishes in South India.

Fish and seafood, which are so plentiful along the vast southern coastline and the Kerala backwaters, are often cooked in coconut milk. Giant prawns and fish *molees* are delicacies in Kerala. Madras is known for its magnificently colored cotton fabrics, designed as everything from sport coats to bikinis. But it is also the place to go for an assortment of shrimp dishes.

Desserts in South India are usually made from vermicelli, rice, or lentils, boiled in milk or coconut milk. Sugar or molasses are often used as sweeteners.

South India is fertile with a variety of tropical fruits such as pineapple, papayas, mangos, and bananas. Coconut water is an ever-popular thirst slaker.

Breakfast in South India is very light, but wholesome and delicious. It often consists of *idlis*, steamed rice cakes that are light as air. They are eaten with coconut or sambar. Another breakfast food is *dosa*, a lacy rice pancake served with fresh coconut chutney. Both idlis and dosa are also eaten as snacks. They are washed down with coffee, which is freshly ground and roasted each day. Naturally, South Indians are great coffee drinkers and very proud of their famous aromatic and wickedly thick brews, always served with lots of milk and sugar.

Now on to the region of Bombay in the West, the final leg of a visitor's trip. The metropolis of Bombay, capital of the state of Maharashtra, is located on the palm-fringed shores of the Arabian Sea. This gateway to India was the dowry of Portuguese princess Catherine of Braganza when she married Charles II in 1661.

A visitor entering Bombay sees skyscrapers contrasting with ancient temples and thatched huts in a merger of Western and Eastern lifestyles. It is also a city of many faiths—Hindus,

Parsees, Jews, Buddhists, Catholics, Moslems, and Jains, to name a few.

Crawford Market offers pyramids and bushels of colorful fruits and vegetables from all over India. In stalls and shops throughout the city, one can find bargains in ivory, silks, silver, gin—everything available in India.

The cuisine of West India represents a wide range of delicacies not found in other regions. In Bombay alone, a visitor can dine on savory repasts from all other regions: idlis from the South, tandoori dishes from the North, and rich milk sweets from Bengal.

Vegetarian foods in the West are influenced by inhabitants of the states of Gujarat and Maharashtra. Nonvegetarian dishes reflect the influence of the people of Goa and the Parsees (descendants of Persians who ventured to India) who live throughout the western region, but mostly in the Bombay area.

When served Maharashtrian and Gujarati meals, it is customary to be offered a sweet dish as the first course, which is eaten with hot *poori*, a wheat bread, and various vegetable and lentil preparations. Most Maharashtrian and Gujarati vegetable curries are seasoned with dried herbs and mustard seeds. Drumsticks, a gourd cooked with fresh grated coconut, is a popular dish. The Gujarati add a pinch of jaggery (a coarse brown sugar made from palm sap) to their curries, which enhances the natural sweetness of the foods.

While Maharashtrians begin and end the meal with rice, the Gujarati eat wheat preparations, such as *bhakhri*, first and the rice last. On the whole, less rice is eaten in West India than in the South or the East.

Basundi, a sweet dish from Gujarat, is made with milk, sugar, fruit seeds, cardamom and almonds, boiled together. *Doodh pak* is similar to North India's rice kheer. Thick, sweetened yogurt seasoned with cardamom and saffron is a favored sweet known as *shrikhand*.

The Parsees and Goans are the epicures of meat dishes in West India. Goa is noted for its hot and sour *vindaloo* curries, in which lots of red peppers and spices are ground with vinegar. They were created by the Portuguese, who introduced the red pepper to India in the 1500s, and were perfected by their Goan descendants. They are best when made with fish and rich meats such as duck or pork. Lamb chili fry is another of their popular meat preparations, which are hot, but very tasty. Country Captain is a hot, dry Goan curry made with chicken and chilies, or with other already cooked meats.

Coconut usually goes into the preparation of Goan vegetable curries. Cucumber mixed with vinegar or lime juice and salt often accompany rice dishes.

Many restaurants in Bombay serve the spicy Parsee specialty *dhan sak*, prepared with meats, lentils, vegetables, spices, and nuts. Bombay duck, actually a white fish much like sole, is served curried or fried. *Patrami machi* is another fish dish, prepared with chilies, coriander leaves, and fresh coconut. Pomfret and *ravas*, Indian salmon, are other regional food fish.

When it comes to sweet dishes and desserts, the Goans and Parsees prepare both Indian and Western versions. They are well known for their *burfi*, a fudge-like sweet.

Many West Indians drink neora, a refreshing non-fermented beverage taken from the coconut. It is sold at railroad stations and streetside bazaars. Coffee, tea, lemon juice, and other fruit juices are also popular drinks in West India.

Now that curiosity and appetites are whetted, indulge in the following selection of subcontinental recipes for an endless Indian food adventure in your own homeland. Dine and drift off to the land of sari silks, Hindu temples, elephant bells, erotic sculptures, and self-realization shrines.

the BENGAL LANCERS INDIAN COOKBOOK

1
Indian Dining

An Indian meal can be an exotic and dramatic experience; it can also be a lot of comfortable fun. Orthodox Indians sit on the floor on colorful mats or low wooden seats. If the meal happens to be a holiday feast, the air is permeated with the heavenly aroma of biryanis and a mild incense. Foods are served in the best hand-tooled copper, brass, and silver pieces; and colorful flower arrangements add to the festive mood.

Both everyday meals and feasts are served in individual *thalis*, circular trays with a high lip. They are from twelve to fourteen inches in diameter and made from silver, brass, copper, or stainless steel. Rice and breads are placed in the middle. *Katoris* (small cups holding dahls, vegetables, meats, chutneys, and yogurts) line the inside edges of the thalis. This arrangement, which can be compared to the American plate and bowl combination, provides an excellent way of serving the buffet dinners to which Indian meals lend themselves so well.

Food is eaten with the hand. Indian meals are not eaten in courses as they often are in America. Indian hostesses, instead, serve small portions of a variety of dishes at once. Like an orchestra conductor, the diner mixes and blends flavors to the perfect symphony. Pieces of bread are used for dunking and scooping up food, sandwich-style. Water is served in metal tumblers. It is the only beverage taken with meals. *Chai* (Indian milk tea) is drunk afterwards. Fresh fruit is served after a meal.

A complete everyday meal consists of the following basic foods: dahl, vegetable, rice, bread, raita, chutney, and pickle. Tiny bowls of melted butter (ghee) and salt accompany every meal. There are, of course, variations. Moslems, for instance, always include meat dishes. The menu depends a great deal on religion and on what is regionally grown and available in local markets.

From fifteen to twenty dishes will be prepared for holiday and religious feasts. They will include at least two vegetable dishes—one dry and one with sauce—special breads, papads, basmati rice, colorful biryanis, pulaos, and appetizers. Sweet dishes are served with fresh fruit and nuts.

When planning an Indian buffet for a horde, first read the recipes through carefully. Determine the amount of cooking time required for each item and plan so that all dishes will be ready for serving at their proper time. Sweets can be cooked a day ahead of time. Dahls should usually be cooked first, since they take the longest. They can be reheated just before serving. Breads and appetizers should be cooked last, since they are served warm.

Just before the feast, a prayer is paid in honor of Agni, God of Fire. A piece of food is also tossed into the fire as an offering to him, in hope that he will grant many more feast celebrations.

The following are a few basic menu suggestions. You can add more dishes for lavish buffets.

1
Bhoona Raan
Alu Dum
Matar Pulao
Cucumber Salad
Suji Halva • Fruit

2
Samosa
Tandoori Chicken
Onion Rings and Lemon Wedges
Dahl Palak
Sada Pulao
Nan
Kheer

3
Shrimp Molee
Lemon Rice
Eggplant Kottu
Papads
Kela Raita
Jalebi

4
Bhara Mirch Subji
Sukha Gobhi
Palak Tomatar
Saffron Rice
Pooris
Lemon-Mango Pickle
Chum Chum

2

Spices and Other Basic Ingredients

The use of spices by Indian chefs predates the beginning of the Aryan period, the sixth century B.C. The temperature in many areas of the subcontinent can climb to over 110 degrees in the shade. Through the centuries, Indians have discovered that marinating and cooking perishable foods in certain combinations of spices keeps them from spoiling for days or, in some cases, months. Each seasoning has either an antiseptic or a preservative quality. Snappy chilies are rich in Vitamin C, which is good for the complexion. Golden turmeric is used to cure skin diseases and leech bites. Sweet cinnamon is a powerful germicide. Aromatic aniseed is the basis of many throat lozenges, and perfumey cardamom aids digestion.

Anyone can pick flowers and place them in a vase. But only a few people know how to arrange a selection so that it is artistically pleasing to the eye. When it comes to Indian cookery, it is not so much what spices are used, as how one cooks with them. The true art lies in the delicacy of spicing to accentuate latent flavors or disguise unpalatable ones.

Just as geometric balance figures in the art of flower arranging, there is a mingling of science with Indian cookery. Spices such as cardamom and pepper render aroma more than flavor when they are used whole in cooking. When they are ground or crushed, however, they render flavor more than aroma. Whole cumin sautéed in butter or oil will have a mild aroma and licorice flavor. Cumin roasted whole and then crushed will be very aromatic and will darken the food as well as give it a nutty flavor. Ground, unroasted cumin imparts its mildest taste to food. Saffron renders its most vibrant color when lightly roasted, then soaked in warm milk.

Pay special attention to the order in which spices and herbs are added when cooking, because it can make a difference in taste. Since turmeric burns easily and turns bitter, it should be added when a sufficient amount of liquid is present or when the skillet has been removed from the heat. If dry hot red peppers are first sautéed in oil and then added to a cooked main ingredient, they will have a more subtle flavor.

Indian cooks do not use commercial curry powders. They prefer to create their own *masalas* (combinations of spices). They grind fresh spices daily on a rectangular grindstone known as a *sil*, with a half-moon-shaped stone called a *batta*. The people of Punjab, rather than grind their spices, crush them with a mortar and pestle. This method is fine when crushed spices are required. Otherwise, American cooks can use an electric blender.

Curry powder is an Anglo-Saxon invention. It consists of a standard blend of spices and herbs. The usual ones are cayenne pepper, coriander, cumin, cloves, cinnamon, fenugreek, ginger, mace, black pepper, and turmeric. They are labeled "Indian Curry" or "Madras Curry—Hot," and they render the same taste to everything.

Fillers such as stems and rice flour are added to these powders, marring their flavor and bouquet. All herbs and spices contain oil, which gives the herb or spice its characteristic aroma and flavor. The packaged ground herbs and spices sold in grocery stores lose their character rapidly because the precious oils have already been released during the crushing and grinding process.

If possible, try to buy herbs and spices in whole form, because they retain aroma and flavor much longer. Grind them as needed and store in glass, screw-top bottles away from the light in a dry, cool place. Do not add them in a lump, but spread them evenly over the item being cooked.

The word *curry* has come to be a vague and oversimplified term for Indian foods cooked in spicy sauces. It conjures up images of yellow or green sauces that are exceedingly hot and all taste alike. *Curry* was coined by the Anglo-Saxons. One theory holds that when the English first heard the Indian word *kari*, during the sixteenth century, they translated it as *curry*. That word never existed in the Indian vocabulary until then. There are some Indians even today who have never heard it. *Kari*, a word that comes from the southern state of Tamil Nadu, means "sauce." *Kadhi* is a sauce made from yogurt and chickpea flour to which fried mustard and cumin seeds are added. Perhaps the word *curry* is derived from *Kari* or *Kadhi*.

Herbs and Spices

Following is a list of the most common herbs and spices and their proper use in Indian cooking. You will notice that curry is not among them.

Aniseed: Licorice-tasting aniseed is the fruit of an annual herb, indigenous to Egypt and the Mediterranean. It is used as a spice for pickles. Kashmiri chefs use it in meat dishes.

Asafoetida: Asafoetida is a resin known as *hing* in India. It is used in minute quantities. This accent for curry and lentil dishes is taken from the roots of the *ferula foetida* plant, indigenous to Eastern Persia and Afghanistan. Stores sell it as a lump, a powder, or as tiny pebbles. Keep it in a tightly covered jar.

Caraway seeds: These are the aromatic seeds of the caraway herb, named after Caria in Asia Minor. They resemble the black cumin in appearance. Caraway is used in masalas and vegetable dishes.

Cardamom: This aromatic eucalyptus-scented seed is a member of the ginger family. Cardamom is usually used as a flavoring in pulaos, biryanis, and sweet dishes. It comes from the fruit of an herbaceous plant grown in India and Ceylon. The green pod and white pod varieties are available in American stores. The green pods are the most fragrant. There is also a large brown cardamom used in certain rice and meat dishes, but it is more difficult to find in this country. The cardamom pod can be used whole or the skin can be discarded and the seeds ground to powder. In order to retain their aromatic character, it is best not to grind them until just before using them.

Cinnamon: This spice comes from the bark of the cinnamon tree, a member of the laurel family that grows along the Malabar coast of India and Ceylon. Indians use stick cinnamon in certain rice and meat dishes. Ground cinnamon is usually included in meat sauces and vegetables dishes. One of the earliest spices known to man, cinnamon is mentioned in the Old and New Testaments.

Cloves: Cloves are the dried aromatic flower buds of the clove tree, which grows in such areas as Zanzibar, Indonesia, and Madagascar. They are used whole or ground in Indian dishes. Chinese writings as early as 266 to 220 B.C. mention that officers of the court sucked on cloves. Indians use the ball tops as breath fresheners. The English derived the world *clove* from the French *clou,* meaning "nail," which the clove resembles.

Coriander seeds: These sweet-smelling, bead-shaped brown seeds come from an herbaceous annual grown mostly in North India and native to the Mediterranean area. The Bible and Sanskrit writings refer to it as very similar to manna. The seeds are used whole, roasted, or ground in many meat and vegetable curries as well as sweet dishes. To roast coriander seeds, heat them over medium-low heat in a heavy skillet several minutes, until they turn a few shades darker. Be careful not to burn them.

Coriander leaves: Coriander leaves (*hara dhania*) (known as *cilantro* in Spanish stores and as Chinese parsley in Chinese stores) are used extensively as a seasoning and garnish in curries. They make an excellent herb garden plant. The leaves are ready for use when the plant is 10 inches tall.

Cumin: The banana-shaped cumin is about ¼ inch long and grayish-brown. It is the sweet aromatic dried fruit of a small plant grown throughout Europe, Mexico, and Kashmir. Cumin is used whole, roasted, or ground in curries and savories. Cumin seeds are roasted in the same manner as coriander seeds. North Indians sprinkle ground, roasted cumin over their vegetables, snacks and yogurt.

Dry red pepper: The Spanish traveled to the New World and discovered chili peppers. They carried the seeds to India in the 1500s. Dry red peppers are usually more pungent the smaller they are. The smallest ones are used for cayenne, the hottest spice. Paprika and chili powder are made from the larger red peppers. Be careful to buy only pure chili powder. Some commercial chili powders are actually a mixture of chili powder, cumin, oregano, garlic, and salt. If whole red chili peppers are used in cooking, it is best to remove them before serving time.

Fennel seeds: Indians roast fennel and use it as a mouth freshener. It looks like a large aniseed and smells stronger. Fennel is also used in many vegetable curries as an excellent accent.

Fenugreek: This flat yellow seed is really a leguminous herb. However, because of its aroma it is used as a spice in chutneys and curries. Fenugreek is especially compatible with eggplant and potatoes. Barely more than a pinch at a time is used, since the taste is almost bitter.

Ginger: Marco Polo discovered this silvery tan-skinned knobby rhizome growing in India and China around 1271. Gingerroot can be purchased in Chinese, Indian, Japanese, and Puerto Rican stores. It is often the most frequently used spice in chutneys and in meat and vegetable dishes. Ginger is usually peeled, chopped, and then grated or ground. You can use a blender for the grinding. Gingerroot should be wrapped and stored in the refrigerator. You can also plant it in sand and cut off what you need as it grows.

Green chilies: Since green chilies vary in hotness, it is a good idea to sample them before you use them. The hottest part is the seeds, which can be removed for a milder taste. You can substitute green sweet peppers for the taste without the fire.

Mace: Mace is the hard shell covering the nutmeg seed. Its aroma is similar to that of the seed. It is included in betel nut spices and sweetmeats such as halvas.

Mango: Dried, ground raw mango lends food a sour and tangy taste, much like that of lemon. It is used extensively in North India, where it is called *amchoor.*

Mustard seeds: Indians usually cook with black mustard seeds. They are more pungent than the yellow variety, which can serve as a milder substitute. In recipes calling for crushed mustard seeds, it is best to do the crushing with a mortar and pestle.

Nutmeg: This spice is the seed of the fruit from the nutmeg tree, grown in the West Indies, Malaya, Indonesia, and New Guinea. Nutmeg is grated and added to puddings and some curries. It is best to buy whole nutmeg and store it in an airtight jar.

Poppy seeds: Indians use white poppy seeds for cooking. They are usually ground, and it is best to roast them before grinding.

Saffron: From 300,000 to 400,000 stigmas of the crocus flower are required to produce one pound of dried saffron, which explains why it is so costly. It is believed that saffron originally came from Asia Minor. Saffron has been growing in Spain for centuries and is cultivated in Kashmir. The orange-red spice is used to flavor and color Mogul rice and meat dishes and some desserts. It is best to roast it first, then soak it in warm milk. Saffron is also used as a dye. Indians use it to color monks' robes and bridal veils.

Turmeric: Turmeric is a boiled-down root from the ginger family. After it is pulled, it is heated in a pot, then set in the sun

Spices and Other Basic Ingredients

to dry. Turmeric is sold in small lumps in India but is available only in ground form in America. Indians are among the major consumers of turmeric. It lends a yellow color to curries and rice dishes. Most of it is grown in Tamil Nadu and Bengal.

Garam Masalas

A *garam masala* is a mixture of hot spices. You can prepare the mixture in advance and use it in recipes that call for it. Garam masalas vary in degrees of spicing and hotness. Following are three basic recipes.

Bengal Lancers Garam Masala

This masala is mildly spiced.

3 ounces coriander seeds
1 ounce cumin seeds
¼ ounce fenugreek seeds
1 ounce cloves
2 ounces cardamom seeds (preferably brown cardamom)
¼ teaspoon mace
¼ teaspoon nutmeg
1 ounce cinnamon
1 ounce black pepper

1. Roast coriander seeds, cumin, and fenugreek seeds separately for a few minutes until their rich aroma is given off. Combine with all other ingredients and grind.
2. Pass the mixture through a sieve and store in an airtight jar. Yield: about 20 tablespoons.

NOTE: Roasting the ingredients separately is important, since each gives off its characteristic aroma at a different time.

Madras Garam Masala

This is spicier than the Bengal Lancers Garam Masala because of the amount of red chilies.

4 ounces coriander seeds

2 ounces cumin seeds
½ ounce fenugreek seeds
2 bay leaves or coriander leaves
2 ounces black pepper
1 ounce dry red chilies
¼ ounce turmeric
1 ounce cinnamon
1 ounce poppy seeds
½ ounce cloves
1 ounce cardamom seeds (preferably brown cardamom)

1. Roast coriander, cumin, fenugreek, and bay leaves or coriander leaves separately until you smell their aroma.
2. Grind all the ingredients and store in an airtight jar. Yield: 30 tablespoons.

Sambar or Rasam Masala

This masala is used for seasoning the dahl or rasam of South India. Use it with any vegetable curry or soup for a spicy accent.

1 tablespoon vegetable oil
¼ teaspoon asafoetida
½ tablespoon turmeric
5 ounces coriander seeds
1 ounce dry red chilies
2 ounces urad dahl (split black peas) or chana dahl (split chickpeas) or split yellow peas
1 ounce black pepper
½ ounce mustard seeds
½ ounce fenugreek seeds
1 ounce cumin seeds

1. Coat skillet with vegetable oil. Cook asafoetida 10 to 15 seconds. Repeat with turmeric and keep the heat low.
2. Fry the other ingredients separately in the same manner for a minute or two.
3. Grind and store in an airtight jar. Yield: 25 tablespoons.

Other Ingredients

The following ingredients are as basic to Indian cookery as herbs and spices.

Ghee: Use ghee in all recipes in this book that call for butter. Ghee is clarified butter. The primary cooking medium in North India, ghee is also used in other regions. Hot mustard seed oil is the cooking medium of the East, and strong-smelling coconut oil is used in the South. Of these, ghee is the most palatable. To clarify butter, melt it in a saucepan over medium heat; then skim the foam off the top and remove from heat. Strain the clear liquid and discard the milky residue in the bottom of the pan. Store in a covered container in the refrigerator.

Coconut and Coconut Milk: When selecting a coconut, shake it to be sure that it has liquid inside and that the meat is moist. Punch a hole in one of the eyes of the coconut and drain off and discard the liquid. Hit the shell with a hammer and pry it open. To remove the meat, slide a sharp knife between the meat and the shell. Before grating the meat, cut off the inner brown skin. To roast the grated coconut, put it in a skillet over medium heat and stir until it begins to brown.

Use only unsweetened or fresh coconut to prepare coconut milk. These are readily available in health food stores. Coconut milk is used as a base and thickening agent in many South Indian curries. For milk of average thickness, soak ½ cup shredded coconut in ½ cup water for 30 minutes to 1 hour. This will yield ¾ cup coconut milk when strained. For thick milk, soak 1 cup shredded coconut in 1 cup water. For thin milk, soak ½ cup shredded coconut in 1 cup water.

Tamarind: This "date of India" is the pulpy, acid-flavored fruit of the tropical tamarind tree. It is usually peeled, seeded, and pressed into a lump, which is available in American gourmet shops. As a rule, use twice as much water as tamarind. Soak in warm water for at least 1 hour; then strain the pulp.

3

Appetizers and Snacks

From the crowded, noisy bazaars in cities like Calcutta and New Delhi to the many thatched-hut villages in remote areas, sidewalk vendors and wayside stands offer an array of snacks cooked while one waits. The air seems endlessly permeated with spicy aromas and the sounds of hawkers peddling their stacks of food—from curry puffs to savory nuts galore.

Indians from Kashmir to Kerala love to snack throughout the day on finger-food munchables. During the early 1900s, the English acquainted Indians with their tradition of afternoon tea, a custom still followed by many—especially in the northern half of the subcontinent. South Indians usually wash down savory snacks with one of their famous thick coffee brews.

Those dainty little tea cakes and cress sandwiches one associates with English tea are cast aside for more enticing nibbles. As a rule, Indian savories are deep-fried and made from lentils, cereals, vegetables and meats. They can assume many forms: fritters, filled pastry pockets, kababs, kofta (meatballs) and pancakes, just to name a few. Snacks range on the flavor scale from bland to spicy, and they are almost always dipped in chutneys.

In Indian homes snacks are not eaten to whet the appetite before a meal. Nor are they savored with alcoholic beverages—taboo for very orthodox Hindus and Buddhists. Although there are some who follow the drinking habits long ago introduced by the French, the British, and the Portuguese, one really must visit a major hotel for sunset hour cocktails and appetizers.

Indian snack foods can easily be adapted to Western entertaining and dining. Merely dub them *hors d'oeuvres* and serve them as exotic accompaniments with the usual party drinks.

Move on to an Indian dinner. Or be eclectic and serve an entrée from France, China, or Greece, for example. Try blending Indian snacks with those from other lands—for a United Nations flair. In any combination, however, keep in mind the basic taste essences and be sure that the flavors are complementary.

Vada

Vadas are deep-fried fritters shaped like doughnuts or small cakes. In this mildly spiced recipe they are made of seasoned ground urad dahl, a leguminous herb often used in Indian food. It is common to see vadas sold by vendors in Madras foodstalls.

1½ cups urad dahl (husked split black peas)
2 green chilies
1 tablespoon chopped fresh ginger
1 teaspoon cumin seed
1 tablespoon chopped fresh coriander
1 teaspoon salt
pinch of baking soda
vegetable oil for deep frying

1. Clean, wash, and soak urad dahl in 2 cups water overnight.

2. Drain the dahl. Grind it in an electric blender, using as much water as necessary to form a very thick and smooth paste. You might have to do this in several batches. Pour into a large bowl.
3. Grind chilies, ginger, cumin seed, and coriander to a smooth paste. Add to the dahl paste. Add salt and mix thoroughly. Add baking soda and mix well again. Cover and set aside 1 hour.
4. Heat vegetable oil for deep frying. Scoop up some of the paste between your fingers (as much as you can conveniently hold). Drop it carefully into the hot oil. You can fry 8 to 10 vada at a time. Fry until golden. Serve immediately with Imli Chutney (see index) and yogurt. Yield: 20 to 25 vadas.

NOTE: If the dahl paste becomes thin, squeeze some of the mixture out, using a piece of cheesecloth. Do this before adding any spices.

Kajoo Vada

These nutty-flavored cashew vadas are mildly seasoned.

1 cup chopped unsalted cashew nuts
2 green chilies or 1 tablespoon chopped sweet pepper (optional)
2 tablespoons chopped fresh coriander leaves
1 tablespoon chopped fresh ginger
½ teaspoon salt
vegetable oil for deep frying

1. Soak cashew nuts in 1 cup water for 1 hour. Drain.
2. Grind cashew nuts, green chilies or sweet pepper, coriander leaves, and ginger to a very thick paste, using as much water as necessary.
3. Transfer to a bowl. Add salt and mix well.
4. Heat vegetable oil for deep frying and make the vadas as in the previous recipe. Yield: 10 to 15 vadas.

Alu Vada

These batter-dipped potato vadas are popular in North India, where lots of potatoes grow. They have a crisp chick-pea crust and a spicy potato filling.

1½ cups chick-pea flour
1 teaspoon ground coriander
⅛ teaspoon red pepper (optional)
1 cup warm water
1½ pounds potatoes
1 tablespoon vegetable oil
1 small onion, finely chopped
pinch of ground asafoetida (*hing*)
1 teaspoon finely chopped ginger
1 teaspoon mustard seed
½ teaspoon coriander seed
2 green chilies, chopped (optional)
½ teaspoon turmeric
1 teaspoon sugar
1 tablespoon dried mango powder or lemon juice
salt to taste
2 tablespoons chopped fresh coriander leaves
pinch of baking soda
vegetable oil for deep frying

1. Sift chick-pea flour and mix in a bowl with ground coriander, red pepper, and enough water to make a smooth, thick batter. Cover and set aside.
2. Boil potatoes; then set aside to cool. Peel and squash them completely with hands. Set aside.
3. Heat 1 tablespoon vegetable oil in a skillet. Add onions and sauté 2 to 3 minutes. Add asafoetida, ginger, mustard seed, and coriander seed. Cook 2 minutes. Add green chilies, turmeric, and potatoes. Continue cooking and mix well for a few minutes. Add sugar, mango powder or lemon juice, and salt to taste.
4. Remove from heat and cool. Sprinkle with coriander leaves. Mix and cool a little longer. Divide potato mixture into 10 to 12 balls.

5. Add baking soda and salt to taste to chick-pea batter and mix well.
6. Heat vegetable oil for deep frying. When quite hot, dip potato balls into batter and fry until golden. Serve with Khajoor Chutney and Podina Chutney (see index).

Samosa

Samosas are deep-fried pastry pockets, filled with regional delicacies—a favorite snack throughout the subcontinent. They are often carried on long trips. This recipe calls for the medium-hot potato and green pea filling popular among Hindu vegetarians. Reduce the amount of green chilies and garam masala for a milder flavor.

1 cup all-purpose flour
1 tablespoon melted butter
1 tablespoon ground coriander
1 teaspoon salt
¾ cup warm water
1 pound potatoes
½ pound (1 cup) green peas (fresh or frozen)
1 tablespoon vegetable oil
1 onion, finely chopped
1 teaspoon chopped fresh ginger
1 teaspoon cumin seed
2 green chilies, chopped (optional)
2 tablespoons chopped fresh coriander leaves
1 teaspoon garam masala (see index)
1 tablespoon dry mango powder or lemon juice
1 tablespoon all-purpose flour mixed with ½ cup water
vegetable oil for deep frying

1. Sift flour and mix with melted butter, ground coriander, and ½ teaspoon salt. Rub butter into flour well. Use about ¾ cup warm water to prepare a stiff but smooth dough. Knead about 5 minutes. Cover with a damp cloth and set aside for 30 minutes.

2. Clean and wash potatoes. Boil with green peas in 2 cups water until potatoes are cooked. Drain and cool. Peel potatoes and cut into small cubes.
3. Heat 1 tablespoon vegetable oil in a skillet. Add onions and sauté 2 minutes. Add ginger, cumin seed, green chilies, peas, potatoes, chopped coriander leaves, garam masala, remaining ½ teaspoon salt, and mango powder or lemon juice. Cook 5 minutes. Cool.
4. Mix 1 tablespoon flour with ½ cup water. Set aside.
5. Knead dough a few minutes. Divide into 12 equal parts. Shape into 12 balls. Roll into disks as thin as possible. Cut each disk in half. Moisten edges of the semicircles with the flour and water mixture. Fold them into cones. Fill each cone with the potato mixture. Do not overstuff. Seal the top and all other openings completely.
6. Heat vegetable oil for deep frying. Fry samosa until golden and crisp. Serve with a sweet and hot chutney. Yield: 24 samosas.

Kheema Samosa

These rich *Kheema* (groundmeat)) samosas are a favorite with nonvegetarian North India. Samosas vary in shape and fillings. In Deccan and in the South, they are semicircular. In the North, they are triangular or circular.

Samosa pastry (see preceding recipe)
2 green chilies, chopped (optional)
5 cloves garlic, chopped
1 teaspoon chopped fresh ginger
¼ cup chopped fresh coriander leaves
1 tablespoon vegetable oil
1 small onion, chopped
1 pound ground lamb or beef
½ teaspoon turmeric
1 teaspoon salt
¼ teaspoon ground cloves
¼ teaspoon cinnamon

½ teaspoon ground cardamom
1 tablespoon dry mango powder or lemon juice
1 tablespoon garam masala (see index)
vegetable oil for deep frying
chopped coriander leaves for garnish

1. Prepare samosa pastry as in the preceding recipe and set aside.
2. Grind the chilies, garlic, ginger and coriander leaves to a smooth paste. Add about 1 tablespoon water if necessary.
3. Heat 1 tablespoon vegetable oil in a skillet. Lightly sauté onions. Add seasoned paste and cook 2 minutes. Add meat, turmeric, salt, cloves, cinnamon, and cardamom. Simmer on low heat until all the liquid dries up. Break up any lumps that may have formed. Add mango powder or lemon juice and garam masala. Set aside to cool.
4. Fill and fry the samosas as in the previous recipe. Sprinkle with chopped coriander leaves before serving. Yield: 24 samosas.

Baigan Pakora

This spicy eggplant pakora, an Indian version of tempura, is popular in the North, where eggplant is widely grown.

2 cups chick-pea flour
1 cup warm water
1 small eggplant
1 teaspoon salt
1 teaspoon garam masala (see index)
½ teaspoon turmeric
1 teaspoon ground coriander
¼ teaspoon red pepper (optional)
2 tablespoons chopped fresh coriander leaves
pinch of baking soda
2 cups vegetable oil for deep frying

1. Sift chick-pea flour into a mixing bowl. Gradually add 1 cup warm water, stirring constantly until a thick and smooth batter is formed. Set aside for 30 minutes.
2. Clean and wash eggplant and cut it in half. Then quarter and slice it into semicircles ⅛ inch thick. Sprinkle ¼ teaspoon of the salt over the slices.
3. Add garam masala, turmeric, ground coriander, red pepper, coriander leaves, baking soda, and remaining ¾ teaspoon salt to batter. Beat well for 5 minutes.
4. Heat vegetable oil for deep frying. Dip sliced eggplant pieces, a few at a time, into the batter and deep fry them. Serve with Dhania Chutney or Imli Chutney (see index) and yogurt. Yield: 15 to 20 servings.

NOTE: You may also use any of the following vegetables or a combination of them for pakora:

Cauliflower: separated into flowerets
Potatoes: thinly sliced rounds
Sweet peppers: sliced thinly, lengthwise
Onions: thinly sliced, or whole cocktail onions
Cabbage: finely chopped
Bananas: sliced
Okra: whole or chopped
Apple: sliced

Panir Pakora

Panir is an Indian cream cheese similar to ricotta, which is used as a substitute in this recipe. Panir is considered an indulgence among Indians, since milk products are so scarce. For Panir Pakora, a rich North Indian snack, panir is dipped in a mildly flavored batter and deep-fried.

Pakora batter (see preceding recipe)
1½ cups ricotta cheese
1 teaspoon garam masala (see index)
½ teaspoon salt

1 teaspoon lemon juice
vegetable oil for deep frying

1. Prepare pakora batter as in the preceding recipe and set aside.
2. Heat ricotta cheese in an ungreased skillet over medium heat, stirring constantly, until all the liquid dries up. Add remaining ingredients and cook a few minutes until the cheese is completely dry. Remove from heat and cool.
3. Knead the cheese mixture well. Roll into a ¼-inch thick pancake. Cut into cubes 1½ inch by 1½ inch.
4. Heat vegetable oil for deep frying. Dip the cheese cubes into the batter and fry until golden on both sides. Serve with Podina Chutney (see index). Yield: about 20 balls.

NOTE: Instead of rolling the cheese out, you can also divide it into equal parts to form balls the size of walnuts.

Chicken Pakora

Chicken Pakora is a snack eaten by well-to-do nonvegetarians, since poultry is expensive. This version is spicy and medium hot.

1 small onion, chopped
6 cloves garlic
1 tablespoon chopped fresh ginger
2 teaspoons garam masala (see index)
salt to taste
1½ pounds chicken legs
pinch baking soda
½ cup chick-pea flour
½ cup fresh coriander leaves
¼ teaspoon chili powder
½ teaspoon ground cumin
1½ cups vegetable oil for deep frying

1. Grind the onions, garlic, and ginger to a smooth paste.
2. Place in a saucepan. Add 1 teaspoon of the garam masala,

salt to taste, chicken, and just enough water to cover the chicken. Boil, covered, 7 to 10 minutes. Set aside to cool.
3. Separate the meat from the bone. Cut large pieces into small ones. Set aside in a mixing bowl.
4. Mix baking soda with chick-pea flour. Break up any lumps. Add remaining teaspoon garam masala, coriander leaves, chili powder, and cumin. Mix well, adding only enough water to form a thick paste. Form the entire mixture into a lump. Divide into 15 to 20 small lumps.
5. Heat vegetable oil for deep frying. Fry pakoras until golden. Serve with a sweet and spicy chutney. Yield: 15 to 20 pakoras.

Fish Pakora

These deep-fried hot fish puffs are a favorite Indian snack.

½ pound fish (fleshy), boiled
1 tablespoon butter
1 tablespoon chick-pea flour or all-purpose flour
4 tablespoons cream
1 egg, beaten
1 teaspoon freshly ground black pepper
½ teaspoon garam masala (see index)
¼ teaspoon turmeric
salt to taste
vegetable oil for deep frying

1. Flake the fish fine and set aside.
2. Heat butter in a skillet. When melted, add flour and blend well. Add cream and stir. Add fish and cook 3 to 5 minutes.
3. Add all other ingredients. Blend until batter is thick. Set aside to cool.
4. Heat vegetable oil for deep frying. Drop a spoonful of mixture into oil and fry until golden. Yield: 15 to 20 pakoras.

Oopma

This is a popular South Indian cereal-like breakfast dish and tea snack, made from cream of wheat. It is dry and very hot.

1 tablespoon split chick-pea and urad dahl (combination)
3 tablespoons butter
1 large onion, finely chopped
1 tablespoon chopped cashew nuts
1 tablespoon chopped peanuts
2 tablespoons fresh coconut, shredded
1 teaspoon mustard seed
3 bay leaves
3 green chilies (optional)
2 tablespoons chopped fresh coriander leaves
1½ cups semolina or cream of wheat
2½ cups water
¼ teaspoon turmeric
½ teaspoon sugar
salt to taste
1 tablespoon lemon juice

1. Wash, clean, and soak the split chick-pea/urad dahl mixture for 1 hour. Drain.
2. Heat butter in a heavy skillet. Add the onions and sauté until translucent. Add cashew nuts, dahl mixture, peanuts, and coconut. Cook a few minutes until cashew nuts are light brown. Add mustard seed. When seeds stop popping, add bay leaves, chilies, and coriander leaves. Cook 1 minute.
3. Add semolina or cream of wheat and cook a few minutes until light brown. Gradually pour in 2½ cups water, stirring constantly so that no lumps form. Add turmeric, sugar, and salt. Bring to a boil. Lower heat and simmer covered until almost all the liquid dries up. Remove from heat. Sprinkle on lemon juice. Stir and serve immediately with plain yogurt. Yield: 4 to 6 servings.

Muruku

Muruku is a doughnut-shaped and mildly spiced South Indian snack with the hard texture of a pretzel.

2 cups rice flour
½ cup chick-pea flour
¼ teaspoon turmeric
⅛ teaspoon red pepper (optional)
¾ teaspoon salt
1 teaspoon ground or finely chopped cashew nuts
1 teaspoon ground or finely chopped peanuts
½ teaspoon sesame seed
1 tablespoon butter
vegetable oil for deep frying

1. Mix well all the dry ingredients and the butter. Add just enough water to prepare a stiff dough. Knead well.
2. Divide into 25 equal parts. Shape each part into a ball. Roll as thin as possible. Using a sharp knife, make a hole the size of a dime in the center of each muruku.
3. Heat vegetable oil for deep frying. Fry the murukus until golden. Serve with Spicy Coconut Chutney (see index). Yield: 25 murukus.

Coconut Muruku

The South Indian shores are graced with coconut palms, and coconut milk accents the flavor of these big, rope ring murukus.

2 cups rice flour
½ cup chick-pea flour
¾ teaspoon salt
pinch of ground asafoetida
⅛ teaspoon red pepper (optional)
½ cup shredded coconut, soaked in ½ cup warm water for 30 minutes
vegetable oil for deep frying

1. Mix together all the ingredients except the water-soaked coconut and the vegetable oil.
2. Gently rub the coconut in the water. Strain to obtain the coconut milk.
3. Add just enough coconut milk to the flour mixture to form a stiff dough. Knead well. Divide into 25 equal parts. Roll each into an 8-inch rope. Bring the two ends together, making a big ring, and press the ends.
4. Heat vegetable oil for deep frying. Fry the murukus until golden. Serve with Spicy Coconut Chutney (see index). Yield: 25 murukus.

NOTE: Murukus are made in different shapes by using muruku molds.

Rava Dosa

This is a lacy, feather-light lentil and farina pancake. It is a favored South Indian breakfast food and tea snack, lightly seasoned with cumin and mustard seed.

1 cup urad dahl (husked, split black peas) soaked in 1½ cups water for 8 to 10 hours
½ cup cream of wheat
½ teaspoon cumin seed
½ teaspoon mustard seed
salt to taste
¼ cup vegetable oil for frying

1. Using a colander, strain the urad dahl. Reserve the water. Blend the dahl into a smooth, thin paste, adding as much water as necessary.
2. Add cream of wheat, cumin seed, mustard seed, and salt. Add more water, if necessary, so that the mixture remains a smooth, thin paste. Mix well and set aside in a warm place for 6 to 8 hours.
3. Beat the mixture well again. It should be of pouring consistency. If too thick, add water and beat again for a few minutes.

4. Heat a flat, heavy skillet over medium-low heat. Grease it with few drops of oil. Pour a ladleful of the batter into the middle of the skillet and quickly spread it into a thin pancake. Cook for a few minutes. Add a few more drops of oil around the dosa. When the top is almost dry, turn the dosa and cook 1 to 2 minutes. Fold the dosa twice. If dosa is very thin, cook it on one side only. Serve with Spicy Coconut Chutney and Sambar (see index). Yield: 10 to 12 dosas.

Masala Rava Dosa

In this stuffed version, potatoes and onions spiced with hot masala are wrapped inside the dosa.

Rava Dosa batter (see preceding recipe)
2 large potatoes, boiled
2 tablespoons vegetable oil
1 tablespoon shredded coconut
pinch of asafoetida
½ teaspoon cumin seed
1 tablespoon finely chopped fresh ginger
1 teaspoon mustard seed
2 green chilies, chopped (optional)
1 large onion, chopped
3 bay leaves
1 tablespoon ground coriander
¼ teaspoon turmeric
salt to taste
¼ cup vegetable oil for frying

1. Prepare dosa batter as in preceding recipe and set aside.
2. Peel potatoes and crumble them into small bits with hands or fork.
3. Heat 2 tablespoons vegetable oil in a skillet. When hot, add coconut and cook 1 minute. Add asafoetida, cumin seed, ginger, mustard seed, chilies, onions, bay leaves, ground coriander, and turmeric. Sauté 3 to 4 minutes. Add potatoes and salt to taste. Mix well. Cook 2 minutes.

4. Cook the dosas as in the previous recipe. After they are cooked, put a few tablespoons of seasoned potatoes in the center of each dosa and fold it twice. Serve with Spicy Coconut Chutney and Sambar (see index). Yield: 10 to 12 dosas.

Papads

Papads, as they are called in the North, and *pappadums,* as they are called in the South, are savory paper-thin wafers made out of dahl or rice dough. They can be found in American gourmet shops and large supermarkets. While some papads are plain, others are spiced with crushed black pepper. They come in different sizes and are usually round.

Since making papads requires some expertise and a great deal of time, they are usually not prepared at home by Indian cooks but purchased from grocery markets. After opening the package, store the papads in an airtight container and do not refrigerate them.

Papads can be cooked on an open fire, baked, or deep-fried. Since they expand considerably, use a large skillet when you fry them, or break each papad into four pieces. Cook them until puffed and crisp. Drain on absorbent paper. They cannot be prepared very far in advance, since moisture in the air makes them go limp.

Bombay Duck

The Bombloe is a fish found in the Arabian Sea along the West coast of India, mostly around Bombay. It floats on the water's surface like a duck, which is probably how the bombloe fish got its nickname, Bombay Duck. These fish are dried, salted, canned, and exported to Europe and America.

While cooking, the fish has an unpleasant odor. It may be necessary to use an air freshener afterward. To cook Bombay Duck, fry on both sides in hot oil for several seconds or bake in a preheated 350-degree oven until golden and crisp.

Machi Kabab:

Kababs are a finger food first introduced to North Indians centuries ago by Moguls. Machi (fish) Kababs are eaten by many living on the East coast and in the lake areas of Punjab. In this version they are tenderized and flavored in a mildly spiced yogurt paste.

1 pound firm-fleshed fish, fresh or thawed
1 small onion, roughly cut
2 cloves garlic
1 teaspoon chopped fresh ginger
1 teaspoon garam masala (see index)
⅛ teaspoon red pepper
¼ teaspoon ground cardamom
½ cup yogurt
1 teaspoon lemon juice
salt to taste
4 tablespoons butter, melted
1 tablespoon chopped coriander leaves
1 lemon, cut into wedges

1. Cut fish into cubes and set aside.
2. Grind all ingredients except fish, butter, coriander leaves, and lemon wedges to a smooth paste. Pour into a bowl. Add fish cubes and marinate 1 hour.
3. Thread fish cubes on skewers and grill 10 to 15 minutes, basting with butter and turning frequently. Place kababs on a serving plate. Sprinkle with coriander leaves and serve with a chutney and lemon wedges. Yield: 4 servings.

Chicken Tika Kabab

This is a mildly spiced Mogul kabab dating back to the eighth century.

1 small onion, chopped
4 cloves garlic
1 teaspoon chopped fresh ginger

6 peppercorns
1 tablespoon salt
2 teaspoons garam masala (see index)
1½ pounds chicken breasts
2 tablespoons butter
½ teaspoon garlic powder
⅛ teaspoon red pepper
salt to taste
1 lemon, cut into wedges

1. Blend onions, garlic, ginger, and peppercorns, adding two to three tablespoons of water.
2. Place in a small saucepan. Add 1 tablespoon salt, 1 teaspoon garam masala, chicken, and just enough water to cover the chicken. Stir a few times. Boil, covered, for 5 minutes.
3. Cool; then separate the meat from the bones. Discard the liquid and cut chicken into small cubes.
4. Mix butter, garlic powder, red pepper, remaining teaspoon garam masala, and salt to taste. Skewer the chicken and baste with the seasoned butter. Grill until done, 7 to 10 minutes. Serve with lemon wedges. Yield: 4 to 6 servings.

Beef Kabab

This beef kabab is hot and spicy.

1 small sweet pepper
½ pound finest quality beef or lamb, cut into ½-inch cubes
¼ teaspoon red pepper
1 teaspoon freshly ground black pepper
¼ teaspoon ground ginger
¼ teaspoon garlic powder
1 tablespoon lemon juice
4 tablespoons butter
salt to taste
1 lemon, cut into wedges

1. Cut the sweet pepper into as many cubes as you have cubes of meat.
2. Alternate the meat and sweet pepper on skewers.
3. Mix together all the remaining ingredients except the lemon wedges.
4. Baste the meat with the seasoned butter; then broil. Continue turning and basting until cooked to desired degree of doneness. Serve with lemon wedges. Yield: 4 servings.

Shrimp Kofta

These mildly spiced shrimp *koftas* (balls) are served with a coconut-fringed yogurt sauce. They are a favorite along the coastal areas of Bengal and Tamil in the South.

1 small onion, chopped
1 cup cooked shrimp
½ teaspoon ground coriander
¼ teaspoon turmeric
½ teaspoon ground cumin
⅛ teaspoon red pepper
salt to taste
1 egg, beaten
4 tablespoons flour
4 tablespoons vegetable oil or butter
3 tablespoons grated fresh coconut
¾ cup yogurt, beaten
2 tablespoons fresh coriander leaves

1. Blend onions and shrimp. Place in a bowl and add coriander, turmeric, cumin, red pepper, and salt to taste. Mix well.
2. Shape into 16 to 20 small balls. Roll them in egg and flour.
3. Heat vegetable oil or butter in a skillet. Cook the kofta 5 to 7 minutes, turning frequently.
4. Dry roast coconut and add to yogurt. Add salt to taste. Pour this mixture over the shrimp koftas. Sprinkle with coriander leaves. Yield: 4 to 5 servings.

Appetizers and Snacks 33

Lobster Kofta

This is a rich but mildly hot seafood kofta.

1 small lobster (about ¾ cup), boiled
1 small onion, minced
½ teaspoon ground coriander
½ teaspoon ground cumin
½ teaspoon ground ginger
½ teaspoon garlic powder
1 teaspoon lemon juice
1 egg, beaten
salt to taste
½ cup bread crumbs
3 tablespoons butter

1. Mince the lobster meat. Add to it all the ingredients except bread crumbs and butter.
2. Shape into about 20 small balls. Roll them in the bread crumbs.
3. Heat the butter in a skillet and cook koftas, uncovered, until golden, about 10 minutes. Serve with chutney. Yield: about 20 balls.

Sukha Kofta

Sukha means "dry," and that is exactly what these spicy meatballs are.

½ pound finely ground lamb or beef
1 small onion, chopped
2 cloves garlic, chopped
⅛ teaspoon red pepper
⅛ teaspoon ground cloves
⅛ teaspoon ground cardamom
1 teaspoon salt
1 teaspoon chopped fresh ginger
¼ cup chopped fresh coriander leaves
1 tablespoon tomato sauce

4 tablespoons vegetable oil
1 lemon, cut into wedges

1. Mix together all ingredients except vegetable oil and lemon wedges. Shape into 15 to 20 balls.
2. Heat vegetable oil in a skillet. Cook meatballs, turning frequently. If skillet is not large enough, cook the meatballs in 2 batches, using half the oil each time. Serve with lemon wedges and a spicy chutney.

Lamb or Pork Chops

Before cooking, the meat is tenderized in a spicy, but not hot, yogurt marinade.

1 teaspoon garam masala (see index)
⅛ teaspoon chili powder
½ cup yogurt, beaten
½ teaspoon garlic powder
½ teaspoon crushed black pepper
1 teaspoon lemon juice
salt to taste
1 pound lamb or pork chops
vegetable oil for deep frying
2 eggs, beaten
1 tablespoon chopped fresh coriander leaves

1. Mix garam masala, chili powder, yogurt, garlic powder, black pepper, lemon juice, and salt in a bowl. Add meat and coat thoroughly. Marinate 2 hours.
2. Heat vegetable oil for deep frying. Dip each chop into beaten eggs and fry until golden, about 20 minutes. Sprinkle with coriander leaves. Serve with a yogurt chutney. Yield: 4 to 6 servings.

Dahi Anda

These hard-cooked eggs are served with a mildly spiced yogurt (*dahi*) sauce for an interesting appetizer or brunch entrée.

½ cup yogurt, beaten
1 teaspoon lemon juice
1 teaspoon freshly ground black pepper
1 teaspoon garam masala (see index)
1 teaspoon butter
¼ teaspoon cumin seed
salt to taste
4 to 5 large hard-cooked eggs, shelled

1. Using a cheesecloth, squeeze out all the water from yogurt. Place in a mixing bowl. Add lemon juice, black pepper, and ½ teaspoon garam masala. Beat to a smooth paste.
2. Heat butter in a skillet and sauté cumin seed 1 to 2 minutes. Add to yogurt mixture. Add salt to taste and mix.
3. Cut eggs in half and arrange on a serving plate. Pour yogurt over them and sprinkle with remaining ½ teaspoon garam masala. Yield: 4 to 5 servings.

4

Soups and Salads

Indian soups are usually made from a base of one of about fifty lentil varieties grown in the subcontinent. These soups tend to be thin but full-bodied in flavor. They are taken with breads and dry curries throughout a meal as a gravy to moisten the rice. Try chilling these soups a day or two. When you reheat them, you will find that the flavor has been greatly enhanced.

Mixed ripe vegetables and fruits are tossed to create pungent, salty, and even sweet salads. These are eaten as side dishes throughout a meal. Chopped or sliced onions, tomatoes, and cucumbers sprinkled with lemon juice, vinegar, salt, and red pepper are eaten with meals throughout North India. Bananas and coconut are favorite South Indian salad ingredients. All over India, fruits and vegetables are combined with whipped yogurt and served chilled as a refreshing and thirst quenching salad that is eaten during or at the end of a meal.

These soups and salads harmonize easily with American cuisine as well as with foods from other lands. Feel free to use these recipes as inspirations for your own creations.

Chicken Mulligatawny Soup

Mulligatawny is a soup that was created over a century ago by British living in South India. Its name comes from the Tamil words *molliga* and *tunni,* meaning "pepper water." There are many versions of this soup, but all are blendings of a British idea with Indian ingredients. This one features chicken in a mildly hot and spicy broth.

7 cups water
1 pound of chicken pieces (with bones)
½ teaspoon salt
1 tablespoon butter
1 medium-sized onion, chopped
¼ teaspoon turmeric
1 teaspoon ground coriander
¼ teaspoon red pepper
1 teaspoon ground cumin seed
¼ teaspoon ground ginger
salt to taste

1. Boil 2 cups of the water in a small pan. Add chicken and ½ teaspoon salt. Turn heat to low and cook, covered, until chicken is tender. Then cool.
2. Remove meat from bones and cut into small pieces. Set aside. Reserve any stock in the pan.
3. Heat butter in a saucepan. Sauté onions lightly. Add turmeric, coriander, red pepper, cumin, and ginger. Cook 1 minute.
4. Add stock and 5 cups water. Bring to a boil. Turn heat to medium-low and simmer 45 minutes.
5. Add chicken and salt to taste. Simmer 15 minutes. Serve with boiled rice. Yield: 5 to 6 servings.

Pepper Water

Yet another version, hotter than the preceding recipe and tart, because it calls for the tamarind juice used in South Indian cooking. Pepper Water is often served with **dry** curries to moisten the rice. When people of Tamil Nadu are stricken with malaria, they drink this soup made with *karavat,* a salt fish.

7 cups meat or vegetable stock
1 mint twig
¼ teaspoon red pepper
¼ teaspoon turmeric
1-inch stick cinnamon
10 peppercorns
5 whole cardamom pods
5 cloves
5 cloves garlic, crushed
1 small onion, chopped
¼ cup tamarind soaked 1 hour in ½ cup water
salt to taste

1. Bring 7 cups stock to a boil in a saucepan. Add all ingredients except tamarind and salt. Boil 5 minutes. Turn heat to medium-low and simmer 1 hour.
2. Strain tamarind juice and discard pulp. Add juice to stock. Simmer 5 minutes. Strain and season with salt to taste. Serve with boiled rice. Yield: 4 to 6 servings.

Rasam

Rasam is a tart, spicy South Indian soup, usually made with tamarind juice and a lentil base. This one has a hot, spicy, soup stock base.

½ teaspoon ground cumin seed
10 black peppercorns
5 cloves garlic
¼ cup tamarind soaked 1 hour in ½ cup water
7 cups water
½ cup chopped fresh coriander leaves
1 tablespoon chopped fresh mint leaves
1 tablespoon butter
½ teaspoon mustard seed
2 bay leaves
salt to taste

1. Grind cumin, peppercorns, and garlic together, adding a few drops of water.
2. Strain tamarind juice and discard pulp. Place juice in a saucepan. Add the seasoned paste and 7 cups water. Boil 15 minutes.
3. Add coriander leaves and mint leaves. Boil another 10 minutes.
4. Heat butter in a skillet. Add mustard seed and bay leaves. Sauté 9 minutes. Add this to rasam with salt to taste. Serve alone or with boiled rice. Yield: 4 to 6 servings.

Dahl Rasam

Coconut water and split peas form the base of this thick and spicy soup.

½ cup split peas
1 small onion, chopped
½ teaspoon salt
1 cup fresh shredded coconut, soaked 1 hour in 2 cups water
2 tablespoons butter
1 small onion, sliced
½ teaspoon black pepper
½ teaspoon ground mustard seed
½ teaspoon ground fenugreek seed
½ teaspoon ground cumin seed
salt to taste
3 tablespoons lemon juice

1. Boil 3 cups water in a saucepan. Add split peas, chopped onion and ½ teaspoon salt. Cook over medium heat until peas are done and most of the liquid has been absorbed. Then cool and grind.
2. Gently rub coconut in the water. Strain to obtain the milk and set aside.
3. Heat butter in a saucepan. Add sliced onion and sauté lightly. Add all the ground spices and cook 1 minute.

4. Add ground dahl (split peas), 3 cups water, salt to taste, and coconut milk. Simmer 15 minutes over medium-low heat. Add lemon juice. Yield: 4 to 6 servings.

Shrimp Rasam

A popular soup in the coastal areas where seafood and fresh fish are caught daily, Shrimp Rasam is tart and hot. Eliminate the chilies and reduce amount of tamarind if you desire a milder taste.

½ pound shrimp, fresh or thawed
1 teaspoon cumin seed
5 cloves garlic
½ teaspoon turmeric
4 green chilies (optional)
¼ cup tamarind soaked 1 hour in ½ cup water, or 3 tablespoons lemon juice
salt to taste
2 tablespoons butter
1 teaspoon mustard seed
1 large onion, sliced

1. Boil shrimp in 7 cups water in a saucepan for 10 minutes.
2. Mince the shrimp. Then return it to same water.
3. Grind cumin, garlic, turmeric and chilies together. Add to minced shrimp.
4. Strain the tamarind juice and discard pulp. Add juice to minced shrimp. Add salt to taste. Bring to a boil and continue boiling 5 minutes.
5. Heat butter in a skillet. Add mustard seeds and sauté a few minutes. Add onions and sauté lightly.
6. Add this to rasam and simmer a few minutes. Yield: 4 to 6 servings.

Tomato Rasam

This thick yellow split pea and tomato purée rasam is pungent with asafoetida.

½ cup yellow split peas
½ teaspoon salt
pinch of ground asafoetida
6 medium-sized ripe tomatoes
1 cup chopped fresh coriander leaves
½ teaspoon garlic powder
½ teaspoon cumin seed
½ teaspoon black pepper
¼ teaspoon chili powder
salt to taste
2 tablespoons lemon juice
1 tablespoon butter
1 teaspoon mustard seed

1. Bring 2 cups water to a boil in a saucepan. Add split peas, ½ teaspoon salt, and asafoetida. Cook over medium heat until peas are cooked, about 20 to 25 minutes. Drain and cool. Then grind. Return to saucepan.
2. Meanwhile, scald the tomatoes in boiling water. Remove skins and purée tomatoes in an electric blender.
3. Add tomato purée to ground split peas in saucepan. Add all ingredients except lemon juice, butter, and mustard seed. Add 5 cups water and mix well. Bring to a boil. Turn heat to medium-low and simmer 15 minutes. Add lemon juice.
4. Heat butter in a skillet and cook mustard seeds a few minutes. Add to soup. Yield: 4 to 6 servings.

Curry Soup

Turmeric, red pepper, ginger, and garlic season this hot, thin soup. It is an excellent partner for boiled rice.

2 tablespoons butter

1 small onion, chopped
¼ teaspoon ground garlic
¼ teaspoon ground ginger
¼ teaspoon red pepper
½ teaspoon turmeric
salt to taste
10 cups meat stock
¼ cup tamarind soaked 1 hour in ½ cup water, or 3 tablespoons lemon juice

1. Heat butter in a saucepan. Add onions and garlic. Sauté 2 minutes. Add all other ingredients except meat stock and tamarind juice. Cook 1 minute.
2. Add stock and bring to a boil. Turn heat to medium-low. Simmer 45 minutes to 1 hour.
3. Strain tamarind juice and discard pulp. Set aside.
4. Strain or pass soup through a sieve. Add tamarind juice or lemon juice. Yield: 4 to 6 servings.

Masoor Dahl Soup

Masoor dahl are tiny, round, and shiny salmon-colored lentils that turn yellow when cooked. This is a mild soup that is good served hot or cold.

¼ teaspoon turmeric
5 cloves garlic, chopped
10 black peppercorns
1 small onion, chopped
¾ cup lentils
1 teaspoon salt
2 tablespoons lemon juice
salt to taste

1. Boil 2½ cups water in a saucepan. Add turmeric, garlic, peppercorns, onions, lentils, and 1 teaspoon salt. Bring to a boil again. Turn heat to medium-low and simmer until lentils are cooked and most of the water has dried up, about 20 minutes.

2. Mash or grind lentils, completely, using a little water if necessary.
3. If they were ground in a blender, return lentils to saucepan. Pour in 6 cups water and bring to a boil. Turn heat to medium-low and simmer 10 to 15 minutes.
4. Strain or pass lentils through a sieve.
5. Return lentils to soup. Add lemon juice and salt to taste. Eat this soup with boiled rice or as it is. Yield: 4 to 6 servings.

Cucumber Salad

Cucumbers are a popular salad vegetable in all regions of India. Lemon juice often serves as a dressing base, especially in the South. This is a refreshing salad sprinkled with a favorite garnish, coriander leaves.

1 small carrot
3 medium-sized cucumbers
2 tablespoons lemon juice
½ teaspoon black pepper
⅛ teaspoon chili powder
1 tablespoon butter
salt to taste
1 tablespoon fresh coriander leaves

1. Peel and shred the carrot. Peel and slice the cucumber.
2. Blend lemon juice, black pepper, chili powder, butter, and salt.
3. On a salad plate, arrange cucumbers in two layers. Pour seasoned lemon juice over each layer. Sprinkle top layer with carrots and coriander leaves. This salad could be eaten with any Indian meal. Yield: 4 servings.

Carrot Salad

This carrot, radish, and red cabbage combination is mildly seasoned with sautéed mustard seeds.

½ pound carrots, peeled and grated

½ pound radishes, grated
½ pound red cabbage, grated
1 teaspoon vinegar
salt to taste
1 tablespoon butter
1 teaspoon mustard seed
1 tablespoon chopped sweet pepper

1. Mix carrots, radishes, red cabbage, vinegar, and salt in a bowl.
2. Heat butter in a sauté pan and sauté mustard seeds. Pour over the mixed vegetables. Sprinkle with sweet peppers. Serve with any Indian meal. Yield: 4 to 5 servings.

Kachumbar

This hot mixed vegetable salad includes fresh coconut and is popular fare in the South. Beware of the chilies.

4 ripe tomatoes
1 cucumber
1 small carrot
1 medium-sized onion, chopped
3 green chilies, chopped (optional)
2 tablespoons shredded fresh coconut
½ teaspoon sugar
½ teaspoon chopped fresh ginger
2 tablespoons lemon juice
1 cup chopped red cabbage
1 teaspoon black pepper
salt to taste
coriander leaves
1 teaspoon garam masala (see index)

1. Cut tomatoes roughly into small pieces. Peel cucumber and chop. Pare carrot and grate.
2. Mix all the ingredients except the coriander leaves and garam masala in a large bowl. Sprinkle with coriander leaves and garam masala. Yield: 4 to 6 servings.

Cucumber Raita

Raitas are an indispensable companion to North Indian meals. They consist of a seasoned whipped yogurt base to which is added fresh or cooked vegetables or fruits. This version is mild. Always serve chilled.

1 medium-sized cucumber
2 cups yogurt, whipped
½ teaspoon black pepper
⅛ teaspoon chili powder (optional)
1 teaspoon salt
⅛ teaspoon ground mustard

1. Peel and shred the cucumber. Place it in a colander to drain off the water. This takes about 1 hour.
2. In a bowl, combine the cucumber and all other ingredients except mustard. Then sprinkle with ground mustard.
3. Place in the refrigerator until ready to use. Serve with any Indian meal. Yield: 4 to 6 servings.

Alu Raita

Potatoes are a versatile North Indian vegetable, often seasoned with cumin.

1 large potato, boiled
2 cups yogurt, whipped
⅛ teaspoon chili powder
1 teaspoon salt
½ teaspoon butter
½ teaspoon mustard seed
½ teaspoon cumin seed
1 tablespoon chopped fresh coriander leaves

1. Peel the potato and cut into small cubes.
2. Mix yogurt, potato, chili powder, and salt in a bowl.
3. Heat butter in a skillet. Add mustard seeds and cumin seeds. Sauté 1 to 2 minutes.

4. Add to the yogurt mixture. Sprinkle with coriander leaves. Refrigerate until serving time. Yield: 4 to 6 servings.

Kela Raita

Kela is North Indian for bananas. Sweet bananas combined with a whisper of black pepper make an unusual tasting raita.

1 large ripe banana
2 cups yogurt, whipped
½ teaspoon black pepper
1 teaspoon lemon juice
½ teaspoon sugar
⅛ teaspoon chili powder (optional)
1 teaspoon salt
coriander leaves

1. Peel the banana and slice into rounds ⅛ inch thick.
2. In a bowl, combine banana and all other ingredients except coriander leaves. Sprinkle with coriander leaves and refrigerate until you are ready to serve. Yield: 4 to 6 servings.

Onion Raita

This is a thick raita that is sweet and pungent.

½ teaspoon ground cumin
½ teaspoon ground coriander
2 cups yogurt, whipped
1 small carrot, grated
1 small onion, finely chopped
1 teaspoon grated fresh ginger
2 tablespoons finely chopped fresh coriander leaves
1 tablespoon finely chopped fresh mint leaves
2 green chilies, chopped (optional)

⅛ teaspoon chili powder (optional)
1 teaspoon lemon juice
¼ teaspoon sugar
1 teaspoon salt
⅛ teaspoon paprika

1. Lightly dry roast cumin and ground coriander. Cool.
2. In a bowl, combine all ingredients except paprika. Sprinkle with paprika and refrigerate until you are ready to serve. Yield: 4 to 6 servings.

Palak Raita

Palak is Indian for spinach, a much eaten vegetable in North India. It is mildly seasoned in this raita.

1 pound fresh spinach, finely chopped
2 cups yogurt, whipped
½ teaspoon black pepper
⅛ teaspoon chili powder (optional)
2 green chilies, chopped
½ teaspoon grated fresh ginger
⅛ teaspoon cinnamon

1. Clean the spinach and drain.
2. In a bowl, combine all ingredients except cinnamon. Sprinkle with cinnamon and refrigerate until serving time. Yield: 4 to 6 servings.

Baigan Raita

Eggplant and onion combine with garam masala for a spicy raita.

1 medium-sized eggplant
2½ cups yogurt, whipped
1 small onion, finely chopped
1 teaspoon garam masala (see index)

⅛ teaspoon chili powder
1 teaspoon lemon juice
1¼ teaspoons salt

1. Preheat oven to 300° F. Place eggplant on rack in oven and bake 20 to 30 minutes.
2. Peel away the skin and mash the pulp fine.
3. Combine all ingredients in a bowl and refrigerate until you are ready to serve. Yield: 4 to 6 servings.

Banana Pachadi

Pachadi is the South Indian equivalent of raita. Like ice cold water, it soothes the palate when taken with hot South Indian curries.

2 cups yogurt
1 tablespoon butter
½ teaspoon mustard seed
1 tablespoon lemon juice
⅛ teaspoon red pepper
2 tablespoons grated coconut
1 teaspoon black pepper
½ teaspoon sugar
salt to taste
2 large bananas

1. Beat the yogurt well in a bowl.
2. Heat butter in a skillet and sauté mustard seeds. Add to yogurt.
3. Add all ingredients except bananas. Mix well. Add bananas and stir a few times. Serve with any Indian meal. Yield: 4 to 6 servings.

Tomato-Onion Pachadi

This is a very mild pachadi accented with coconut, typical of South Indian food.

1½ cups yogurt
3 tomatoes, chopped

1 small onion, chopped
2 green chilies, chopped
2 tablespoons grated coconut
1 teaspoon sugar
2 tablespoons chopped fresh coriander leaves
1 teaspoon garam masala (see index)
salt to taste

1. Beat the yogurt well.
2. Add all ingredients and mix well. Yield: 4 to 6 servings.

5

Meat Dishes

In India mutton is not sheep meat. It is very fresh goat meat and is usually quite tough. It was dubbed mutton by the English living in India, perhaps because mutton chops sounded more appetizing than goat chops. While goat is the common table meat in the villages, lamb is the meat most commonly eaten in restaurants and homes by Indians in metropolitan areas.

There are no goat dishes in this chapter. Instead, there are recipes for rich but not hot lamb and beef curries, the kinds that typically come from North India and are reminiscent of the sumptuous dishes enjoyed by ancient Mogul royalty.

Orthodox Moslems are forbidden to eat pork, ham, or bacon. The Hindus, who account for the majority of India's population, consume pork and lamb but not beef. To them, the cow is an animal symbolizing life-giving nourishment and the fertility of the earth.

Although religious beliefs still figure prominently in Indian diets today, education is fostering new attitudes. As Indians become more educated, they tend to rationalize their rejection of social taboos associated with certain foods. However, many orthodox Hindus still maintain the old social attitudes. But Moslems and Christians in India, who number about seventy-five million, can and do eat beef.

The lamb curries in this chapter can be kept a few days after cooking. Just add a little water (1 to 2 tablespoons) and warm; do not boil a curry. Beef can be substituted for lamb in most of the recipes. Beef, however, does not keep very well, because it dries out faster than lamb. Also, its texture changes too much when it is reheated. Because American beef has a higher water content compared to Indian beef, the amount of water called for in the beef recipes has been reduced. If you desire a really dry curry, do not add any water. In every recipe, the meat should be washed and patted dry before cooking.

The amount of cooking time allowed for the meats in these recipes has been reduced because of the high quality of meats available in the United States. Most Indian meats are fairly tough and must be cooked slowly for a long time. Crushed green papaya, vinegar marinades, and yogurt are common tenderizers for grilled and fried meats.

Only in large cities can good quality meat be purchased, and it is expensive. Since refrigeration is still a luxury available only to the wealthy, meats are usually cooked within 24 hours after slaughter.

For centuries, Indians have been cooking meats and other perishable foods in spicy sauces to keep them from spoiling in the intense heat. It was the English who dubbed these dishes curries.

Americans associate Indian meat dishes almost exclusively with curries. Tandoori cooking, however, is a keen competitor. A *tandoori* is a simple cylindrical clay oven, usually standing from four to five feet in height, two feet in diameter at the bottom, and one foot at the top. When a fire is properly burning in a tandoori oven, the coals are banked to one side for the cooking process. The sand and ashes covering the bottom absorb most of the fat drippings without smoking or flaming. Spiced meat, fish, or poultry, whole or in kabab form, are skewered and quickly thrust into the oven. The heat is so intense that a tandoori cook can always be identified by the lack of hair on his arms. Tandoori dishes can also be prepared on a barbecue grill or a revolving spit.

Many Indian meat dishes reflect a blending with Middle Eastern foods—kofta, korma (rich, thick braised meat), kheema, and kababs, for example.

Indian cooks will spend an entire day preparing a superb entrée—grinding spices and marinating tough meat for many hours, then simmering it a long time. But with modern techniques and equipment these dishes can be prepared in a relatively short period of time.

Feel free to experiment with the meat recipes in this chapter and learn to create your own symphony of spices to accommodate your palate. It is not necessary to accompany these entrées with Indian bread and vegetables, but they are best served over rice.

Kofta Curry

Yogurt is the binding agent for this North Indian version of spicy meatballs simmered in a thick, rich tomato-based sauce. Split peas and chick-pea flour are other common binding agents, and sometimes a raw egg (a British touch). This dish can be prepared the day before and reheated just prior to serving.

5 cloves garlic
2 tablespoons chopped fresh ginger
3 tablespoons chopped fresh coriander leaves
1 medium-sized sweet pepper, chopped
8 tablespoons yogurt
2 pounds ground lamb
2 teaspoons salt
½ teaspoon ground cardamom
¼ teaspoon cinnamon
¼ teaspoon ground cloves
pinch of red pepper (optional)
5 tablespoons vegetable oil
5 whole cardamom pods

1-inch stick cinnamon
3 large onions, finely chopped
½ teaspoon turmeric
1 tablespoon ground coriander
1 tablespoon ground cumin
½ cup tomato sauce
1 cup hot water

1. Grind the garlic, 1 tablespoon of the chopped ginger, 2 tablespoons of the chopped coriander leaves, ½ of the chopped sweet pepper, and 2 tablespoons of the yogurt to a smooth paste. Transfer to a bowl and combine with the meat. Add 1 teaspoon of the salt, the ground cardamom, ground cinnamon, ground cloves, and a pinch of red pepper. Mix well. Set aside.
2. Heat vegetable oil in a saucepan. Add whole cardamom and 1-inch stick cinnamon. Cook 2 minutes. Add chopped onion, remaining tablespoon chopped ginger, and remaining chopped sweet pepper. Cook until onion is golden. Add turmeric, a pinch of red pepper, ground coriander, and ground cumin. Cook 2 minutes. Add tomato sauce and cook 5 minutes. Pour in hot water and bring to a boil. Lower heat; add 1 teaspoon salt and simmer 10 minutes.
3. Meanwhile, knead the meat mixture to a smooth dough. Divide into 15 to 20 equal parts. Shape into balls (koftas). Add to the sauce and simmer, covered, 30 minutes or until they are cooked.
4. Beat the remaining 6 tablespoons yogurt and add it to the koftas. Simmer a few minutes. Sprinkle with remaining tablespoon of chopped coriander leaves. Yield: 4 to 6 servings.

Nargisi Kofta

These hard-cooked eggs coated with spicy ground meat are called "nargisi" because when cut in half they resemble the yellow and white narcissus flower.

5 cloves garlic

Meat Dishes 55

2 tablespoons chopped fresh ginger
2 green chilies (optional)
1 small onion, coarsely chopped
8 tablespoons yogurt
1½ pounds finely ground lamb or beef
½ teaspoon ground cardamom
¼ teaspoon cinnamon
¼ teaspoon ground cloves
⅛ teaspoon ground nutmeg
⅛ teaspoon ground mace
1 teaspoon turmeric
2½ teaspoons salt
2 teaspoons garam masala (see index)
3 tablespoons chopped fresh coriander leaves
1 egg, beaten
8 to 10 medium-sized hard-cooked eggs, shelled
2 tablespoons chick-pea flour or all-purpose flour
5 tablespoons vegetable oil
2 large onions, finely chopped
½ cup finely chopped sweet pepper
5 whole cardamom pods
½ teaspoon cumin seed
10 black peppercorns
4 medium-sized tomatoes, chopped
1½ cups warm water

1. Grind the garlic, 1 tablespoon of the ginger, chilies, 1 coarsely chopped onion, and 1 tablespoon of the yogurt to a smooth paste. Mix the paste with the ground meat. Add ground cardamom, cinnamon, cloves, nutmeg, mace, ½ teaspoon of the turmeric, 1 teaspoon of the salt, 1 teaspoon of the garam masala, and 1 tablespoon of the chopped coriander leaves. Mix well. Add beaten egg and knead the mixture thoroughly. Set aside.
2. Dust hard-cooked eggs with flour. Divide the meat mixture into 8 to 10 equal parts. Flatten each and place an egg in the center. Then wrap the seasoned meat around the egg, coating completely and evenly.

3. Heat vegetable oil in a skillet. When hot, add meat-coated eggs and cook until brown all over. Remove from the skillet, using a slotted spoon. Set them on paper toweling to drain.
4. To the same oil, add the 2 finely chopped onions, remaining tablespoon of ginger, and chopped sweet pepper. Sauté until the onions are translucent. Add the whole cardamom, cumin seed, and peppercorns. Cook 2 minutes. Add remaining ½ teaspoon turmeric, 1½ teaspoons salt, 1 teaspoon garam masala, and chopped tomatoes. Simmer until tomatoes are tender. Mix in the remaining 7 tablespoons yogurt and cook a few minutes. Pour in the warm water and bring to a boil. Lower heat and simmer 10 to 15 minutes over medium heat.
5. Add koftas and simmer until they are completely cooked. Cut each in half and pour some of the sauce on the halves. Just before serving, sprinkle on the remaining 2 tablespoons chopped coriander leaves. Yield: 4 to 6 servings.

Rogan Josh

This dish is everyday fare for upper-class Moguls in North India—especially Kashmir. Lamb is simmered in a thick, deep red, nutty-flavored sauce—with a whisper of saffron to give it a dramatic color.

6 tablespoons vegetable oil
2 pounds lamb, cubed
2 large onions, finely chopped
4 tablespoons blanched almonds
5 cloves garlic, chopped
2 tablespoons chopped fresh ginger
1 teaspoon poppy seed
1 tablespoon ground coriander

Meat Dishes 57

1 tablespoon ground cumin
½ teaspoon ground cloves
¼ teaspoon cinnamon
¼ teaspoon red pepper
½ teaspoon ground cardamom
¼ teaspoon saffron
½ teaspoon turmeric
pinch of nutmeg
pinch of mace
2 tablespoons cold water
½ cup yogurt, well beaten
½ cup tomato sauce
salt to taste
1½ cups water
¼ cup chopped fresh coriander leaves

1. Heat vegetable oil in a skillet. Add meat and brown well. Remove meat and use paper toweling or colander to drain away grease.
2. Put onions in same oil and sauté until golden. Meanwhile, dry roast the almonds.
3. Grind the almonds, garlic, ginger, poppy seed, ground coriander, cumin, cloves, cinnamon, red pepper, cardamom, saffron, turmeric, nutmeg, and mace to a smooth paste, with 2 tablespoons water. This is the masala.
4. Add masala to the sautéed onions. Cook over medium-low heat until oil separates from masala, about 5 minutes.
5. Gradually add well-beaten yogurt, stirring constantly. Cook 5 minutes.
6. Gradually add tomato sauce, stirring constantly. Cook until oil separates from mixture, about 5 minutes.
7. Add meat and cook a few minutes. Add salt to taste and 1½ cups water. Bring to a boil over high heat. Lower heat. Cook covered until meat is tender, about 1 hour. Sprinkle with coriander leaves. Serve with rice and Indian bread. Yield: 4 to 6 servings.

Lamb Do Pyaza

Pyaza is the North Indian word for onion, and this recipe includes lots of them. Some Indian chefs believe the amount of onions used in this recipe should be twice (*do*) the weight of the meat. The onion flavor in Lamb Do Pyaza is tamed with a hint of ginger.

3 large onions, finely chopped
5 cloves garlic
2 tablespoons chopped fresh ginger
5 whole cardamom pods (use seeds only)
1 teaspoon cumin seed
½ teaspoon turmeric
¼ teaspoon cayenne pepper (optional)
2 tablespoons cold water
2 pounds lamb, cubed
6 tablespoons vegetable oil
3 medium-sized tomatoes, chopped
1 cup hot water
1½ teaspoons salt
2 tablespoons chopped fresh coriander leaves
1 tablespoon garam masala (see index)
lemon juice to taste

1. Grind ⅓ of the chopped onions with garlic, ginger, cardamom, cumin seed, turmeric, and cayenne pepper to a smooth paste, adding 2 tablespoons cold water. Marinate the lamb in the paste for 1 to 2 hours.
2. Heat vegetable oil in a skillet over medium-high heat. Sauté remaining chopped onions lightly, about 3 minutes.
3. Add the lamb and marinade. Brown the meat lightly. Add chopped tomatoes and cook 5 minutes. Add 1 cup hot water and salt. Lower heat and cook covered until meat is tender. Add fresh coriander leaves, garam masala, and lemon juice. Yield: 4 to 6 servings.

Gobhi Gosht

Gobhi gosht is a North Indian cauliflower-meat curry. Typical of northern curries, this one is rich and spicy.

4 tablespoons vegetable oil
2 large onions, chopped
6 cloves garlic, chopped
1 tablespoon chopped fresh ginger
1 tablespoon ground coriander
¼ teaspoon red pepper (optional)
½ teaspoon turmeric
½ teaspoon cumin seed
1 tablespoon garam masala (see index)
4 tomatoes, chopped
2 pounds lamb, cubed
1 cup water
4 tablespoons yogurt
1½ teaspoons salt
1 pound cauliflower, separated into flowerets
2 tablespoons chopped fresh coriander leaves
1 tablespoon lemon juice

1. Heat vegetable oil in a skillet. Add onions, garlic, and ginger. Cook until onions are golden. Add ground coriander, red pepper, turmeric, cumin seed, garam masala, and tomatoes. Cook until the tomatoes are completely mixed and the oil separates, about 15 to 20 minutes. If mixture is dry, add a few tablespoons of water.
2. Add meat and brown on all sides. Add 1 cup water and simmer, covered, 15 minutes. Add beaten yogurt and salt. Simmer 30 minutes.
3. Add cauliflower and simmer until the meat and cauliflower are tender. Sprinkle with coriander leaves and lemon juice before serving. Yield: 4 to 6 servings.

Kashmir Gosht

Most North Indian curries are thick. This one is dry and calls for saffron, cardamom, cloves, and almonds—typical Mogul seasonings.

4 bay leaves
5 whole cardamom pods
2 tablespoons almonds, dry roasted until light brown
4 cloves
8 black peppercorns
1-inch stick cinnamon
1½ teaspoons salt
¼ cup yogurt
1 tablespoon chopped fresh ginger
pinch of ground asafoetida
2 pounds lamb, cubed
4 tablespoons vegetable oil
2 large onions, finely chopped
1 cup water
¼ teaspoon saffron, crushed in 2 tablespoons warm milk or cream
1 tablespoon garam masala (see index)

1. Grind bay leaves, cardamom, almonds, cloves, peppercorns, cinnamon, and salt to a paste. Set aside.
2. Beat the yogurt. Add the ginger, asafoetida, and meat. Mix well and set aside.
3. Heat vegetable oil in a skillet. Add onions and cook lightly. Add meat and yogurt mixture. Cook over medium-high heat, stirring constantly, 5 minutes. Then turn heat to medium-low and cook until all the liquid dries up.
4. Add ½ cup water. Cook until the liquid dries up. Add the ground paste. Cook 2 minutes. Add remaining ½ cup water and cook until meat is tender.
5. Add the saffron soaked in warm milk. Cook 2 minutes. Sprinkle with garam masala. Serve with Paratha or Nan (see index). Yield: 4 servings.

Dahl Gosht

The meat in this northern curry is simmered in a thick, rich dahl-based sauce.

2 cups lentils soaked in 2½ cups water
4 tablespoons vegetable oil
3 onions, chopped
5 cloves garlic, chopped
2 green chilies, sliced (optional)
1 tablespoon chopped fresh ginger
1 tablespoon ground coriander
1 tablespoon ground cumin seed
½ teaspoon ground cardamom
½ teaspoon turmeric
⅛ teaspoon red pepper (optional)
½ cup chopped fresh coriander leaves
1 tablespoon garam masala (see index)
1½ teaspoons salt
2 pounds lamb, cubed
½ cup tomato sauce or 6 medium-sized tomatoes, chopped
3 cups warm water
1 tablespoon lemon juice

1. Soak the lentils in 2½ cups cold water for 1 hour.
2. Heat vegetable oil in a skillet. Add onions, garlic, chilies, and ginger. Cook until onions are golden. Add ground coriander, ground cumin, and ground cardamom. Cook 1 minute. Add the turmeric, red pepper, coriander leaves, garam masala, and salt. Cook 3 minutes.
3. Add the meat and brown. Add drained lentils and tomato sauce. Stir a few times.
4. Pour in 3 cups warm water and bring to a boil. Then lower heat and cook, covered, until the meat and lentils are completely cooked. Sprinkle on lemon juice just before serving. Yield: 4 to 6 servings.

Bhoona Raan

Golden-orange boned leg of lamb laid out flat in the shape of a butterfly is a typical Moslem specialty in the state of Hyderabad. It is usually cooked in a clay tandoori oven and is great for outdoor grilling. Chilled leftovers have a superb flavor.

½ cup yogurt
1 tablespoon ground coriander
10 cardamom seeds
½ teaspoon turmeric
1 tablespoon salt
5 cloves
10 black peppercorns
2 tablespoons chopped fresh ginger
3-inch stick cinnamon
6 cloves garlic
½ teaspoon orange or red food coloring
½ cup lemon juice
5- to 6-pound leg of lamb, boned
5 tablespoons butter, melted
1 teaspoon dry mint leaves, crumbled

1. Grind yogurt, coriander, cardamom seeds, turmeric, salt, cloves, peppercorns, ginger, cinnamon stick, and garlic to a paste. Transfer to a bowl and add orange or red food coloring and ¼ cup of the lemon juice.
2. Spread the boned meat out flat so that it resembles the shape of a butterfly. Using a sharp knife, make deep cuts all over.
3. Rub the paste over the meat and into the deep cuts. Place in refrigerator to marinate 5 to 6 hours.
4. Combine remaining ¼ cup lemon juice and melted butter. Add crumbled dry mint leaves. Place the meat on a grill, 3 inches above a medium charcoal fire (or oven broiler). Grill 30 minutes on each side, brushing frequently with the lemon butter. Cut the meat across the grain into ¼-inch slices. Yield: 6 to 8 servings.

Lamb with Spinach

The spinach-based sauce in this old Mogul recipe is touched with a faint aroma and flavor of cardamom.

6 tablespoons vegetable oil
1-inch stick cinnamon
5 whole cardamom pods
3 bay leaves
2 medium-sized onions, finely chopped
½ cup yogurt
1 teaspoon ground ginger
1 teaspoon garlic powder
1 teaspoon salt
1 teaspoon ground cumin
1 teaspoon ground cardamom
¼ teaspoon red pepper (optional)
½ teaspoon turmeric
2 pounds lamb, cubed
1 pound spinach, fresh or thawed
4 cups water
2 tablespoons lemon juice

1. Heat vegetable oil in a skillet. Add cinnamon stick, cardamom pods, and bay leaves. Cook 1 minute. Add onions and sauté 2 minutes.
2. Beat yogurt well and mix with ginger, garlic powder, salt, ground cumin, ground cardamom, red pepper, and turmeric.
3. Slowly add this paste to the onions. Cook 2 minutes. Add the meat and brown on all sides. Cook over medium-low heat until most of the liquid dries up.
4. Meanwhile, clean the spinach (if fresh) and chop. Boil in 4 cups water a few minutes. Drain off all water and purée the spinach.
5. Pour puréed spinach over the meat. Mix and cook for 5 minutes on low heat. Add lemon juice. Yield: 4 to 6 servings.

Dhan Sak

This is a dish made famous by the Parsees, descendents of the Persians, who live in the Bombay region. Traditionally, it is composed of meat, numerous vegetables, and Indian lentils—sort of an Indian goulash. This version is rich and hot.

1 cup lentils, or ½ cup lentils and ½ cup channa dahl (split chick-peas)
6 cups water
2 sprigs mint
1 onion, coarsely chopped
2 medium-sized potatoes, cubed
1 medium-sized eggplant, cubed
1 cup chopped spinach
2 pounds chopped tomatoes
2 pounds lamb, cubed
½ teaspoon mustard seeds
5 cloves garlic, chopped
1 tablespoon chopped fresh ginger
2 green chilies (optional)
2 tablespoons fresh coriander leaves
4 tablespoons butter
2 onions, finely chopped
1 teaspoon ground coriander
1 teaspoon ground cumin
¼ teaspoon turmeric
⅛ teaspoon red pepper (optional)
¼ teaspoon cinnamon
¼ teaspoon ground cloves
salt to taste
3 tablespoons fresh lemon juice

1. Clean and wash the lentils and/or channa dahl. Place in a large saucepan with 6 cups water, mint, and 1 coarsely chopped onion. Turn on heat and bring to a boil.
2. Add potatoes, eggplant, spinach, tomatoes, and lamb. Lower heat and cook until meat is tender, about 1½ hours.

3. Remove meat pieces and set aside. Pass the liquid through a sieve and discard the residue. Return the meat and strained sauce to the saucepan. Cook over low heat.
4. Meanwhile, grind mustard seed, garlic, ginger, chilies, and coriander leaves to a smooth paste. Set aside.
5. Heat butter in a skillet. Add finely chopped onions and cook until golden. Add the seasoned paste and cook 2 minutes. Add ground coriander, ground cumin, and turmeric. Cook 2 minutes.
6. Add this to the meat and sauce mixture. Add red pepper, cinnamon, cloves, and salt to taste. Stir a few times and cook 15 to 20 minutes, or until a thick sauce is formed. Add lemon juice. Serve with fried rice and Kachumbar (see index). Yield: 4 to 6 servings.

Kheema Curry

Kheema is Indian for ground meat. In this northern version, it is spiced with cinnamon, cloves, and cardamom in a mild, thick sauce. This recipe features chopped tomatoes. Sometimes green peas, cubed potatoes, or chopped, hard-cooked eggs are added to kheema.

2 pounds ground lamb
1 teaspoon turmeric
¼ teaspoon red pepper (optional)
¼ teaspoon ground nutmeg
¼ teaspoon ground mace
½ teaspoon cinnamon
½ teaspoon ground cloves
1 cup chopped fresh coriander leaves
½ teaspoon ground cardamom
4 tablespoons vegetable oil
2 large onions, chopped
1 tablespoon chopped fresh ginger
5 cloves garlic, chopped
1 teaspoon cumin seed
4 tomatoes, chopped

1½ teaspoons salt
1 tablespoon garam masala (see index)
2 tablespoons lemon juice

1. Mix ground lamb with turmeric, red pepper, nutmeg, mace, cinnamon, cloves, ¾ cup of the coriander leaves, and cardamom. Set aside.
2. Heat vegetable oil in a skillet. Add onions, ginger, and garlic. Cook until golden. Sprinkle in cumin seed and cook 1 to 2 minutes longer.
3. Add spiced meat and brown. Add chopped tomatoes and salt. Stir. Bring to a boil.
4. Lower heat and simmer until meat is cooked. Add garam masala and lemon juice. Sprinkle with remaining ¼ cup chopped coriander leaves. Yield: 4 to 6 servings.

Madras Kheema Curry

Cashew nuts and coconut accent this South Indian kheema recipe, which tends to be a little on the hot side. The use of whole cardamom, cloves, and cinnamon creates a sweet aroma. Kheema is often used to stuff sweet peppers and eggplant.

4 tablespoons vegetable oil
1 tablespoon finely chopped fresh ginger
8 cloves garlic, finely chopped
2 large onions, finely chopped
5 whole cardamom pods
5 cloves
1-inch stick cinnamon
2 pounds ground lamb
½ teaspoon turmeric
1½ teaspoons salt
¼ teaspoon red pepper
¼ cup cashew nuts
2 tablespoons shredded coconut (preferably unsweetened fresh)

1. Heat vegetable oil in a skillet. Add ginger, garlic, and onion. Sauté until onions are golden. Add cardamom, cloves, and cinnamon. Cook 2 minutes.
2. Add meat, turmeric, salt, and red pepper. Cook until meat is brown.
3. Meanwhile, dry roast the cashew nuts and coconut to a light brown. Add this to meat and cook 5 minutes. Yield: 4 to 6 servings.

Madras Lamb Curry

Lamb is simmered in an aromatic and sweet coconut sauce.

2 cups coconut milk (see index)
5 cloves garlic, minced
2 bay leaves
4 cloves
1-inch stick cinnamon
2 tablespoons chopped coriander leaves
¼ teaspoon red pepper
5 whole green cardamom pods
1 teaspoon salt
½ teaspoon turmeric
2 pounds lamb, cubed
5 tablespoons vegetable oil
2 large onions, finely chopped
1 tablespoon lemon juice

1. Combine coconut milk, garlic, bay leaves, cloves, cinnamon, coriander leaves, red pepper, cardamom, salt, turmeric, and lamb in a large pot. Bring to a boil. Lower heat and simmer, half-covered, until meat is tender.
2. Meanwhile, heat vegetable oil in a skillet. Sauté onions until translucent.
3. Add cooked onions to meat. Mix and simmer 5 minutes. Add lemon juice. Yield: 4 to 6 servings.

Beef Curry

Beef broth blends with coconut milk in this beef curry enjoyed by nonvegetarians.

2 pounds beef, cubed
1 tablespoon ground coriander
¼ teaspoon ground ginger
½ teaspoon turmeric
½ teaspoon ground cardamom
½ teaspoon black pepper
½ teaspoon ground cumin
½ teaspoon chili powder (optional)
2 tablespoons water
3 tablespoons vegetable oil
1 onion, finely chopped
5 cloves garlic, finely chopped
1 cup coconut milk (see index)
1½ teaspoons salt
lemon juice to taste

1. Simmer beef in 2 cups water until tender. Reserve broth.
2. Grind coriander, ginger, turmeric, cardamom, black pepper, cumin, chili powder, and 2 tablespoons water to a smooth paste. Set aside.
3. Heat vegetable oil in a large skillet. Add onions and garlic. Sauté until onions are translucent. Add seasoned paste and cook 3 minutes longer.
4. Add beef and ½ cup broth. Gradually bring to a boil. Add 1 cup coconut milk. Simmer until meat is tender. Add salt and lemon juice to taste before serving. Yield: 4 to 6 servings.

Moslem Beef Curry

Blanched almonds, grated coconut, cardamom, and garam masala enhance this rich and handsome meat dish.

2 cups yogurt, beaten
¼ teaspoon red pepper

½ teaspoon turmeric
2 pounds beef, of high quality
5 cloves garlic, chopped
1 tablespoon chopped fresh ginger
2 tablespoons blanched almonds, soaked in water for 1 hour
1 teaspoon poppy seed
4 tablespoons vegetable oil
5 cardamom pods
1-inch stick cinnamon
5 cloves
1 large onion, chopped
2 cups water
salt to taste
¼ cup grated fresh coconut, dry roasted
1 tablespoon garam masala (see index)

1. Mix the yogurt, red pepper, and turmeric. Marinate the beef in this mixture 1 hour.
2. Grind the garlic, ginger, almonds, and poppy seeds. Set aside.
3. Heat vegetable oil in a large skillet. Add cardamom, cinnamon, and cloves. Cook 1 minute. Add onions and sauté until golden. Add the ground paste. Cook until oil separates, about 5 minutes.
4. Add marinated meat and brown. Add 2 cups water and boil 4 minutes. Simmer over low heat until meat is tender.
5. Add salt, coconut, and garam masala. Stir and cook 2 minutes. Serve with rice and Indian bread. Yield: 4 to 6 servings.

Beef Liver Curry

Tomatoes and yogurt form a thick, rich sauce for the beef liver in this recipe.

6 tablespoons vegetable oil
2 large onions, chopped
5 cloves garlic, crushed

1 tablespoon chopped fresh ginger
1 pound calf or beef liver, cut into small pieces
½ teaspoon ground cardamom
½ teaspoon caraway seeds
¼ cup chopped coriander leaves
¼ teaspoon red pepper (optional)
salt to taste
5 tomatoes, chopped
½ cup yogurt, beaten
2 cups water

1. Heat vegetable oil in a large skillet. Add onions, garlic, and ginger. Sauté until onions are translucent.
2. Add the liver. Cook 1 to 2 minutes on each side.
3. Add all other ingredients except the yogurt and water. Cook 2 minutes.
4. Add yogurt and 2 cups water. Bring to a boil. Then simmer on low heat until cooked, about 45 minutes. Serve with rice and Chapatis (see index). Yield: 4 to 5 servings.

Anglo-Indian Beef Liver

This is a favorite recipe of the British living in India. It is a spicy mingling of the two cultures.

¼ teaspoon salt
⅛ teaspoon black pepper
⅛ teaspoon red pepper (optional)
⅛ teaspoon turmeric
2 pounds calf or beef liver, cut into 4 to 5 slices
all-purpose flour, for dredging
5 tablespoons vegetable oil
1 medium-sized onion, minced
1 teaspoon chopped fresh ginger
1 cup chicken or beef broth
salt to taste
¼ cup chopped fresh coriander leaves

1. Mix ¼ teaspoon salt, black pepper, red pepper, and turmeric.

2. Rub the liver slices with this mixture and dredge them in the flour. Set aside.
3. Heat 3 tablespoons of the vegetable oil in a skillet. Add onions and ginger. Sauté until onions are translucent.
4. Add the broth and boil until liquid is reduced by half. Add salt to taste, if necessary.
5. In another skillet, heat remaining 2 tablespoons vegetable oil and sauté liver slices until brown on both sides.
6. Pour reduced onion broth sauce over the liver. Sprinkle with coriander leaves and serve with rice and Chapatis (see index). Yield: 4 to 5 servings.

Beef Vindaloo

Vindaloos are hot and sour curries that originated in Goa on the West coast of India. The Portuguese are believed to have created them in the 1500s when they introduced the red chili to India. As a rule, rich meats and fish are marinated and cooked in a spiced vinegar paste with red chilies. Adjust the amount of pepper to suit your taste.

1 tablespoon ground coriander
½ teaspoon ground ginger
½ teaspoon ground cumin
½ teaspoon black pepper
½ teaspoon turmeric
½ teaspoon chili powder (optional)
½ teaspoon ground mustard
3 tablespoons vinegar
4 tablespoons vegetable oil
1 large onion, chopped
5 cloves garlic, chopped
2 chilies, finely chopped (optional)
1½ pounds beef, cut into large pieces
salt to taste
lemon juice to taste

1. Grind coriander, ginger, cumin, pepper, turmeric, chili powder, mustard, and vinegar to a paste. Set aside.

2. Heat vegetable oil in a skillet. Add onion, garlic, and chilies. Sauté 4 minutes. Add paste and cook 3 minutes.
3. Add meat and simmer until tender. Before serving, add salt and lemon juice to taste. Yield: 4 servings.

Lamb Vindaloo

This version of vindaloo features lamb, seasoned with cardamom, fenugreek, cloves, and cinnamon and simmered in a thick tomato-based sauce.

2 tablespoons vinegar
1 tablespoon ground coriander
1 tablespoon ground cumin
½ teaspoon ground turmeric
1 teaspoon ground mustard
½ teaspoon ground cardamom
1 teaspoon ground fenugreek
½ teaspoon ground cloves
1 teaspoon red pepper
½ teaspoon cinnamon
6 tablespoons vegetable oil
1 large onion, chopped
5 cloves garlic, finely minced
1 tablespoon finely chopped fresh ginger
2 pounds lamb, cubed
½ cup tomato sauce, diluted with ½ cup warm water
1½ teaspoons salt
½ teaspoon sugar
2 tablespoons tamarind juice or lemon juice
2 tablespoons chopped fresh coriander leaves

1. Mix vinegar, coriander, cumin, turmeric, mustard, cardamom, fenugreek, cloves, red pepper, and cinnamon to a paste. Set aside.
2. Heat vegetable oil in a skillet. Add chopped onions, garlic, and ginger. Sauté onions lightly. Add the paste and cook 2 to 3 minutes.

3. Add meat and brown on all sides. Add tomato-water mixture, salt, and sugar. Bring to a boil over low heat. Simmer, half-covered, until the meat is tender. Add lemon juice or tamarind juice to taste. Mix lightly. Sprinkle with coriander leaves. Yield: 4 to 6 servings.

Lamb Molee

Molees are popular in South India, Malay, and Ceylon, where coconuts grow abundantly. Coconut milk is the base of the thick creamy molee sauce, which is mildly spiced. Do not cover the pan at any time during cooking, and bring the milk to a boil very slowly so it will not turn oily.

6 tablespoons vegetable oil
2 pounds lamb, cut into thin slices
1 large onion, thinly sliced
4 cloves garlic, thinly sliced
1 tablespoon minced fresh ginger
½ teaspoon turmeric
¼ teaspoon red pepper (optional)
4 whole cardamom pods
4 cloves
1-inch stick cinnamon
1 teaspoon ground fenugreek
½ teaspoon ground mustard
2 cups coconut milk (see index)
½ teaspoon sugar
salt to taste
1 small eggplant, sliced
lemon juice to taste

1. Heat 4 tablespoons of the vegetable oil in a skillet. Sauté the lamb until brown on all sides. Remove from skillet.
2. To the same oil, add onions, garlic, and ginger. Sauté until the onions are translucent.
3. Remove skillet from heat. Add turmeric and red pepper. Stir a few times.

4. Return skillet to heat. Add cardamom, cloves, cinnamon, fenugreek, and mustard. Cook ½ minute.
5. Add 2 cups coconut milk and sugar. Bring to a boil. Simmer, uncovered, 10 minutes over medium-low heat. Add browned meat and salt to taste. Simmer over low heat until meat is tender.
6. Just before serving, cook eggplant slices in remaining 2 tablespoons vegetable oil until brown and crisp. Add these to meat. Sprinkle with lemon juice. Yield: 4 to 6 servings.

Pork Cutlets

These meat cutlets—strictly a British influence—are brushed with spicy Indian seasonings.

1½ pounds finely ground pork
2 medium-sized onions, minced
1 tablespoon garam masala (see index)
3 tablespoons fresh coriander leaves
¼ teaspoon red pepper or 3 green chilies, chopped
1 slice bread, soaked in ½ cup milk
⅛ teaspoon cinnamon
salt to taste
3 tablespoons vegetable oil
4 eggs, well beaten

1. Mix all ingredients except eggs and vegetable oil. Shape into 4 to 6 patties.
2. Heat vegetable oil in a skillet. Dip patties into beaten egg and place in skillet. Cook until golden. Serve with Nan or Chapatis (see index) and spicy chutneys.

Kashmiri Lamb or Pork Chops

Mildly spiced chops are cooked with quartered, juicy tomatoes. Potatoes or carrots can be added as well.

1 tablespoon vegetable oil
2 pounds lamb or pork chops

2 medium-sized onions, sliced
1 tablespoon ground coriander
1 teaspoon ground ginger
5 tomatoes, quartered
½ teaspoon ground cardamom
½ teaspoon caraway seed
pinch of nutmeg
salt to taste
1 tablespoon lemon juice
3 tablespoons fresh coriander leaves

1. Heat vegetable oil in a large skillet. Spread oil so it covers entire surface of skillet. Cook the chops until lightly browned.
2. Add all remaining ingredients except coriander leaves. Be sure to sprinkle the ground spices over each meat piece. Cook covered over low heat until chops are done. Check frequently to see that meat does not stick to skillet. If so, add a few tablespoons water. Sprinkle with coriander leaves and serve with rice and Chapatis (see index). Yield: 4 to 6 servings.

Madras Lamb or Pork Chops

This South Indian dish has a whisper of coconut and outspoken, snappy chilies.

2 pounds lamb or pork chops
4 cups water
1 medium-sized onion, sliced
1-inch stick cinnamon, broken into small pieces
5 green chilies (optional)
1 tablespoon chopped fresh ginger
¼ cup grated fresh coconut or packaged unsweetened coconut
5 cloves garlic
3 cloves
½ cup chopped fresh coriander leaves

½ teaspoon cumin seeds
salt to taste
½ cup vegetable oil for frying

1. Boil chops in 4 cups water 10 minutes.
2. Meanwhile, grind all remaining ingredients except oil to a smooth paste.
3. Marinate chops in paste for 1 hour.
4. Heat vegetable oil in a skillet and fry chops until golden and oil separates. Fry only a few chops at a time so that they will brown properly. Yield: 4 to 5 servings.

Goanese Pork Curry

This is a really hot and spicy curry, concocted by descendants of the Portuguese living in Goa.

15 dry red chilies
15 cloves garlic
2 tablespoons vinegar
2 tablespoons chopped fresh ginger
¼ teaspoon ground cardamom
⅛ teaspoon ground cinnamon
⅛ teaspoon ground cloves
4 tablespoons vegetable oil
2 large onions, chopped
2 pounds pork, cubed
2 cups water
salt to taste
½ cup chopped fresh coriander leaves

1. Soak chilies and garlic in vinegar 2 hours.
2. Grind chilies, garlic, vinegar, ginger, cardamom, cinnamon, and cloves to a paste.
3. Heat vegetable oil in a skillet. Add onions and sauté until golden. Add ground paste and cook until oil separates.

4. Add pork and brown on all sides. Add 2 cups water and bring to a boil. Simmer over low heat until meat is tender. Add salt to taste and coriander leaves. Serve with rice. Yield: 4 to 6 servings.

Pork Korma

This is a dark, rich curry, thickened with yogurt.

5 tablespoons vegetable oil
3 large onions, chopped
6 cloves garlic, chopped
1 teaspoon ground ginger
1 teaspoon cumin seed
2 to 3 bay leaves
5 whole cardamom pods
6 cloves
1 teaspoon freshly ground black pepper
½ cup chopped fresh coriander leaves
1½ pounds pork, cubed
½ cup tomato sauce
½ cup water
2 cups yogurt
salt to taste

1. Heat vegetable oil in a skillet and cook onions and garlic until golden.
2. Add all remaining ingredients except pork, tomato sauce, water, yogurt, and salt to taste. Cook 2 minutes.
3. Add pork and brown on all sides. Cook covered 10 minutes.
4. Add tomato sauce and ½ cup water. Bring to a boil. Lower heat and simmer covered until meat is done.
5. Beat the yogurt and add to the meat along with salt to taste. Stir a few times. Simmer 5 minutes. Serve with rice and Chapatis (see index). Yield: 4 to 5 servings.

Sheekh Kabab

It is not uncommon to see these mildly spiced ground-meat kababs prepared over charcoal fires in the marketplaces of Kashmir and Agra near the Taj Mahal. They are great for outdoor barbecues.

1 tablespoon minced fresh ginger
1 green chili, finely chopped
1 tablespoon finely chopped coriander leaves
8 black peppercorns
1 teaspoon cumin seed
½ cup yogurt
2 tablespoons melted butter
1 pound ground beef or lamb
vegetable oil for greasing skewers
1 onion, thinly sliced
1 lemon, sliced

1. Grind ginger, green chili, coriander leaves, peppercorns, and cumin seed to a smooth paste. Add yogurt and melted butter. Mix well. Combine well with the ground meat.
2. Grease the skewers well with vegetable oil. Press the meat mixture around the skewers in thick 2½-inch lengths.
3. Broil kababs until brown and crisp on the outside and soft and juicy inside. Serve with slices of onion and lemon. Yield: 2 to 4 servings.

Goanese Sheekh Kababs

Cubed lamb and pork are cooked with a vindaloo sauce for these hot and sour kababs.

1 teaspoon ground coriander
1 teaspoon turmeric
¼ teaspoon ground cumin seed
¼ teaspoon chili powder
¼ teaspoon ground ginger

¼ teaspoon ground mustard seed
pinch of ground fenugreek
pinch of black pepper
2 tablespoons vinegar
1 pound lamb, cubed
1 pound pork, cubed
thin slices of green ginger
2 ounces butter
1 large onion, finely chopped
4 cloves garlic, sliced
6 green chilies, cut lengthwise
1 tablespoon tomato paste
1 tablespoon lime juice

1. Preheat oven to 350° F. To make the vindaloo paste, combine coriander, turmeric, cumin seed, chili powder, ground ginger, mustard seed, fenugreek, pepper, and vinegar. Mix well. Set aside.
2. Thread lamb and pork on skewers alternately with ginger slices. Place in baking pan and set aside.
3. Heat butter in a skillet. Add onions, garlic, and chilies. Sauté 3 minutes. Add vindaloo paste and tomato paste. Stir and blend well. Gradually sprinkle with lime juice and stir until a thick sauce forms.
4. Pour over the kababs in baking pan. Place in preheated oven and bake until meat is brown and done. Turn and baste occasionally. Yield: 4 servings.

Hoosaini Kababs

This dry curry consists of spiced oval-shaped ground-meat patties, either fried in a skillet or threaded on a skewer with vegetables and grilled.

3 tablespoons vegetable oil or butter
1 large onion, minced
2 teaspoons finely chopped fresh ginger
6 cloves garlic, minced

1 tablespoon grated fresh coconut
1 teaspoon each, ground: cloves, cumin, cinnamon, almonds, split-pea flour, turmeric, cardamom, coriander
¼ teaspoon chili powder (optional)
2 pounds ground lamb or beef
2 teaspoons salt
1 tablespoon finely chopped fresh mint or coriander
1 tablespoon lemon juice
2 eggs, lightly beaten

1. Heat vegetable oil in a skillet over medium-low heat. Add onions, ginger, garlic, and coconut. Cook 5 minutes. Add cloves, cumin, cinnamon, almonds, split-pea flour, turmeric, cardamom, coriander, and chili powder. Cook 5 minutes.
2. Add meat and salt and continue cooking over medium-low heat until mixture dries up. Add fresh coriander or mint; stir a few times and cool.
3. Grind the cooled, seasoned mixture into a fine paste. Add lemon juice and eggs. Form the mixture into oval-shaped patties, about 20 of them. Fry in a skillet containing 2 to 3 tablespoons vegetable oil, or thread patties on skewers alternately with a piece of ginger, garlic, and onion. Then baste with butter and grill. Yield: 4 to 6 servings.

Irani Kababs

The Moguls picked up this recipe long ago when they tramped through Persia, which is now Iran.

1 medium onion, finely chopped
1 egg, well beaten
1 teaspoon salt
¼ teaspoon red pepper (optional)
¼ teaspoon ground cloves
¼ teaspoon ground cinnamon
1 tablespoon chick-pea flour (or regular flour)
1 tablespoon chopped fresh coriander leaves

1 tablespoon chopped fresh mint
½ teaspoon ground cardamom
2 pounds ground lamb
2 large tomatoes

1. Thoroughly mix all ingredients (except tomatoes) with the lamb until a smooth paste is obtained. Refrigerate 2 hours.
2. Mix well again. Divide into 8 parts and shape into 8 oblong patties. Thread the patties on skewers, alternating with slices of tomatoes, and broil or grill until browned on all sides. Serve with Lemon Rice (see index). Yield: 4 servings.

Boti Kabab

This is a lemon-butter glazed kabab, made from small pieces of very tender meat that have been marinated several hours in a spiced yogurt. If the meat is grilled too rare, the spices will have a raw taste.

juice of 1 lime
5 cloves garlic, crushed
2 teaspoons poppy seed
1 teaspoon ground ginger
2 teaspoons turmeric
4 teaspoons ground coriander
¼ teaspoon cayenne pepper
1 teaspoon mustard seed
½ cup yogurt (plain or natural)
2 pounds sirloin or leg of lamb, cut into 1½-inch pieces
¼ cup melted butter plus juice of 1 lime

1. Grind the juice of 1 lime, garlic, poppy seed, ginger, turmeric, coriander, cayenne pepper, mustard seed, and yogurt to form a paste. Prick meat pieces with a fork and add to paste. Marinate 2 hours.
2. Thread meat on skewers and broil 15 minutes or until meat is done and glazed. Baste frequently with mixture of melted butter and lime juice. Yield: 8 servings.

Shami Kabab

Unlike other kababs, these spicy ground-meat patties are dipped in batter and deep fried.

3 tablespoons butter or vegetable oil
2 medium-sized onions, finely chopped or minced
5 cloves garlic
1 tablespoon ground or fresh chopped ginger
¼ teaspoon red pepper or chili powder (optional)
½ cup chopped coriander leaves or sweet pepper
1 tablespoon salt
¼ teaspoon turmeric
4 medium-sized tomatoes, sliced
2 pounds minced lean meat (beef, pork, or lamb)
2 tablespoons split peas
½ cup warm water
2 tablespoons lemon juice
1 teaspoon black pepper
1 teaspoon allspice
Shami Batter (recipe follows)
½ cup vegetable oil for frying

1. Heat 3 tablespoons butter or oil in a saucepan. Add onions, garlic, ginger, red pepper or chili powder, and chopped coriander leaves or sweet pepper. Sauté lightly. Add salt and turmeric and stir.
2. Add sliced tomatoes and cook 5 minutes. Add meat and split peas and cook 5 minutes. Add ½ cup warm water and bring to a boil. Lower heat and cook 45 minutes.
3. Add lemon juice, black pepper, and allspice. Remove from heat. Mix; then mash well. Mash a second time. Shape into 15 patties. Prepare Shami Batter.
4. Heat the ½ cup vegetable oil in a skillet. Coat each patty thoroughly in the batter and fry over medium heat until brown and crisp. Drain on paper towels. Serve with Dhania Chutney (see index) and wedges of lemon.

Shami Batter
4 tablespoons chick-pea or split-pea flour

4 tablespoons milk
½ teaspoon salt

Mix the chick-pea or split-pea flour with the milk and salt. Beat until batter is smooth.

Kathi Kabab

In Bengal, the meat pieces for this hot East Indian kabab are brushed with mustard oil, the eastern cooking medium.

1 teaspoon ground ginger
1 tablespoon ground cardamom
2 medium onions, finely chopped
2 teaspoons salt
½ teaspoon chili powder (optional)
1 tablespoon cumin seed
1 tablespoon red pepper (optional)
¼ teaspoon cinnamon
¼ teaspoon ground cloves
2 pounds leg of lamb, cubed
3 tablespoons vegetable oil
1 lime, sliced
1 onion, thinly sliced

1. Combine ginger, cardamom, onions, salt, chili powder, cumin seed, red pepper, cinnamon, and cloves in a large bowl. Add lamb cubes and marinate 2 hours.
2. Brush meat cubes with oil and thread them on skewers. Broil 10 minutes or until meat is brown on the outside and done on the inside. Serve garnished with lime and onion slices. Yield: 6 to 8 servings.

Rabbit Curry

This is a spicy, dry curry that is made with fresh tomatoes.

2 pounds rabbit meat, disjointed
3 tablespoons vegetable oil

7 cloves garlic, chopped
1 tablespoon chopped fresh ginger
3 large onions, chopped
½ teaspoon turmeric
1 tablespoon ground coriander
½ teaspoon red pepper (optional)
1 tablespoon garam masala (see index)
salt to taste
5 fresh tomatoes, chopped
2 tablespoons lemon juice
¼ cup chopped fresh coriander leaves

1. Soak rabbit meat in acidulated water (water to which 1 or 2 tablespoons of vinegar has been added) for a few hours. Rinse and dry carefully.
2. Heat vegetable oil in a saucepan. Add garlic, ginger, and onion. Cook 5 minutes. Add turmeric, ground coriander, red pepper, garam masala, and salt to taste. Cook 2 minutes. Add tomatoes. Cook until oil separates.
4. Add rabbit and cook 5 minutes. Lower heat and cook, covered, 1½ to 2 hours, until meat is done. If more sauce is desired, add 1 cup stock or water and simmer 5 to 7 minutes longer. Sprinkle with lemon juice and garnish with coriander leaves. Yield: 4 to 6 servings.

6

Poultry and Egg Dishes

Chicken and other poultry may very well be considered the filet mignon of India, since fowl is an expensive indulgence reserved for the wealthy.

Most Indians buy their fowl live in metropolitan marketplaces or from the poultry man who makes his rounds with his cart through the neighborhoods and rural areas. Fresh chickens and ducks can be found hanging from hooks in the few specialty stores having refrigeration.

Indian chicken is frequently tough and requires long, slow cooking. Since American chicken is much more tender, the cooking period is much shorter. Most of the recipes in this section require skinning the chicken and, in some cases, cutting the meat into small pieces in order to allow the spices to penetrate the meat. Fryers are the best choice for these dishes, as they are young and tender.

Eggs, an excellent source of protein, are enjoyed by Indians throughout the subcontinent. As a rule, they are hard-cooked first, then chopped and served with curry sauces mixed with vegetables. Several popular egg dishes can be found at the end of this section.

Tandoori Chicken

Tandoori Chicken, a specialty in Agra, has been acclaimed by many as the exotic jewel of Indian culinary art. It is reserved for special festive occasions. If the cooking is timed correctly, the crisp outside is an exquisite red-orange color, which is achieved with a combination of a dozen spices and colorings, and the inner meat is so tender and moist it falls from the bone.

1 tablespoon ground coriander
1 tablespoon ground cumin
1 tablespoon garlic powder
1 tablespoon ground ginger
1 tablespoon salt
1 teaspoon ground cardamom
1 teaspoon black pepper
¼ teaspoon turmeric
½ teaspoon red or orange food coloring
¼ teaspoon cinnamon
¼ teaspoon red pepper (optional)
¼ teaspoon ground nutmeg
¼ teaspoon mace
¼ teaspoon ground cloves
½ cup lemon juice
½ cup yogurt
1 tablespoon vinegar
1 tablespoon vegetable oil
3-pound fryer or 3 pounds legs and breasts
3 tablespoons butter
¼ teaspoon saffron
1 tablespoon ground dry mango powder mixed with
    ¼ teaspoon salt
1 onion, sliced into rings
lemon wedges

1. Mix well all ingredients except chicken, butter, saffron, mango powder, onion rings, and lemon wedges. Set the paste aside.

2. Skin, wash, and clean the chicken. Pierce all over with a fork. Make deep cuts in the breasts. Rub the paste all over chicken and refrigerate for 25 to 48 hours. While marinating, turn chicken pieces a few times and rub in paste gently.
3. One hour before cooking, remove chicken from refrigerator and let sit at room temperature. Preheat broiler to 350° F.
4. In a small saucepan, warm butter and add saffron. Set aside.
5. Place chicken in a baking tray. Broil for 10 minutes. Baste with saffron butter.
6. Broil for another 10 minutes. Baste again with saffron butter and broil a few minutes more, until chicken is tender. Sprinkle mango powder over chicken and serve with onion rings and lemon wedges. Yield: 4 servings.

Chili Chicken

This recipe features snappy capsicum—cayenne pepper—introduced to India by the Portuguese. Eventually, it journeyed to the Orient. This version follows the Chinese method of cooking.

2-pound fryer
½ teaspoon black pepper
½ teaspoon cayenne pepper
1 teaspoon salt
1 tablespoon flour
2 egg whites
1 cup vegetable oil
pinch of salt
5 medium-sized mushrooms
2 tablespoons onions, finely chopped
1 medium-sized capsicum, cut into 8 lengthwise pieces
6 cloves garlic

½ teaspoon chopped fresh ginger
1 teaspoon salt
Curry Sauce (recipe follows)

1. Skin chicken and remove bones. Cut into 1-inch pieces.
2. Dust pieces with mixture of black pepper, cayenne pepper, and 1 teaspoon salt.
3. Beat the flour with egg whites until they froth. Coat chicken with the mixture.
4. Heat vegetable oil in a skillet and fry chicken, several pieces at a time, until golden brown. Remove from skillet and set aside.
5. Place salt, mushrooms, onions, capsicum, garlic, and ginger in the same oil used for chicken and sauté 15 minutes. Meanwhile, prepare Curry Sauce.
6. Add chicken and curry sauce. Cook 5 minutes. Serve hot with boiled rice or noodles and vegetables. Yield: 4 servings.

Curry Sauce:

1 teaspoon flour
½ teaspoon white pepper
½ teaspoon salt
1 teaspoon sugar
½ cup chicken stock
1 tablespoon vinegar
1 tablespoon soy sauce

Mix together all ingredients, blending well. Add to cooked, diced chicken and seasonings.

Chicken Korma

This chicken korma is very mellow. It was brought to India by the Mogul emperors.

3 tablespoons yogurt
¼ teaspoon turmeric

2 cloves garlic, crushed
3-pound fryer, disjointed and skinned
2 ounces butter
1 large onion, halved and sliced into thin wedges
2 cloves garlic, sliced lengthwise
6 whole cardamom pods
1-inch piece ginger, finely sliced
6 cloves
2-inch stick cinnamon
1 teaspoon ground coriander
1 teaspoon ground almonds
¼ teaspoon ground cumin seed
pinch of ground chilies (optional)
¼ teaspoon black pepper
salt to taste
lemon juice to taste

1. Mix yogurt with turmeric and crushed garlic. Rub the marinade over chicken pieces and set aside 1 hour at room temperature.
2. Heat butter in a skillet. Add onions, 2 sliced cloves garlic, cardamom, ginger, cloves, and cinnamon. Sauté 5 minutes. Add coriander, almonds, cumin seed, chilies, and black pepper. Cook over low heat 4 minutes.
3. Add the chicken and marinade. Mix gently. Cover and simmer 1 hour, until chicken is tender. Do not add any liquid. The korma will form a thick, rich sauce of its own. Before serving, add salt and lemon juice to taste. Yield: 4 servings.

Murg Musallam

This subtly spiced, dry chicken curry is prepared by one of two methods: with the chicken whole or cut into pieces, as in the recipe below.

5-pound fryer or 5 pounds legs and breasts, skinned
1 cup yogurt
1 tablespoon salt

1 teaspoon ground ginger
½ teaspoon turmeric
1 teaspoon garlic powder
¼ teaspoon cayenne pepper (optional)
1 cup vegetable oil
2 large onions, chopped
1 tablespoon ground coriander
1 tablespoon ground cumin
1 tablespoon ground almonds
½ cup desiccated coconut (fresh)
¼ teaspoon ground nutmeg
¼ teaspoon ground mace
½ teaspoon ground cinnamon
½ teaspoon ground cloves
1 tablespoon ground cardamom
1 cup warm water
2 tablespoons milk
¼ teaspoon saffron
½ cup finely chopped fresh coriander leaves
lemon juice to taste

1. Separate drumsticks from thighs. Pierce chicken pieces with a fork. Make a few deep cuts in the breasts.
2. Mix yogurt with salt, ginger, turmeric, garlic powder, and cayenne pepper. Rub this paste over the chicken and marinate 2 hours.
3. Heat vegetable oil in a large, heavy, deep skillet and fry onions until golden. Remove onions and set aside to cool.
4. Dry roast the following at medium-low heat for 2 to 3 minutes: ground coriander, cumin, almonds, coconut, nutmeg, and mace.
5. Place the fried onions and all roasted ingredients in a blender and grind to a fine paste. Transfer to a bowl and add cinnamon, cloves, and cardamom. Mix well. This is your masala.
6. Reheat oil in which onions were fried and brown marinated chicken. Pour the ground masala paste over the chicken and stir. Pour in 1 cup warm water. Simmer until chicken is tender.

7. In a small saucepan, warm the milk and add saffron. Gradually add to chicken, stirring slowly. Cook 2 more minutes. Sprinkle coriander leaves and lemon juice over chicken. Yield: 4 to 6 servings.

Country Captain

This Goanese dry curry is popular all the way up the West coast to Bombay. One story has it that *captain* is a corruption of *capon*. Another explanation is that during early British occupancy, many people visiting India were lodged in dak bungalows. One of the only available foods was chicken, cooked quickly in the few available spices. Since most sahibs were military men then, this chicken dish was dubbed Country Captain.

3 tablespoons vegetable oil
3-pound fryer, disjointed
1 large onion, finely chopped
2 tablespoons finely chopped fresh ginger
3 red chilies, cut lengthwise (optional)
¼ teaspoon black pepper
1 teaspoon salt
1 cup water
1 tablespoon chopped fresh coriander

1. Heat vegetable oil in a skillet. Add chicken pieces and cook until lightly browned. Remove chicken and set aside.
2. In same skillet and oil, sauté onions until translucent. Add ginger, chilies, and black pepper. Stir and cook a few minutes.
3. Add the chicken, salt, and 1 cup water. Simmer until tender, about 1 hour. Sprinkle with chopped coriander before serving. Yield: 4 servings.

Chicken Molee

Chicken is simmered in a subtle coconut sauce for this South Indian dish, often made with leftover cooked chicken.

1 tablespoon butter
1 large onion, chopped
1 clove garlic, sliced
3 chilies, cut lengthwise, seeds removed
6 thin slices fresh ginger
2-inch stick cinnamon
1 teaspoon turmeric
6 cloves
2 cups coconut milk (see index)
salt to taste
2½ to 3 pounds cooked chicken pieces, skinned

1. Heat butter in a skillet. Add onions and sauté 2 minutes. Add garlic, chilies, ginger, and cinnamon. Stir and cook until onions are golden. Add turmeric and cloves. Lower heat and cook 4 minutes.
2. Gradually pour in coconut milk and sprinkle in salt to taste. Slowly bring to a boil.
3. Add cold chicken and heat thoroughly. Do not cover the pan at any time or the molee will turn oily. Yield: 4 to 6 servings.

Chicken Vindaloo

A spice and vinegar paste is fried with chilies and chicken for this spicy, fiery curry, popular with South and West Indians.

½ cup vinegar
½ teaspoon ground cloves
¼ teaspoon ground cinnamon
½ teaspoon turmeric
1 teaspoon ground ginger
1 teaspoon black pepper
½ teaspoon red pepper

1 teaspoon ground mustard seed
1 tablespoon cumin seed
2 tablespoons ground coriander
3 chilies, cut lengthwise, with seeds removed
4 tablespoons vegetable oil
2 large onions, finely chopped
4 cloves garlic, chopped
3-pound fryer, disjointed and skinned
1 tablespoon salt
1 cup warm water

1. Mix vinegar, cloves, cinnamon, turmeric, ginger, black pepper, red pepper, mustard seed, cumin seed, coriander, and chilies to a paste. Set aside.
2. Heat vegetable oil in a skillet. Add onions and garlic. Sauté until golden. Add the paste and cook 5 minutes over medium-low heat.
3. Add chicken, salt, and 1 cup warm water. Mix well and simmer, covered, until chicken is tender, about 1 hour. Yield: 4 to 5 servings.

Malabari Chicken

A thin coconut curry, this South Indian dish is softly seasoned.

½ cup vegetable oil
3 medium-sized onions, chopped
1 tablespoon ground cumin
1 tablespoon ground coriander
1 tablespoon unsweetened desiccated coconut
5 cloves garlic
1 tablespoon fresh chopped ginger
1 cup chopped fresh coriander leaves
3-pound fryer, disjointed and skinned
½ teaspoon ground cloves
½ teaspoon ground cardamom
½ teaspoon black pepper
¼ teaspoon ground cinnamon
½ cup warm water

salt to taste
2 cups thin coconut milk (see index)
2 tablespoons lemon juice

1. Heat vegetable oil in a skillet and sauté ⅔ of the chopped onions until golden. Remove from skillet with slotted spoon and remove skillet from heat.
2. Dry roast cumin, ground coriander, and coconut for 2 minutes. Grind dry-roasted ingredients with the sautéed onions. Blend to a smooth paste. Transfer to a bowl.
3. Grind garlic, ginger, and coriander leaves to a smooth paste, using a little water.
4. Heat oil again. Add remaining chopped onions and sauté 3 minutes. Add garlic-ginger-coriander paste and cook 5 minutes.
5. Add chicken and cook 3 minutes.
6. Add ground onion paste and stir a few times. Add cloves, cardamom, black pepper, cinnamon, ½ cup warm water, and salt to taste. Cover and cook until chicken is almost done.
7. Add coconut milk and lemon juice. Cook 5 minutes. Yield: 4 servings.

Malai Chicken

For this tasty dish, chicken is marinated in a hot and spicy yogurt, then simmered in a creamy tomato sauce.

3 pounds chicken breasts and legs
½ cup yogurt
½ cup lemon juice
1 tablespoon salt
1 teaspoon ground cardamom
½ teaspoon ground cloves
½ teaspoon ground cinnamon
1 teaspoon black pepper
¼ teaspoon red pepper
1 tablespoon vinegar

Poultry and Egg Dishes 95

1 tablespoon vegetable oil
Tomato-Cream Sauce (recipe follows)
4 tablespoons butter
1 tablespoon chopped fresh ginger
½ teaspoon cumin seed
1 teaspoon garam masala (see index)
½ cup chopped fresh coriander leaves

1. Skin chicken pieces and pierce all over with a fork.
2. Mix yogurt, lemon juice, salt, cardamom, cloves, cinnamon, black pepper, red pepper, vinegar, and vegetable oil to a paste. Rub it over the chicken and marinate 3 to 4 hours.
3. One hour before removing chicken from marinade, prepare Tomato-Cream Sauce.
4. Place chicken in a baking pan and broil for 20 minutes, or until the chicken is tender, turning it several times.
5. Heat butter in a skillet. Add broiled chicken and fry. Remove from skillet.
6. In same butter, sauté the ginger and cumin seed for ½ minute. Add to the tomato-cream sauce and heat a few minutes.
7. Add the chicken pieces to sauce and heat 10 minutes. Sprinkle with garam masala and coriander leaves. Yield: 4 servings.

Tomato-Cream Sauce:
6 tablespoons butter
7 medium-sized tomatoes, coarsely chopped
¼ teaspoon red pepper
1 teaspoon salt
1 teaspoon sugar
½ cup whipping cream
2 tablespoons lemon juice

1. Heat butter in pot. Add tomatoes and cook over medium-high heat for 15 minutes, or until a thick tomato sauce forms.

2. Add red pepper, salt, and sugar. Mix well and pass through a strainer.
3. Beat cream well and mix it with the tomato sauce. Add lemon juice. Return to pot and simmer for a few minutes.

Fowl Curry

This recipe calls for a mature hen which is heavier and less tender than a roasting chicken.

10 cloves garlic
1 tablespoon chopped fresh ginger
1 teaspoon cumin seed
½ teaspoon red pepper
1 teaspoon turmeric
4-pound fowl, disjointed
2½ cups water
2 medium-sized potatoes, boiled and cubed
salt to taste
2 tablespoons vegetable oil
1 small onion, chopped
1 cup freshly shredded coconut
1 tablespoon lemon juice

1. Grind garlic, ginger and cumin to a paste.
2. Place in a bowl and mix with red pepper and turmeric. Rub this paste over the chicken.
3. Place chicken in a saucepan. Add 2½ cups water. Bring to a boil and cook over low heat until meat is tender.
4. Add potatoes and salt to taste. Stir a few times.
5. Heat vegetable oil in a skillet and sauté onions until golden.
6. Grind shredded coconut, adding a little water.
7. Add sautéed onions and ground coconut to chicken. Bring to a boil; then simmer 5 minutes. Add lemon juice and mix well. Yield: 4 to 6 servings.

Chicken Liver Curry

These chicken livers, simmered in a spicy but not hot curry, are good with rice and Nan or Chapatis (see index).

3 tablespoons vegetable oil
5 whole cardamom pods
3 bay leaves
1 teaspoon cumin seed
1 tablespoon chopped fresh ginger
5 cloves garlic, chopped
2 large onions, chopped
½ teaspoon turmeric
2 cups chicken broth
1 pound chicken livers, washed and dried
2 tablespoons vinegar
2 tablespoons chopped fresh coriander leaves

1. Heat vegetable oil in a skillet. Add cardamom and bay leaves. Cook 1 minute. Add cumin, ginger, garlic, and onions. Sauté until onions are golden.
2. Remove skillet from heat. Add turmeric and stir a few times.
3. Return skillet to heat. Add chicken broth and bring to a boil. Simmer over medium-low heat 20 minutes.
4. Add livers and vinegar. Simmer until livers are done. Garnish with coriander leaves and serve. Yield: 4 servings.

Parsee Chicken Curry

The Parsees are known for their hot and highly seasoned chicken and meat curries.

3- to 4-pound fryer, cut up
1 tablespoon chopped ginger
1 teaspoon cumin seed
2 green chilies (optional)
8 cloves garlic

¼ teaspoon ground cloves
¼ teaspoon cinnamon
¼ teaspoon ground cardamom
salt to taste
2 tablespoons vinegar
2 tablespoons Worcestershire Sauce
1 tablespoon black pepper
2 tablespoons all-purpose flour
vegetable oil for deep frying
4 eggs, beaten

1. Pierce chicken pieces lightly with a fork and set aside.
2. Grind ginger, cumin seed, chilies, and garlic to a fine paste, adding a few drops of water.
3. Pour paste into a bowl and mix with cloves, cinnamon, and cardamom.
4. Add remaining ingredients, except oil and eggs. Rub chicken pieces with the paste and marinate 1 hour.
5. Heat vegetable oil for deep frying. Dip chicken pieces into beaten eggs and fry until golden. Serve with any Indian bread. Yield: 4 to 6 servings.

Sour Chicken Curry

This curry gets its pucker from the tamarind juice used so often in South Indian foods.

3- to 4-pound fryer, cut up
½ teaspoon ground ginger
1 tablespoon freshly ground black pepper
½ teaspoon turmeric
1 tablespoon ground coriander
¼ teaspoon red pepper
¼ teaspoon ground cardamom
¼ cup tamarind soaked 1 hour in ½ cup water
salt to taste
2 tablespoons butter
2 onions, sliced
lemon wedges

1. Place chicken pieces in a saucepan with just enough water to cover the chicken. Bring to a boil. Then simmer 5 minutes.
2. Make a paste with all the ground spices, adding a few drops of water.
3. Add this paste to the chicken. Simmer until chicken is tender.
4. Strain the tamarind juice and discard the pulp. Add juice to chicken along with salt to taste. Simmer 5 minutes.
5. Heat butter in a skillet and sauté onions until golden.
6. Add onions to chicken. Stir and bring to a boil. Remove from heat. Serve with plain boiled rice and lemon wedges. Yield: 4 to 6 servings.

Duck Korma

Kormas are aromatic, rich curries with lots of hearty character. Rich duck meat enhances this sauce.

1 cup yogurt
½ teaspoon salt
1 tablespoon ground coriander
1 tablespoon ground cumin
1 tablespoon red pepper (optional)
¼ teaspoon turmeric
½ teaspoon black pepper
1 teaspoon ground almonds
pinch of mace
3- to 4-pound duck, disjointed
2 tablespoons vegetable oil
5 whole cardamom pods
1-inch stick cinnamon
5 cloves
2 to 3 bay leaves
1 large onion, chopped
salt to taste
1 tablespoon lemon juice
3 tablespoons chopped fresh coriander leaves

1. Mix yogurt with ½ teaspoon salt, ground coriander, cumin, red pepper, turmeric, black pepper, almonds, and mace. Marinate duck in this mixture 2 to 3 hours.
2. Heat vegetable oil in a large skillet. Add cardamom, cinnamon, cloves, and bay leaves. Cook 1 minute or until cinnamon expands.
3. Add onion and cook until golden. Add duck and marinade. Cook 2 to 3 minutes. Add salt to taste and cook covered over low heat until tender. Sprinkle with lemon juice and garnish with coriander leaves. Serve with any Indian bread. Yield: 4 to 5 servings.

Duck Curry

The coconut sauce in this curry is tart with tamarind and snappy with peppers, as South Indian chefs prepare it.

4 tablespoons vegetable oil
2 large onions, chopped
2 cloves garlic, crushed
½ teaspoon turmeric
1 teaspoon ground cumin
1 teaspoon ground fenugreek
1 teaspoon ground ginger
½ teaspoon red pepper
3- to 4-pound duck, disjointed
1½ cups water
salt to taste
2 tablespoons lemon juice
½ cup shredded fresh coconut soaked 1 hour in 1 cup water

1. Heat vegetable oil in skillet and sauté onions until translucent. Add garlic and cook 1 minute longer.
2. Add turmeric, cumin, fenugreek, ginger, and red pepper. Cook 2 minutes.
3. Add duck and sauté until browned.
4. Add 1½ cups water. Bring to a boil; then simmer over low heat until duck is tender.

5. Add salt and lemon juice.
6. Strain coconut milk, discard coconut, and add milk to duck. Simmer 2 to 3 minutes. Serve with rice and Chapatis (see index). Yield: 4 to 6 servings.

Bhuna Batak

Roast duck is filled with a typically northern stuffing of potatoes, onions, and garam masala.

3- to 4-pound duck
¼ teaspoon turmeric
1 teaspoon black pepper
¼ teaspoon red pepper (optional)
½ teaspoon salt
¼ cup butter
1 large potato, boiled and mashed
salt to taste
2 large onions, chopped
1 teaspoon garam masala (see index)
3 slices bread, soaked in ½ cup milk

1. Chop giblets and set aside. Preheat oven to 350° F.
2. Combine turmeric, black pepper, red pepper, ½ teaspoon salt, and butter. Smear the mixture all over the duck.
3. Combine potato, giblets, salt to taste, onions, garam masala, and crumbled bread. Stuff the duck with the mixture. Then close the vent and truss the bird.
4. Place duck breast side up in a roasting pan and prick all over with a fork. Bake 15 minutes.
5. Turn the bird on one side and prick all over with a fork. Roast 15 to 20 minutes.
6. Turn bird to other side. Prick all over and roast 15 minutes.
7. Turn bird breast side up and roast 15 minutes.
8. Lift bird out of pan and pour juices into a bowl.
9. Place duck back in pan. Baste with a little butter and roast 30 minutes, basting occasionally with its own juices. Serve with Parathas (see index). Yield: 4 to 5 servings.

Duck Vindaloo

Rich duck meat is an ideal base for a hot and sour Goanese vindaloo.

2 tablespoons vinegar
10 cloves garlic
1 tablespoon chopped fresh ginger
½ teaspoon turmeric
6 dry red chilies, whole
10 black peppercorns
1 teaspoon cumin seed
4 tablespoons vegetable oil
1-inch stick cinnamon
2 large onions, chopped
3- to 4-pound duck, disjointed
salt to taste
½ cup tomato sauce
1 cup water
2 tablespoons sugar
2 tablespoons vinegar

1. Grind together 2 tablespoons of the vinegar, garlic, ginger, turmeric, red chilies, peppercorns, and cumin seed to a smooth paste.
2. Heat vegetable oil in a large skillet. Add cinnamon stick. When it expands, add onion and sauté until golden.
3. Add spice paste and cook until oil separates, 5 to 7 minutes.
4. Add duck pieces. Cook until browned.
5. Add salt, tomato sauce, and 1 cup water. Bring to a boil. Then simmer over medium-low heat until duck is tender. Add sugar and remaining 2 tablespoons vinegar. Cook 5 minutes. Serve with rice and Parathas (see index). You can use the same recipe for making goose curry. Yield: 4 to 5 servings.

Pheasant or Partridge, Indian Style

A relatively uncomplicated dry curry, this dish is mildly spiced.

4-pound pheasant or partridge
1 small onion, chopped
½ teaspoon turmeric
½ teaspoon red pepper (optional)
4 tablespoons butter
salt to taste
1 tablespoon black pepper

1. Wipe the bird with a damp cloth and cut it into serving pieces.
2. Grind onion, turmeric, and red pepper to a paste. Rub the paste over the meat pieces and set aside.
3. Heat butter in a saucepan. Add meat, except breasts, and cook until half done.
4. Add breasts and salt to taste. Add a few tablespoons water if meat starts to stick to pan. Cook until tender, about 1½ hours. Sprinkle with black pepper. Yield: 4 to 5 servings.

Madras Egg Curry

Indian egg curries are popular throughout the subcontinent. The eggs are usually hard-cooked and added to a thick sauce.

1 cup shredded fresh coconut
3 green chilies (optional)
½ teaspoon mustard seed
6 cloves garlic, chopped
½ teaspoon cumin seed
½ teaspoon black pepper
1 teaspoon ground coriander

¼ teaspoon cinnamon
½ teaspoon turmeric
⅛ teaspoon red pepper
1 tablespoon water
3 tablespoons vegetable oil
2 large onions, sliced
2 large potatoes, boiled and cubed
salt to taste
7 to 8 medium-sized hard-cooked eggs, shelled and halved
1 tablespoon lemon juice
2 tablespoons chopped fresh coriander leaves

1. Soak coconut in 2 cups lukewarm water 30 minutes, gently rubbing coconut a few times. Strain and reserve coconut milk.
2. Grind together chilies, mustard seed, garlic, cumin seed, black pepper, ground coriander, cinnamon, turmeric, and red pepper, adding 1 tablespoon water. Set aside.
3. Heat vegetable oil in a saucepan. Sauté onions until translucent. Add ground paste and cook until oil separates.
4. Add potatoes and cook 2 minutes. Add coconut milk and salt to taste. Bring to a boil. Then lower heat and simmer 15 to 20 minutes, until a thick sauce is obtained.
5. Add eggs and lemon juice, and simmer until eggs are heated through. Sprinkle with chopped coriander leaves and serve with rice and Indian bread. Yield: 4 to 6 servings.

Tandoori Eggs

In North India, these eggs would be baked in a cylindrical clay tandoori oven.

1 tablespoon butter
4 tablespoons yogurt
¼ teaspoon cinnamon
4 whole cardamom pods

5 black peppercorns
½ teaspoon ground coriander
5 cloves
5 cloves garlic
pinch of nutmeg
1 teaspoon poppy seeds
⅛ teaspoon red pepper
1 tablespoon chopped fresh ginger
1 tablespoon lemon juice
½ teaspoon cumin seeds
½ cup chopped onions
salt to taste
8 medium-sized hard-cooked eggs, shelled and halved

1. Preheat oven to 400° F. Grind all ingredients together except eggs.
2. Place eggs in a pyrex dish and pour the ground mixture evenly over all the eggs. Bake 5 to 7 minutes. Serve tandoori eggs with Chapatis (see index). Yield: 4 to 6 servings.

Matar Anda Curry

This peas and egg curry is a softly spiced and stunning entrée, worthy of a rajah's table.

3 tablespoons butter
2 whole cardamom pods
2 bay leaves
2 medium-sized onions, sliced
1 tablespoon ground coriander
¼ teaspoon turmeric
1 cup green peas
3 tomatoes, chopped
1½ cups warm water
4 hard-cooked eggs, shelled and quartered
salt to taste
2 tablespoons chopped fresh coriander leaves

1. Heat butter in a saucepan. Add cardamom, bay leaves, and onions. Sauté 5 minutes.

2. Add ground coriander, turmeric, peas, and tomatoes. Cook 5 minutes.
3. Add 1½ cups warm water and bring to a boil. Then simmer over low heat 15 minutes.
4. Add quartered eggs and season with salt to taste. Stir lightly a few times. Heat the eggs through. Sprinkle with coriander leaves. Serve with Parathas or Chapatis (see index) and rice. Yield: 4 to 6 servings.

Omelette Pakaki Curry

This hot but sumptuous curry is flavored with spinach and tomatoes.

5 eggs
salt to taste
1 teaspoon garam masala (see index)
1 tablespoon butter
1 pound fresh or thawed spinach
2 tablespoons butter
1 large onion, sliced
5 cloves garlic
1 tablespoon chopped fresh ginger
2 green chilies (optional)
1 teaspoon ground cumin
3 large tomatoes, chopped
1 cup water
2 tablespoons chopped fresh coriander leaves

1. Beat eggs until yolks are lemon colored. Add salt to taste and garam masala. Beat again.
2. Heat 1 tablespoon butter in a skillet. Pour in egg mixture and cook an omelette ¼-inch thick. Cut into small serving pieces. Set aside and keep warm.
3. Salt spinach and cook in a covered saucepan for 5 minutes. Grind spinach to a paste.

4. Heat 2 tablespoons butter in a saucepan and cook onions, garlic, ginger, and chilies until onions are golden. Add cumin and tomatoes. Cook a few minutes more.
5. Add 1 cup water. Simmer 10 minutes.
6. Add omelette pieces and heat them through. Stir lightly a few times. Garnish with coriander leaves.

7

Fish and Seafood Dishes

India's vast coastline is silvered with the sunbathed waters of the Bay of Bengal in the East, the Indian Ocean in the South, and the Arabian Sea in the West, all of which yield a wealth of fish and seafood. Indians have a choice of more than two thousand varieties of seafood and inland fresh-water fish. Even the most orthodox Hindu living along the coast will eat fish.

Some of the finest shrimp, prawns, lobsters, and crabs in the world are netted in India's coastal waters. The largest prawns weigh one pound, after shelling and cleaning. The catches are so abundant that the surplus is salted and dried. Oysters netted from ancient beds can be as small as a quarter or as large as a dinner plate.

Pomfret is a seafish prepared as a grand offering at festive dinners and official banquets. It resembles a butter fish and is flat and from eight to ten inches long. Striped bass or flounder are excellent substitutes. New Delhi is one of the few inland areas where it is available. Cod is the best stand-in for rahu, an Indian fresh-water delicacy. Sole, flounder, cod, and halibut are comparable to many Indian fish. Substitutes are given in the fish recipes in this section.

Indians prepare their fish in many ways. Since coconut palms fringe most of the warm, sandy beaches, fish caught in these areas are usually cooked in coconut milk or grated coconut. There are koftas, kababs, thick curries, tandooris, and sumptuous stuffed fish. Batter-fried fish is an Indian specialty.

When possible, use fresh fish. Select those with bright eyes and very red gills. Be especially careful not to overcook the fish. Unlike Indian meat dishes, fish entrées require a short cooking time. But like meat dishes, they are often marinated in spiced yogurt or vinegar and lemon juice.

Most of the fish dishes in this chapter are served with rice and accompanied by vegetable curries and breads. They need not be served with Indian accompaniments, however. They may be combined with American dishes as long as the flavors are complementary.

Shrimp Curry Madras

The coconut palms that fringe the Madras shores provide the rich milk for their seafood dishes. This renowned shrimp curry is by no means fiery.

3 tablespoons vegetable oil
3 bay leaves
3 cloves
2 large onions, sliced
5 cloves garlic, chopped
1 tablespoon chopped fresh ginger
¼ teaspoon turmeric
¼ teaspoon red pepper (optional)
2 cups shredded fresh coconut, soaked 1 hour in 4½ cups water
1 pound shrimp, fresh or thawed, shelled
salt to taste
2 tablespoons lemon juice

1. Heat vegetable oil in a skillet. Add bay leaves, cloves, onions, garlic, and ginger. Sauté until onions are translucent. Add turmeric and red pepper. Stir a few times. Remove from heat.

2. Strain coconut milk and discard coconut. Add milk to sautéed onions. Bring to a boil; then simmer over medium-low heat 15 minutes.
3. Add shrimp, salt to taste, and lemon juice. Simmer until done, about 15 minutes. Serve with rice. Yield: 4 to 6 servings.

Shrimp Masala

Not as mild as the previous curry, the coconut sauce in this shrimp dish is tart with the juice of the tropical tamarind fruit, grown in South India.

5 cloves garlic
1 tablespoon garam masala (see index)
1 teaspoon mustard seed
1 tablespoon chopped fresh ginger
1 teaspoon coriander seed
1 teaspoon cumin seed
¼ teaspoon red pepper
3 tablespoons vegetable oil
2 bay leaves
2 medium onions, sliced
2 cups fresh shredded coconut, soaked 1 hour in 3 cups water
1 pound shrimp, fresh or thawed, shelled
2 tablespoons tamarind, soaked 1 hour in ¼ cup water
salt to taste

1. Grind together the garlic, garam masala, mustard seed, ginger, coriander seed, cumin seed and red pepper to a paste.
2. Heat vegetable oil in a skillet. Add bay leaves and onions. Sauté until onions are translucent. Add ground paste and cook until oil separates, about 15 minutes.
3. Meanwhile, strain the coconut milk, discard coconut, and add milk to sautéed onions. Bring to a boil; then simmer over medium-low heat 15 minutes.
4. Add shrimp and simmer until done, about 5 minutes.

5. Strain tamarind juice and discard pulp. Add juice and salt to taste to the shrimp mixture. Cook 9 minutes. Serve with rice. Yield: 4 to 6 servings.

Shrimp Vindaloo

Vinegar, ground spices, and red chilies combine to create hot and sour Goan vindaloos. This dish can be red hot agony with 10 dry red chilies, so adjust the number to your taste.

1 tablespoon grated fresh coconut
1 teaspoon ground coriander
1 teaspoon ground cumin
2 medium onions, chopped
10 cloves garlic
1 teaspoon mustard seed
½ teaspoon sugar
10 dry whole red chilies
¼ cup vinegar
¼ cup vegetable oil
2 cups water
1 pound shrimp, fresh or thawed, shelled
salt to taste

1. Dry roast the coconut lightly. Separately, dry roast the coriander and cumin. Set aside.
2. Grind together onions, garlic, mustard seed, sugar, red chilies, all dry-roasted ingredients, and vinegar to a paste.
3. Heat vegetable oil in a skillet. Add paste and cook until oil separates, about 15 minutes. Add 2 cups water. Bring to a boil; then simmer over medium-low heat 10 minutes.
4. Add shrimp and salt to taste. Cook until the shrimp is tender, about 5 minutes. Serve with rice and Chapatis (see index). Yield: 4 servings.

Fish and Seafood Dishes 113

Shrimp Curry Bengal Lancers

Shrimp in a hot (10 green chilies!) green sauce that also has the bite of tamarind. This recipe has burned a path from South India to the Bengal Lancers restaurant.

4 medium onions, chopped
1 cup chopped fresh coriander leaves
5 cloves garlic
1 tablespoon chopped fresh ginger
10 green chilies
¼ cup vegetable oil
1-inch stick cinnamon
5 green cardamom pods
2 bay leaves
1 teaspoon mustard seed
1 teaspoon fennel seed
1 tablespoon ground coriander
1 tablespoon ground cumin
4 cups water
1 pound shrimp, fresh or thawed, shelled
2 tablespoons tamarind, soaked 1 hour in ½ cup warm water, or 2 tablespoons lemon juice
salt to taste

1. Grind together onions, coriander leaves, garlic, ginger, and green chilies to a paste, adding a few tablespoons water. Set aside.
2. Heat vegetable oil in a skillet. Add cinnamon, cardamom, and bay leaves. Sauté 2 minutes. Add mustard seed and fennel seed. Sauté 1 minute. Add ground paste and cook until oil separates, about 15 minutes. Add ground coriander and cumin. Cook 2 minutes longer.
3. Add 4 cups water. Bring to a boil; then simmer over medium-low heat 15 minutes.
4. Add shrimp and cook until tender, about 15 minutes.
5. Strain tamarind juice, discard pulp, and add juice and salt to taste to the sauce. Cook a few minutes. Serve with rice and Chapatis (see index). Yield: 4 to 6 servings.

Shrimp Molee

A mild coconut milk curry, popular in Tamil Nadu and along the Malabar coast, Shrimp Molee is aromatic with whole cardamom, cinnamon, and bay leaves.

2 tablespoons vegetable oil
1 whole cardamom pod
1-inch stick cinnamon
2 bay leaves
1 pound shrimp, fresh or thawed, shelled
1 large onion, chopped
1 teaspoon chopped fresh ginger
5 cloves garlic, chopped
¼ teaspoon turmeric
2 green chilies (optional)
2 cups shredded coconut, soaked 30 minutes in 3½ cups water
salt to taste

1. Heat vegetable oil in a large skillet. Add cardamom, cinnamon, and bay leaves. Sauté 2 minutes.
2. Add shrimp and sauté 2 minutes. Remove shrimp and set aside.
3. Add onions, ginger, and garlic to the oil and sauté 4 to 5 minutes.
4. Add turmeric and green chilies. Stir a few times.
5. Strain coconut milk and discard coconut. Add milk to seasoned onions. Do not cover pan after adding coconut milk or the dish might become oily. Bring to a boil and simmer over medium-low heat 10 minutes.
6. Add shrimp and salt to taste. Simmer 10 minutes. Serve with boiled rice or pulao (see index) and Indian bread. Yield: 4 to 6 servings.

Malai Jhinga

A whisper of almonds accents these shrimp (*jhinga*) cooked in coconut cream (*malai*).

3 tablespoons vegetable oil
2 bay leaves

Fish and Seafood Dishes 115

1-inch stick cinnamon
5 whole cardamom pods
1½ pounds shrimp, fresh or thawed, shelled
3 cloves garlic, chopped
1 teaspoon chopped ginger
1 large onion, chopped
1 tablespoon flour
3 tablespoons ground almonds
1 cup shredded coconut, soaked 30 minutes in 2½ cups water
⅛ teaspoon red pepper
1 teaspoon sugar
salt to taste
1 tablespoon lemon juice
2 tablespoons chopped fresh coriander leaves

1. Heat vegetable oil in a large skillet. Add bay leaves, cinnamon, and cardamom. Sauté 1 to 2 minutes, or until cinnamon expands.
2. Add shrimp and sauté 2 to 3 minutes. Remove shrimp from oil and set aside.
3. Add garlic, ginger, and onions to skillet. Sauté until onions are translucent.
4. Add flour and almonds. Cook 2 minutes, stirring constantly.
5. Strain coconut milk and discard coconut. Add milk, red pepper, and sugar to seasoned onions and almonds. Bring to a boil. Then simmer on medium-low heat 10 minutes.
6. Add shrimp and salt to taste. Simmer 7 to 10 minutes. Add lemon juice and sprinkle with coriander leaves. Serve with rice and any Indian bread. Yield: 4 to 6 servings.

Jhinga Khasta

Khasta is North Indian for pastry. These sausage-shaped potato and shrimp rolls are dipped in egg and bread crumbs (a British touch) before frying. Serve them with pulaos, vegetable curries, and chutneys. Or offer them as appetizers.

1 pound cooked shrimp
1 medium potato, boiled and mashed

¼ teaspoon red pepper
¼ teaspoon ground coriander
¼ cup chopped fresh coriander leaves
1 teaspoon freshly ground black pepper
¼ teaspoon turmeric
1 tablespoon lemon juice
salt to taste
vegetable oil for deep frying
2 eggs, beaten
1 cup bread crumbs

1. Mince the shrimp very fine and mix it with mashed potatoes.
2. Add red pepper, ground coriander, fresh coriander leaves, black pepper, turmeric, lemon juice and salt. Knead to a smooth dough.
3. Divide into 15 to 20 equal portions. Shape each portion like a sausage. If the dough is too stiff, add a little water.
4. Heat vegetable oil for deep frying.
5. Dip rolls in beaten eggs and bread crumbs. Fry until golden. Yield: 4 to 6 servings.

Tandoori Shrimp

These spicy shrimp are a vibrant red-orange when they come out of the oven. Like many Indian meat dishes, these shrimp are first marinated in seasoned yogurt.

½ small onion, chopped
6 cloves garlic
1 tablespoon chopped fresh ginger
2 tablespoons lemon juice
½ cup yogurt, beaten
2 tablespoons ground coriander
1 tablespoon ground cumin
¼ teaspoon red pepper (optional)
¼ teaspoon cinnamon
¼ teaspoon ground cloves
¼ teaspoon ground cardamom

2 tablespoons butter
few drops of orange or red food coloring
1 teaspoon salt
1½ pounds shrimp, fresh or thawed, shelled

1. Grind together onions, garlic, ginger, and lemon juice to a paste. Place in a large bowl and add all other ingredients except shrimp. Mix well.
2. Add shrimp to the marinade and mix gently so that all shrimp are coated evenly. Marinate 2 hours.
3. Preheat oven to 375° F. Pour shrimp and marinade into a baking dish. Bake 10 minutes. Stir a few times and bake another 10 minutes, or until done. Serve with Nan or Chapatis (see index). Yield: 4 to 6 servings.

Tandoori Fish

The people of the northern states of Punjab and Haryana (Land of the Five Rivers) cook much of their fresh-water fish in the clay tandoori. This dish is a rich, dry curry.

1 cup yogurt
1 small onion, chopped
1 teaspoon poppy seeds
1 teaspoon ground cumin
1 teaspoon ground coriander
¼ teaspoon red pepper
4 cloves garlic
½ teaspoon ground cardamom
¼ teaspoon ground cloves
½ teaspoon ground ginger
¼ teaspoon ground cinnamon
2 tablespoons lemon juice
1 teaspoon salt
1 tablespoon butter
6 fish fillets (halibut, cod, or flounder)
1 tomato, sliced
1 small lemon, cut into wedges

1 small onion, cut into rings
2 tablespoons coriander leaves

1. Blend all ingredients except fish, tomato slices, lemon wedges, onion rings, and coriander leaves.
2. Make cuts on surface of fish. Rub the yogurt paste gently into cuts and on surface. Marinate 2 hours.
3. Bake fish 15 to 20 minutes, or until tender. Garnish with sliced tomatoes, lemon wedges, onion rings, and coriander leaves. Serve with Indian bread and pulao (see index). Yield: 6 servings.

Fish Curry Bengal Lancers

This scorching fish curry in puckery tamarind-tomato sauce is prepared as it is at the Bengal Lancers restaurant.

4 tablespoons vegetable oil
2 pounds fish fillets, cut into serving pieces
3 large onions, chopped
5 cloves garlic
1 teaspoon chopped fresh ginger
10 green chilies, chopped
1 cup fresh coriander leaves
½ teaspoon cumin seed
½ teaspoon mustard seed
½ teaspoon fennel seed
1 teaspoon ground coriander
1 teaspoon ground cumin
3 tomatoes, chopped
2 cups water
salt to taste
2 tablespoons tamarind, soaked 1 hour in ½ cup water, or 2 tablespoons lemon juice

1. Heat 1 tablespoon of the vegetable oil in a large skillet. Add fish and sauté lightly. Remove fish and set aside.
2. Grind onions, garlic, ginger, chilies, and coriander leaves to form a paste, adding 1 tablespoon water if necessary. Set aside.

3. Heat remaining vegetable oil in the same skillet. Add cumin seed, mustard seed, and fennel seed. Sauté 1 minute. Add seasoned onion paste and cook until oil separates, about 15 minutes. Add ground coriander and ground cumin. Cook 1 minute. Add tomatoes and cook 2 to 3 minutes.
4. Add 2 cups water. Bring to a boil; then simmer over medium-low heat 10 minutes.
5. Add fish and salt to taste. Simmer 10 minutes.
6. Strain tamarind juice and discard pulp. Add juice to fish and simmer 5 minutes. Serve with rice and any Indian bread. Yield: 4 to 6 servings.

Malabari Machi

A spicy and hot coconut sauce sparks this fish (*machi*) curry from the Malabar coast.

1 tablespoon shredded coconut
1 teaspoon coriander seed
3 tablespoons vegetable oil
2 large onions, chopped
2 tablespoons chopped fresh ginger
6 cloves garlic
½ teaspoon cumin seed
1 cup fresh coriander leaves
3 green chilies, chopped (optional)
5 whole cardamom pods
2 bay leaves
salt to taste
2 pounds fish fillets (sole or flounder), cut into small pieces
½ cup water
¼ teaspoon ground cloves
¼ teaspoon ground cinnamon
1 teaspoon black pepper
1½ cups shredded coconut, soaked 30 minutes in 3 cups water
1 tablespoon lemon juice

1. Dry roast 1 tablespoon coconut and coriander seeds. Set aside.

2. Heat 2 tablespoons of the vegetable oil in a skillet. Add half of the chopped onions and sauté until golden. Remove onions with a slotted spoon and place them with other roasted ingredients. Reserve oil in skillet.
3. Grind ginger, garlic, cumin seed, coriander leaves, and green chilies in 2 tablespoons water. Set aside. Make a paste of the sautéed onions, roasted coconut, and coriander seeds.
4. Heat remaining 1 tablespoon oil in skillet with reserved oil. Add whole cardamom and bay leaves. Sauté 1 to 2 minutes. Add remaining chopped onions and sauté until translucent. Add ginger-garlic paste and cook 2 to 3 minutes. Add sauteed onion paste and cook 3 minutes.
5. Add fish and salt to taste. Cook 1 minute. Add ½ cup water and simmer 10 minutes. Add cloves, cinnamon, and black pepper.
6. Strain coconut milk and discard coconut. Add milk to fish. Bring to a boil; then simmer gently 5 minutes. Add lemon juice and serve. Yield: 4 to 6 servings.

Dahi Machi

For this softly seasoned, dry fish curry from the Bengal area in eastern India, fish is simmered in yogurt (*dahi*) mingled with cinnamon, cardamom, and cloves.

3 tablespoons vegetable oil
2 medium onions, chopped
½ teaspoon cumin seed
1 teaspoon chopped fresh ginger
2 cloves garlic
½ teaspoon turmeric
½ cup chopped fresh coriander leaves
1½ pounds halibut
salt to taste
¼ teaspoon cinnamon
¼ teaspoon ground cardamom

¼ teaspoon ground cloves
1½ cups yogurt, beaten
2 tablespoons lemon juice

1. Heat vegetable oil in a skillet. Sauté onions until translucent. Remove from heat.
2. Grind together cumin seed, ginger, garlic, turmeric, and coriander leaves to a paste.
3. Add ground paste to sautéed onions and cook 2 minutes.
4. Add fish, salt to taste, cinnamon, cardamom, and cloves. Cook over low heat 1 to 2 minutes.
5. Add well-beaten yogurt and continue to cook over low heat until fish is tender, about 15 to 20 minutes. Add lemon juice and serve. Yield: 4 to 6 servings.

Fish Molee

A delicacy in the southern state of Kerala, this hot dish is usually made with fish caught in the backwater areas.

2 tablespoons vegetable oil
1½ pounds fish fillets (halibut, cod, or flounder)
2 large onions, chopped
1 teaspoon chopped fresh ginger
2 cloves garlic
3 green chilies, chopped
½ teaspoon turmeric
1 teaspoon black pepper
½ fresh coconut, shredded and soaked 1 hour in 2½ cups water
1 tablespoon vinegar
salt to taste

1. Heat 1 tablespoon of the vegetable oil in a skillet. Add fish and sauté a few minutes, until light brown. Remove and set aside.
2. Add the remaining 1 tablespoon oil to skillet and heat. Sauté the onions until golden. Add ginger, garlic, green chilies, turmeric, and black pepper. Cook 2 to 3 minutes.

3. Strain the coconut milk and discard coconut. Add the milk to sautéed onions. Bring to a boil. Then simmer, uncovered, over medium-low heat 10 minutes.
4. Add vinegar, fish, and salt to taste. Cook 10 to 15 minutes and serve. Yield: 4 to 6 servings.

Fish with Tomato Sauce

In addition to yogurt and coconut milk, tomatoes sometimes form rich, thick fish curry sauces.

2 pounds fish fillets (halibut or cod)
2 tablespoons vegetable oil
1 teaspoon chopped fresh ginger
3 cloves garlic
3 cloves
2 whole dry red peppers (optional)
½ teaspoon cumin seed
¼ teaspoon turmeric
½ teaspoon black peppercorns
1 tablespoon lemon juice
2 large onions, chopped
4 cups tomato sauce
2 cups water
3 tablespoons chopped fresh coriander leaves
salt to taste

1. Cut fillets into serving pieces. Heat 1 tablespoon of the vegetable oil in a skillet and brown fish pieces. Remove and set aside.
2. Grind together ginger, garlic, cloves, red peppers, cumin seed, turmeric, peppercorns, and lemon juice to form a paste.
3. Heat remaining 1 tablespoon oil in same skillet. Add onions and sauté until translucent. Add ground paste and cook 2 minutes. Add tomato sauce and cook 5 minutes.
4. Add 2 cups water and coriander leaves. Bring to a boil. Then simmer 15 minutes.

5. Add fish and salt to taste. Simmer until fish is tender, about 30 minutes. Yield: 4 to 6 servings.

Tamatar Machi

Fillet of haddock is simmered in a hot, coconut-flavored tomato sauce.

2 pounds fresh fillet of haddock
flour for dredging
2 tablespoons butter
1 medium onion
12 black peppercorns
1-inch stick cinnamon
5 cloves
5 cloves garlic
1 teaspoon cumin seed
3 green chilies
2 bay leaves
3 tablespoons vegetable oil
1 tablespoon chopped fresh ginger
2 medium onions, chopped
5 tomatoes, skinned and chopped
1 cup shredded coconut, soaked 30 minutes in 2 cups water
salt to taste
2 tablespoons lemon juice
1 teaspoon garam masala (see index)
¼ cup chopped fresh coriander leaves

1. Rinse fish fillets and cut into serving pieces.
2. Roll fish pieces in flour. Then sauté them in butter. Remove fish from skillet and set aside.
3. Grind 1 onion, peppercorns, cinnamon, cloves, garlic, cumin seed, chilies, and bay leaves to a paste.
4. Heat vegetable oil in skillet. Sauté ginger and 2 chopped onions until onions are translucent.
5. Add ground paste and cook 2 to 3 minutes.
6. Add tomatoes and cook 5 minutes, or until a purée is obtained.

7. Strain coconut milk and discard the coconut. Add milk to purée. Bring to a boil; then simmer 10 minutes.
8. Add salt and fish. Simmer 10 minutes. Add lemon juice and garam masala and stir. Sprinkle with coriander leaves. Serve with rice. Yield: 4 to 6 servings.

Machi Palak

Fish is simmered in softly spiced, creamy tomatoes and spinach. This dish is popular in the North and Central regions.

6 large tomatoes
1 pound fish fillets (cod, halibut, or turbot)
¼ cup butter
5 cloves garlic
1 teaspoon chopped fresh ginger
1 small onion, chopped
1 teaspoon ground cumin
¼ teaspoon turmeric
⅛ teaspoon red pepper
1 pound fresh spinach, chopped and cleaned
salt to taste
2 tablespoons lemon juice

1. Scald the tomatoes and remove the skins. Set aside.
2. Slice the fish into serving pieces and set aside.
3. Heat butter in skillet. Add garlic, ginger, and onions. Sauté 2 to 3 minutes.
4. Add cumin, turmeric, red pepper, and tomatoes. Convert mixture to a purée. Cook 5 minutes.
5. Add spinach to purée and cook 10 minutes.
6. Add salt and fish. Simmer until fish is tender, 30 to 45 minutes. Add lemon juice. Serve with any Indian bread and rice. Yield: 4 to 5 servings.

Fish Curry

This is a watery, tart tamarind curry.

1 teaspoon chopped fresh ginger

5 cloves garlic, chopped
5 cloves
1 teaspoon ground coriander
½ teaspoon turmeric
2 green chilies (optional)
2 tablespoons tamarind, soaked 1 hour in 1 cup water
2 tablespoons vegetable oil
2 medium onions, chopped
2 bay leaves
2 cups water
2 tablespoons chopped fresh coriander leaves
salt to taste
1½ pounds halibut or cod, cut into serving pieces

1. Grind ginger, garlic, cloves, ground coriander, turmeric, and chilies to a paste. Set aside.
2. Strain tamarind juice and discard pulp. Reserve juice.
3. Heat vegetable oil in a skillet. Add onions and bay leaves. Sauté until onions are translucent. Add the ground paste and cook 1 to 2 minutes.
4. Add 2 cups water, tamarind juice, coriander leaves, and salt to taste. Bring to a boil; then simmer 15 minutes.
5. Add fish and cook 15 minutes. Serve with rice. Yield: 4 to 6 servings.

Machi Khasta

Delicately spiced fish filling is rolled into a tube-shaped pastry, then dipped in eggs and bread crumbs and fried.

2 cups all-purpose flour
1¾ teaspoon salt
3 tablespoons butter
¾ cup warm water
½ pound fish fillet (cod or perch)
1 cup water mixed with ¼ teaspoon salt
¼ teaspoon red pepper
⅛ teaspoon turmeric
⅛ teaspoon cinnamon
¼ teaspoon caraway seed

1 teaspoon chopped fresh ginger
1 teaspoon garam masala (see index)
4 eggs, beaten
bread crumbs for coating fish
vegetable oil for deep frying

1. Mix flour with ¾ teaspoon of the salt. Gently rub butter into flour, breaking all the lumps. Adding about ¾ cup warm water, knead to a stiff and smooth dough. Cover with a damp cloth and set aside 30 minutes.
2. Meanwhile, boil fish in 1 cup water with ¼ teaspoon salt, 5 to 7 minutes, or until cooked. Remove any bones and mash the fish well.
3. Add red pepper, turmeric, cinnamon, caraway seed, ginger, garam masala and remaining 1 teaspoon salt to mashed fish. Mix well. Set aside.
4. Knead the dough well for a few minutes. Divide it into 25 equal portions. Roll each out into a 3- to 4-inch round. Brush the edges with water and cover them.
5. Divide fish mixture into 25 equal portions and spread over the rounds, leaving ¼ inch at the edges. Carefully roll them into tubes.
6. Roll tubes in beaten egg and then in bread crumbs.
7. Heat vegetable oil in flat-bottomed pan and fry the khasta until golden, turning them gently. Or bake them in a preheated 450° F. oven 10 to 15 minutes. Turn them a few times and brush with butter. Serve with a pulao, chutney, and a vegetable curry. Yield: 6 servings.

Fish Kofta

Kofta (ground-meat balls) were introduced to North India by the East Europeans. In this version, highly seasoned fish balls are served in a creamy, coconut sauce.

1½ pounds fish fillets (cod or perch)
1 cup water plus ¼ teaspoon salt
1 slice of bread, soaked in ½ cup milk

Fish and Seafood Dishes 127

2 tablespoons yogurt
2 tablespoons rice flour
salt to taste
¼ teaspoon turmeric
¼ teaspoon red pepper
½ teaspoon cumin seed
2 teaspoons ground coriander
4 tablespoons chopped fresh coriander leaves
1 teaspoon chopped fresh ginger
2 teaspoons garam masala (see index)
¼ teaspoon ground cardamom
vegetable oil for deep frying
2 tablespoons vegetable oil
3 whole cardamom pods
1 large onion, chopped
1 cup freshly shredded coconut, soaked 30 minutes in 2½ cups water
½ cup water
1 tablespoon lemon juice
coriander leaves

1. Poach the fish in 1 cup water with ¼ teaspoon salt, or just enough water to cover the fish. Simmer 7 to 10 minutes, or until fish flakes with a fork. Drain immediately. Remove any bones and mash the fish.
2. Add bread with all the milk squeezed from it, yogurt, rice flour, salt to taste, ⅛ teaspoon of the turmeric, ⅛ teaspoon of the red pepper, ¼ teaspoon of the cumin seed, 1 teaspoon of the ground coriander, 2 tablespoons of the coriander leaves, ½ teaspoon of the ginger, 1 teaspoon of the garam masala, and ⅛ teaspoon of the ground cardamom to fish. Mix well.
3. Divide mixture into 20 to 25 equal parts. Shape them into balls and set aside 15 to 20 minutes, to dry a little.
4. Heat vegetable oil and deep fry the kofta until golden.
5. Heat 2 tablespoons vegetable oil in a large skillet. Add cardamom and onions. Sauté until onions are translucent.

6. Add remaining ⅛ teaspoon turmeric, ⅛ teaspoon red pepper, ⅛ teaspoon cumin seed, 1 teaspoon ground coriander, 2 tablespoons coriander leaves, ½ teaspoon ginger, 1 teaspoon garam masala, and ⅛ teaspoon ground cardamom to the cooked onions. Sauté a few minutes.
7. Strain the coconut milk and discard coconut. Add milk to the seasoned onions and bring to a boil. Simmer gently 15 minutes.
8. Add the fish balls and ½ cup water. Bring to a boil; then simmer gently 10 minutes. Add lemon juice and garnish with coriander leaves. Serve with boiled rice and Indian bread. Yield: 4 to 6 servings.

Baked Fish Kerala Style

In Kerala, cooks wrap trout in banana leaves and bake them over hot coals.

10 cloves garlic
1 teaspoon red pepper
1 cup grated fresh coconut
½ teaspoon turmeric
1 tablespoon vinegar
1 tablespoon chopped fresh ginger
¼ cup chopped fresh coriander leaves
4 tablespoons butter
salt to taste
4 fresh trout, 1 pound each

1. Grind all ingredients to a paste except the fish. Preheat oven to 375° F.
2. Clean the fish and cut off the heads. Rub the paste inside and outside the fish.
3. Oil 4 pieces of aluminum foil, each large enough to wrap one fish. Close the foil around the fish and crimp the edges.
4. Place wrapped fish in a baking dish and bake 15 to 20 minutes. Check for doneness. Serve with Indian breads and rice. Yield: 4 servings.

Bhuna Kekada

A soft-shell crab is one that has just shed its old, hard shell. The new underdeveloped shell is tender and edible. These mildly spiced, soft-shell crabs are broiled to a rich golden hue.

4 large soft-shell crabs
¼ cup butter
¼ teaspoon red pepper
¼ teaspoon turmeric
¼ cup lemon juice
flour for dredging
freshly ground black pepper to taste
salt to taste

1. Wash crabs several times. Make an incision across the front of the shell behind the eyes. Lift the pointed flaps on each side of back shell and remove the spongy gills and sand bags.
2. Mix together butter, red pepper, turmeric, and lemon juice.
3. Roll crabs in lemon juice mixture and then in flour.
4. Place crabs on broiling rack 2 to 3 inches from heat source. Broil 10 to 12 minutes, turning once. Sprinkle with black pepper and salt to taste and serve. Yield: 4 servings.

Crab Curry

For this uncomplicated yet distinctive dish from the coastal area, onions are mingled with coconut sauce.

4 soft-shell crabs
2 cups freshly shredded coconut, soaked 30 minutes in 4 cups water
¼ cup butter
2 bay leaves
4 large onions, sliced
2 green chilies, chopped

¼ cup lemon juice
salt to taste
3 tablespoons chopped fresh coriander leaves

1. Clean the crabs. Remove and discard legs and sand bags. Place crabs in a large saucepan. Set aside.
2. Strain coconut milk and discard coconut. Set milk aside.
3. Heat butter in a skillet. Add bay leaves and onions. Sauté until onions are translucent. Add chilies and cook a few minutes.
4. Pour the onion mixture over the crabs.
5. Add coconut milk, lemon juice, and salt to taste. Bring to a boil; then simmer until crabs are done, about 20 minutes. Sprinkle with coriander leaves and serve with pulao (see index). Yield: 4 to 6 servings.

Crab Kofta

Almonds and cardamom add a sweet and nutty accent to these crab balls.

1 pound fresh crab meat
5 cloves garlic
½ cup chopped fresh coriander leaves
1 egg, beaten
¼ teaspoon red pepper
3 tablespoons ground almonds
½ teaspoon ground cardamom
¼ teaspoon ground ginger
¾ teaspoon salt
vegetable oil for deep frying
bread crumbs for coating kofta
2 tablespoons butter
2 bay leaves
3 whole cardamom pods
1 teaspoon chopped fresh ginger
2 medium onions, chopped
1 teaspoon ground coriander

1 teaspoon ground cumin
¼ cup tomato sauce
1 cup shredded coconut, soaked 30 minutes in 2 cups water
salt to taste
1 tablespoon lemon juice

1. Grind together crab meat, garlic, and ¼ cup of the chopped coriander leaves.
2. Place seasoned meat in a mixing bowl and add well-beaten egg, ⅛ teaspoon of the red pepper, 1 tablespoon of the ground almonds, ½ teaspoon ground cardamom, ¼ teaspoon ground ginger, and ¾ teaspoon salt. Mix well.
3. Heat vegetable oil for deep frying.
4. Meanwhile, shape the seasoned meat mixture into 18 to 20 balls. Roll balls in bread crumbs and deep fry until golden. Drain and set aside.
5. Heat butter in a skillet. Add bay leaves and cardamom pods. Sauté 1 to 2 minutes. Add chopped ginger and onions. Sauté until onions are translucent. Add ground coriander, ground cumin, remaining ⅛ teaspoon red pepper, and remaining 2 tablespoons ground almonds. Cook 1 minute.
6. Add tomato sauce to seasoned onions and cook 5 minutes.
7. Strain coconut milk and discard coconut. Add milk to onion and tomato mixture. Bring to a boil; then simmer 10 minutes.
8. Add crab balls and salt to taste. Simmer 5 minutes. Add lemon juice. Sprinkle with remaining ¼ cup coriander leaves and serve. Yield: 4 to 5 servings.

Lobster Curry

Bengal is renowned for its lobster dishes. This lobster dish is cooked in a garlicky coconut sauce, hot with green chilies.

2 tablespoons butter
2 bay leaves
1 large onion, chopped

1 tablespoon butter
5 cloves garlic, chopped
1 tablespoon chopped fresh ginger
3 green chilies, seeds removed and chilies sliced lengthwise
¼ teaspoon turmeric
2 cups freshly shredded coconut, soaked 30 minutes in 3 cups water
salt to taste
1½ pounds cooked lobster meat
1 tablespoon lemon juice

1. Heat 2 tablespoons butter in a skillet. Add bay leaves and sauté 2 minutes.
2. Add onions to butter and sauté until golden. Remove onions and set aside.
3. Heat remaining butter in same skillet. Add garlic, ginger, and chilies. Cook 1 minute. Lower heat and add turmeric. Stir a few times.
4. Strain coconut milk and discard coconut. Add milk to garlic mixture. Bring to a boil. Simmer 10 minutes.
5. Add salt to taste, sautéed onions, and lobster meat. Simmer 10 minutes. Add lemon juice. Serve with rice and Indian breads. Yield: 4 to 6 servings.

Broiled Lobster

In Bengal, fish are often rubbed with black pepper and mustard paste to produce a mouth-watering pungency.

4 live soft-shell lobsters, about 1¼ pounds each
½ teaspoon turmeric
½ cup butter
1 teaspoon ground mustard
1 teaspoon salt
1 tablespoon freshly ground black pepper
1 tablespoon chopped fresh coriander leaves

1. Split the live lobsters. Remove and discard stomach sac and intestinal vein. Preheat broiler.
2. Mix all remaining ingredients together.

Fish and Seafood Dishes 133

3. Rub each lobster half with the above mixture and reserve what is left.
4. Place lobster halves 3 to 4 inches from source of heat. Broil 10 to 15 minutes.
5. Pour remaining butter mixture over lobsters before serving. Yield: 4 servings.

8

Vegetable and Dahl Dishes

Indian chefs can start with an unsophisticated vegetable such as the humble potato and magically transform it into a dozen highly individual flavors, textures, and appearances—all royal dishes fit for a rajah's banquet table. Potatoes can be cooked whole in softly flavored yogurt, combined with other vegetables, meats, rice, and dahl in rich or hot sauces, or hollowed out and filled with a number of mouth-watering stuffings. The possibilities are endless.

Indians find it amusing when they are served boiled green beans dotted with a pat of butter in American restaurants. They say to themselves confidently, "This would never happen in India." American vegetables, which are often canned or frozen, are rarely exciting.

Many Indians are still vegetarians. So it is no wonder that some of the most sumptuous vegetarian dishes are prepared by Indian chefs. Anything that can be done with meats and fish can also be accomplished with vegetables.

Basically, there are four ways Indians prepare their vegetable dishes. For dry dishes, the vegetables are first sautéed, then cooked over medium heat with no water. Wet curries are made by first sautéeing the vegetables, then simmering them over medium heat, with water added to form a sauce. Vegetables such as eggplant and sweet peppers are stuffed, then cooked in water over low heat to produce a rich, thick gravy. Vegetables are also cooked with dahls, especially in South India, where vegetable dishes are usually watery and seasoned with coconut and tamarind. Northern dishes are thick and rich.

Vegetable curries nearly always include onions, ginger, chilies, and coriander leaves. The best ginger is the youngest. It should be slightly pink, tender, and easy to cut. Onions are added as raw rings, ground for sauces, or fried.

North India is the main supplier of vegetables to the rest of the subcontinent. Since most of the time it never gets really cold in India, vegetables are grown almost year round. However, there are seasons for some vegetables, such as mushrooms, which thrive during the monsoon season (June to September). The most exotic and expensive mushrooms are grown in the cool Vale of Kashmir. They are heart-shaped, black, and spongy. Cauliflower flourishes in the winter, which is generally the best season for vegetables in India. Most Indian vegetables —okra, eggplant, peas, cauliflower, sweet peppers, and potatoes, for example, are also available in the United States.

Nearly all vegetables in India are purchased fresh. Even in the big cities women go out each day and haggle with the produce man over his colorful assortment of fresh, plump, and shiny vegetables. Canned vegetables are available, but most Indians prefer the taste and nutrition of fresh ones.

You should try to use fresh vegetables when preparing any of the vegetable dishes in this chapter. These vegetable dishes are not prepared with an abundance of herbs and spices by Indian standards; therefore, the natural flavors of the vegetables are played up. If you are serving the vegetables with a highly flavored main dish, play down the aromatics. If the main dish is bland, go ahead and experiment with the spices and herbs.

Dahls (cooked lentils), like vegetables, are very important to the Indian vegetarian diet, since they are a rich source of vitamins, protein, and minerals. The literal meaning of *dahl* is "split lentil." There are about sixty different varieties of dahls grown in India.

Through the centuries, *dahl* has come to mean the soup-like dishes made from the split whole lentil. Throughout the subcontinent these dishes are eaten each day with almost every meal. It is a misconception to think that all Indian dahls are watery. Many excellent ones are thick, especially in the North. In the East and South they are thinner and served with rice.

Dahl dishes get their distinctive flavors from different masala combinations that are first sautéed in oil or ghee, then mixed with the dahl and simmered a long time. Mustard seed, cumin seed, asafoetida, and fenugreek are characteristic dahl masalas.

Split lentils cook much faster than whole grains, which often must soak from five hours to several days before cooking. Small, skinned lentils such as urad dahl, moong dahl, and masoor dahl cook fastest. Leftover dahls keep several days under refrigeration in a covered container. And they often taste even richer after being stored.

Both dahls and vegetables are usually served in a *thali*, a silver or bell metal dish with fluted edges. Small bowls called *katoris* are included in the big dish; these contain an assortment of dahls, chutneys, and salads. In the South, rice is served in the thali, while in the North, bread takes the place of rice. One of the exciting experiences of a thali meal is the different taste combinations that complement each other.

Bhara Baigan

Eggplant is one of the most widely used and versatile vegetables in Indian cooking. In this hearty, stuffed eggplant dish, the mild spices are absorbed by the chick-pea filling.

6 tablespoons vegetable oil
5 cloves garlic, chopped
1 teaspoon chopped fresh ginger
1 tablespoon chopped fresh coriander leaves

3 green chilies, chopped (optional)
1 teaspoon ground coriander
¼ teaspoon turmeric
salt to taste
1 cup chick-pea flour
1 teaspoon garam masala (see index)
salt to taste
1 teaspoon dry mango powder or lemon juice
5 small eggplants
1 teaspoon mustard seed
salt to taste

1. To prepare the filling, heat 2 tablespoons of the vegetable oil in a skillet. Add garlic, ginger, coriander leaves, chilies, ground coriander, turmeric, and salt to taste. Cook 2 minutes, or until garlic is golden. Add chick-pea flour, garam masala, and salt to taste. Cook a few minutes. Add mango powder.
2. Wash eggplants and make a deep lengthwise slit in each. Divide filling into 5 parts. Stuff slit in each eggplant with filling. Tie eggplants with thread so stuffing does not fall out.
3. Heat remaining 4 tablespoons vegetable oil in a large flat-bottomed skillet. Add mustard seed. When seeds stop crackling, carefully add the eggplants and sprinkle on some salt to taste.
4. Cook, covered, over low heat, about 30 minutes, or until cooked. Turn the eggplants occasionally. Yield: 4 to 6 servings.

Baigan Subji

This thick, rich eggplant curry is most popular in the North, but is also found in West and Central India. *Subji* means "dry, cooked vegetables." Many Indians, however, use it to mean simply "vegetables."

5 tablespoons vegetable oil
2 large onions, chopped

1 teaspoon chopped fresh ginger
¼ teaspoon turmeric
1 teaspoon ground coriander
¼ teaspoon red pepper
4 tomatoes, roughly cut
3 large eggplants, cubed
salt to taste
1 cup water
1 tablespoon lemon juice
3 tablespoons chopped fresh coriander leaves

1. Heat vegetable oil in a large skillet. Add onions and ginger. Sauté onions until golden.
2. Add turmeric, coriander, red pepper, and tomatoes. Cook until tomatoes are liquefied and a thick sauce is obtained, about 10 to 15 minutes.
3. Add eggplant, salt to taste, and 1 cup water. Mix. Cook, covered, until eggplant is soft, about 40 minutes. Add lemon juice and sprinkle with coriander leaves. Yield: 4 to 6 servings.

Eggplant Kottu

This dish is eaten along the coastal areas of South India. Eggplant and chick-peas are mashed and mixed with freshly grated coconut. Eliminate the green and red chilies if you prefer a mild dish. Substitute green pepper for the pepper taste without the fire.

½ cup split chick-peas or moong dahl
1½ cups water plus a pinch of salt and ⅛ teaspoon turmeric
4 medium eggplants
2 cups water plus a pinch of salt and ⅛ teaspoon turmeric
1 cup fresh grated coconut
½ teaspoon cumin seed
3 green chilies (optional)
2 tablespoons vegetable oil
1 teaspoon mustard seed
3 bay leaves

3 red chilies, chopped (optional)
1 tablespoon lemon juice
salt to taste
2 tablespoons chopped fresh coriander leaves

1. Boil chick-peas or moong dahl in 1½ cups water with a pinch of salt and ⅛ teaspoon turmeric until done. Then mash them well.
2. Slice the eggplants lengthwise. Boil them in a large saucepan filled with 2 cups water, a pinch of salt and ⅛ teaspoon turmeric. When eggplants are tender, add the mashed dahl.
3. Grind the coconut, cumin seed, and green chilies together.
4. Heat 1 tablespoon of the vegetable oil in a skillet and cook the coconut paste 2 to 3 minutes. Add to eggplant mixture.
5. Heat remaining 1 tablespoon oil in the skillet and add mustard seed, bay leaves, and red chilies. When mustard seeds stop cracking, add this mixture to the eggplants. Add lemon juice. Stir a few times. Add salt to taste and sprinkle with coriander leaves. Yield: 4 to 6 servings.

Bhara Mirch Subji

Indians have created many ways to stuff a green pepper (*mirch*). Choose one to suit your palate.

5 large sweet peppers
For stuffing, prepare one of the following: Alu Vada, Kheema Samosa, or Sukhi Urad Dahl (see index)
2 tablespoons vegetable oil
pinch of salt

1. Cut a hole in the top of each sweet pepper and remove seeds.

2. Prepare the stuffing and fill the sweet peppers.
3. Heat vegetable oil in a skillet. Add stuffed sweet peppers. Sprinkle with a pinch of salt and cook, covered, until peppers are tender, about 25 to 30 minutes. Turn them a few times while cooking. Yield: 5 servings.

Kashmiri Mirch Subji

All sweet peppers in India are grown in the North and they are very popular in Kashmir. Kashmiri cooks add a pinch of asafoetida to many of their vegetable dishes, which are traditionally dry and rich.

5 large sweet peppers
2 medium potatoes
4 tablespoons vegetable oil
½ teaspoon mustard seed
pinch of ground asafoetida
1 teaspoon chopped fresh ginger
½ teaspoon cumin seed
2 green chilies (optional)
¼ teaspoon turmeric
salt to taste
2 tablespoons chick-pea flour
1 tablespoon ground mango powder or lemon juice

1. Cut each sweet pepper lengthwise into 8 to 10 pieces. Remove seeds and wash.
2. Scrape the potatoes. Wash and cut into cubes.
3. Heat vegetable oil in a skillet. Add mustard seed. When seeds stop crackling, add a pinch of ground asafoetida, ginger, cumin seed, chilies, turmeric, and sweet peppers. Cook 5 minutes.
4. Add potatoes and salt to taste. Cook until potatoes and sweet peppers are done, about 25 to 30 minutes.
5. Add chick-pea flour and cook 3 minutes. Add mango powder and serve. Yield: 4 to 6 servings.

Khoya Matar

This pea (*matar*) curry is served by wealthy North Indians, since dried whole milk (*khoya*) is so expensive in India. This thick, mild curry is aromatic with whole cardamom.

4 tablespoons vegetable oil
2 large onions, chopped
½ teaspoon cumin seed
½ teaspoon ground ginger
1 tablespoon ground coriander
5 whole cardamom pods
¼ teaspoon turmeric
⅛ teaspoon red pepper (optional)
½ cup very fine dried whole milk
2 large tomatoes, chopped
3 cups green peas
salt to taste
1 cup water

1. Heat vegetable oil in a skillet. Add onions and sauté lightly.
2. Add cumin seed, ginger, coriander, cardamom, turmeric, and red pepper. Stir a few times.
3. Add dried whole milk and stir continuously 2 to 3 minutes.
4. Add tomatoes and cook 5 minutes.
5. Add peas and salt to taste. Mix well. Add 1 cup water and bring to a boil. Cook, covered, over low heat until peas are tender. Yield: 4 to 6 servings.

Matar Panir

This is a soft Indian cheese (chenna or panir) and green pea curry. It is popular with vegetarians.

½ gallon milk
1 cup whipping cream
juice of 2 lemons

Vegetable and Dahl Dishes 143

¼ cup butter
1 teaspoon chopped fresh ginger
5 cloves garlic, chopped
1 large onion, chopped
2 large tomatoes, scalded, skins removed, and chopped
1 teaspoon turmeric
¼ teaspoon red pepper (optional)
1 teaspoon garam masala (see index)
2 cups green peas
1 teaspoon sugar
salt to taste
¼ cup chopped fresh coriander leaves

1. Mix the milk with half-and-half in a saucepan. Bring it to a boil and add lemon juice. When milk curdles, let it stand for a while.
2. Drain milk in a colander and reserve the liquid (whey) for making the sauce.
3. Hang the solid white soft cheese in a cheesecloth bag over the sink for 6 hours, to drain away any liquid.
4. Knead the cheese well until smooth and creamy.
5. Spread cheese on a flat surface in a ¼-inch thick layer. This can be done by rolling the cheese into a ball, then flattening it, gently, on a piece of aluminum foil. Cut cheese into 1-inch cubes.
6. Heat butter in a skillet. Fry the cheese cubes until light gold. Drain the cubes on paper towels and keep covered until needed.
7. Add ginger, garlic, and onions to the butter. Cook 10 minutes.
8. Add tomatoes, turmeric, red pepper, and garam masala to the above mixture. Cook 5 minutes.
9. Add 4 cups reserved whey and boil 3 minutes. Then simmer 10 minutes over medium-low heat. Stir a few times.
10. Add peas, sugar, salt to taste, and half the coriander leaves. Cook, covered, over medium-low heat until peas are tender, about 15 minutes. Stir a few times during the cooking.

11. Uncover and add the fried cheese cubes. Cook over low heat 6 to 7 minutes. Sprinkle with remaining coriander leaves. Serve with rice, Chapatis (see index) and a meat curry. Yield: 5 to 6 servings.

Gobhi Matar

Cauliflower (*gobhi*) is grown mostly in North and Central India, where this mixed vegetable curry is a regional dish. Softly spiced green peas, cauliflower, and tomatoes are accented with chewy golden raisins and crunchy cashew nuts.

2 cups green peas
4 cups water plus 1 teaspoon salt
2 tablespoons vegetable oil
1 tablespoon golden raisins
2 tablespoons cashew nuts, cut in half
1 teaspoon mustard seed
2 large onions, sliced
4 cloves garlic, chopped
1 tablespoon chopped fresh ginger
½ teaspoon cumin seed
¼ teaspoon turmeric
¼ teaspoon red pepper (optional)
2 pounds cauliflower, fresh or thawed, separated into flowerets
4 large tomatoes, chopped
salt to taste
2 cups water
½ cup chopped fresh coriander leaves

1. Boil the peas in 4 cups water and 1 teaspoon salt 10 minutes. Drain and discard the water.
2. Heat 1 tablespoon vegetable oil in a skillet. Add raisins and cashew nuts and fry lightly. Remove from oil and set aside.
3. Add remaining 1 tablespoon oil to the skillet and heat. Add mustard seed. When seeds stop crackling, add onions, garlic, and ginger. Sauté 3 to 5 minutes.

4. Add cumin seed, turmeric, red pepper, and cauliflower. Cook 3 to 5 minutes.
5. Add tomatoes, raisins, cashew nuts, and salt to taste. Mix well.
6. Pour in 2 cups water. Stir a few times and cook, covered, 15 minutes over low heat.
7. Add peas and cook until cauliflower is tender, about 25 to 30 minutes. Sprinkle with coriander leaves and serve. Yield: 4 to 6 servings.

Gobhi Masalam

Buy cauliflower that is white. A tinge of yellow means it is old. The flowerets should be tight. Cauliflower alone stars in this North Indian dish. It is served with a thick yogurt sauce.

1 large cauliflower
1 tablespoon salt
2 large onions, chopped
1 cup yogurt
½ cup chopped coriander leaves
½ teaspoon ground cardamom
¼ teaspoon turmeric
¼ teaspoon ground cloves
⅛ teaspoon red pepper
1 teaspoon garam masala (see index)
1 tablespoon chopped fresh ginger
1 teaspoon sugar
3 tablespoons vegetable oil
salt to taste
1 tomato, sliced

1. Place the cauliflower in a large saucepan and add enough water to barely cover the cauliflower. Sprinkle 1 tablespoon salt over it. Cover and cook over medium heat 10 minutes. Remove cauliflower and reserve 1 cup of water in the saucepan.

2. Meanwhile, blend onions, yogurt, ¼ cup of the coriander leaves, cardamom, turmeric, cloves, red pepper, garam masala, ginger, and sugar.
3. Heat oil in a skillet and add the ground paste. Cook 5 to 7 minutes; then remove from heat to cool.
4. Gently rub the paste over the cauliflower. Be careful not to break the flowerets.
5. Return the cauliflower to the 1 cup of water in the saucepan in which it was steamed. Pour any remaining paste over the top. Add salt to taste. Cook, covered, over low heat until the cauliflower is done, about 25 to 30 minutes. If the sauce is too thick, add some water and cook for a few minutes more.
6. Place the cauliflower on a serving platter or in a large bowl. Decorate the top with tomato slices. Drizzle the sauce over the cauliflower and sprinkle with remaining ¼ cup coriander leaves. Yield: 4 to 6 servings.

Sukha Gobhi

This is a dry (*sukha*) cauliflower, potatoes, and tomato curry. Serve it with Indian bread and rice.

3 tablespoons vegetable oil
1 large onion, thinly sliced
1 tablespoon chopped fresh ginger
5 cloves garlic, chopped
2 green chilies, chopped (optional)
¼ teaspoon turmeric
1 large potato, scraped, washed, and diced
2 pounds cauliflower, fresh or thawed, separated into flowerets
½ cup chopped fresh coriander leaves
⅛ teaspoon red pepper (optional)
1 teaspoon garam masala (see index)
salt to taste
3 large tomatoes, roughly cut

1. Heat vegetable oil in a skillet. Add onions, ginger, garlic, and chilies. Sauté 2 to 3 minutes.

2. Add turmeric and potatoes. Cook 2 to 3 minutes.
3. Add cauliflower, coriander leaves, red pepper, garam masala, and salt to taste. Cook 5 minutes.
4. Add tomatoes and cook until the liquid dries up and potatoes and cauliflower are tender. Yield: 4 to 6 servings.

Alu Dum

Dum, which means "breathed in," is the Indian method of steam cooking. For this dish, whole potatoes (*alu*) are cooked in a rich yogurt masala.

2 pounds walnut-sized potatoes
1 tablespoon blanched almonds
1 tablespoon fennel seed
½ teaspoon cumin seed
1 teaspoon chopped fresh ginger
½ teaspoon ground cloves
3 tablespoons vegetable oil
¼ teaspoon turmeric
½ teaspoon ground cardamom
1 teaspoon black pepper
⅛ teaspoon red pepper (optional)
1 cup yogurt, well-beaten
salt to taste
1 teaspoon garam masala (see index)
1 tablespoon lemon juice

1. Parboil the potatoes. If small potatoes are not available, use large potatoes, and cut them into small pieces after peeling. Peel and prick potatoes all over with a toothpick. Set aside.
2. Dry roast the almonds until golden. Grind together the fennel seed, cumin seed, ginger, cloves, and almonds to a paste, adding about 1 tablespoon water.
3. Heat vegetable oil in a skillet. Add potatoes and cook until light gold. Remove potatoes from oil and set aside to drain.

4. Reheat the oil. Add the ground spice paste and cook for half a minute.
5. Add turmeric, cardamom, black pepper, red pepper and well-beaten yogurt. Cook 1 to 2 minutes.
6. Add potatoes and salt to taste. Cook, covered, until potatoes are tender, about 20 minutes. Sprinkle with garam masala and lemon juice. Serve with rice or any Indian bread. Yield: 4 to 6 servings.

Palak Tomatar

Tomatoes and spinach are cooked and then ground to a thick, creamy consistency in this mild dish with a hint of ginger.

1 pound fresh or thawed spinach
3 tomatoes, chopped
1 large onion, chopped
¼ teaspoon turmeric
1 tablespoon chopped fresh ginger
2 green chilies (optional)
1 cup water
5 tablespoons butter
salt to taste
1 tablespoon lemon juice

1. Place spinach, tomatoes, onions, turmeric, ginger and chilies in a saucepan with 1 cup water. Cook, covered, 15 minutes over medium-low heat.
2. Remove from heat and cool. Blend in an electric blender to a creamy consistency.
3. Heat butter in a saucepan. Add spinach mixture and salt to taste. Cook 5 minutes over low heat. Add lemon juice and serve. Yield: 4 to 6 servings.

Tomato Foogath

Foogaths are savory dishes made from different kinds of cooked vegetables and freshly scraped or grated coconut.

2 tablespoons vegetable oil
1 teaspoon mustard seeds

1 large onion, chopped
1 teaspoon chopped fresh ginger
3 cloves garlic, chopped
2 green chilies, chopped
2 large tomatoes, skinned and chopped
¼ cup freshly grated coconut
1 teaspoon salt

1. Heat vegetable oil in a skillet. Add mustard seed. When seeds start crackling, add onions, ginger, garlic, and chilies. Sauté 2 to 3 minutes.
2. Add tomatoes, coconut, and salt. Stir gently and cook over low heat, uncovered, until most of the liquid dries up. Serve with rice and any Indian bread. Yield: 4 servings.

Variations: Instead of tomatoes, use 1 small cabbage sliced and parboiled. Or use parboiled cauliflower, carrots, green peas, or any other vegetable or fruit.

Sukhi Bhindi

If using fresh okra, select young and tender pods that snap like green beans. There are no sweet spices in this dry okra dish.

2 pounds okra, fresh or thawed
4 tablespoons vegetable oil
1 teaspoon mustard seed
¼ teaspoon ground asafoetida
¼ teaspoon turmeric
⅛ teaspoon red pepper (optional)
salt to taste
2 tablespoons rice flour
¼ cup chopped fresh coriander leaves
2 tablespoons lemon juice

1. Clean okra gently with a moist kitchen towel. Cut each crosswise into 4 to 6 pieces.
2. Heat vegetable oil in a skillet. Add mustard seed. When seeds start popping, add asafoetida, okra, turmeric, red

pepper, and salt to taste. Cook, covered, until okra is tender, about 15 to 20 minutes.
3. Meanwhile, dry roast the rice flour until light gold.
4. Add rice flour and coriander leaves to okra. Cook 5 minutes over low heat. If the okra starts sticking to the pan, add 1 tablespoon or so of water. Sprinkle with lemon juice and serve. Yield: 4 to 6 servings.

Bhindi Subji

This okra and tomato curry is not as dry as the previous one, but it is spicier.

2 pounds okra, fresh or thawed
4 tablespoons vegetable oil
1 medium onion, minced
4 cloves garlic, chopped
½ teaspoon cumin seed
2 green chilies, chopped (optional)
¼ cup chopped fresh coriander leaves
¼ teaspoon turmeric
2 cans (8 ounces each) stewed tomatoes
2 tablespoons vinegar
½ cup water
1 tablespoon ground black pepper
salt to taste

1. Wipe okra gently with moist kitchen towel. Cut each into 4 pieces and set aside.
2. Heat vegetable oil in a skillet. Add onions, garlic, cumin seed, chilies, and coriander leaves. Sauté 4 to 5 minutes. Add turmeric. Stir once or twice.
3. Add tomatoes, vinegar, and ½ cup water. Bring to a boil. Lower heat and simmer 15 minutes.
4. Add okra, black pepper, and salt to taste. Cover and cook until okra is tender, about 20 minutes. Yield: 4 to 6 servings.

Sukha Bundhgobi

Thinly sliced cabbage is cooked with green peas and potatoes in this dry curry.

1 large white cabbage, about 1½ pounds
2 large potatoes
4 tablespoons vegetable oil
1 teaspoon mustard seed
¼ teaspoon fenugreek seed
1 medium onion, sliced
½ cup green peas
1 teaspoon sugar
salt to taste
⅛ teaspoon red pepper (optional)
2 tablespoons lemon juice

1. Slice the cabbage thin. Wash it and set aside to drain.
2. Scrape the potatoes and dice them. Wash and set aside to drain.
3. Heat vegetable oil in a skillet. Add mustard seed and fenugreek seed. When mustard seeds stop popping, add onions and sauté 3 minutes.
4. Add peas and potatoes. Cook 5 minutes.
5. Add cabbage, sugar, salt to taste, and red pepper. Cook, covered, until vegetables are tender, about 20 minutes. Add lemon juice and serve. Yield: 4 to 6 servings.

Dahl Palak

Vegetables and dahls are cooked together in this easy-to-prepare, softly seasoned North Indian dish.

½ cup split peas
2 cups water
¼ teaspoon turmeric
½ teaspoon salt
1 pound spinach, chopped

3 tablespoons butter
1 tablespoon chopped fresh ginger
4 cloves garlic, chopped
1 tablespoon garam masala (see index)
1 tablespoon lemon juice
salt to taste

1. Soak split peas in 2 cups water 1 hour.
2. Add turmeric and ½ teaspoon salt to split peas. Boil 10 minutes in same water used for soaking peas.
3. Add spinach and cook until most of the liquid has been absorbed and peas are done.
4. Meanwhile, heat butter in a skillet. Add ginger and garlic. Cook until garlic is golden. Add garam masala.
5. Immediately add the seasoned ginger and garlic to the spinach-pea mixture. Add lemon juice and salt to taste and serve. Yield: 4 to 6 servings.

Kabuli Chana

This dahl-based dish found its way to India from Kabul, the capital of Afghanistan. *Chana* are chick-peas, or *garbanzos*, as the Mexicans call them. They grow abundantly in North and East India.

1 pound Kabuli chanas (large chick-peas)
4 cups water
1 tablespoon salt
5 tablespoons vegetable oil
1 small onion, finely chopped
2 green chilies (optional)
1 teaspoon ground coriander
½ teaspoon cumin seeds
½ teaspoon ground ginger
¼ teaspoon ground cloves
½ teaspoon ground garlic
¼ teaspoon red pepper

2 large tomatoes, chopped
1 tablespoon dry mango powder or lemon juice
2 tablespoons chopped fresh coriander leaves

1. Clean and wash the chick-peas. Soak them in 4 cups water overnight. Boil the chick-peas in same water with 1 tablespoon salt, until done, about 40 minutes. Drain and reserve 1 cup of stock.
2. Heat vegetable oil in a skillet. Add onions and chilies. Sauté until onions are golden.
3. Add ground coriander, cumin seed, ginger, cloves, garlic, and red pepper. Fry a few minutes.
4. Add tomatoes and cook until oil separates and tomatoes are converted to a purée.
5. Add boiled chanas, 1 cup of chana stock, and salt to taste. Cook 15 minutes over low heat. Add mango powder or lemon juice and mix. Sprinkle with coriander leaves and serve. Yield: 4 to 6 servings.

Chana Masala

This is a dry, spiced dahl dish.

4 tablespoons vegetable oil
1 teaspoon mustard seed
pinch of asafoetida
1 teaspoon ground coriander
¼ teaspoon ground ginger
3 green chilies, chopped
1 pound canned chick-peas
salt to taste
2 tomatoes, quartered
1 tablespoon ground mango powder or lemon juice
2 tablespoons chopped fresh coriander leaves

1. Heat vegetable oil in a skillet. Add mustard seed. When seeds stop crackling, add asafoetida, ground coriander, ginger, and chilies. Cook a few minutes.

2. Add drained chick-peas and salt to taste. Mix gently. Cook a few minutes.
3. Gently place quartered tomatoes into skillet, making sure they do not break. The tomatoes are used for decoration. Cook, covered, for a few minutes, or until tomatoes are heated through. Add mango powder or lemon juice and sprinkle with coriander leaves. Yield: 4 to 6 servings.

Sambar

This is a South Indian dahl-based dish that has the consistency of a very thick soup. It is usually eaten with plain boiled rice. An endless variety of vegetables and fish can be used for sambars. This one features tomatoes, eggplant, and potatoes mixed with dahl. Sambars make excellent dips.

2 tablespoons tamarind or lemon juice
10 cups water
¾ cup split yellow peas
½ teaspoon turmeric
½ teaspoon salt
4 medium tomatoes, chopped
½ teaspoon cumin seed
5 whole dry red peppers
½ teaspoon black peppercorns
¼ teaspoon fenugreek seed
1 teaspoon ground coriander, dry roasted
2 tablespoons fresh shredded coconut, dry roasted
6 tablespoons butter
1 small eggplant, cut into small cubes
1 medium potato, peeled and cut into small cubes
1 large onion, sliced
salt to taste
½ teaspoon sugar (optional)
½ teaspoon mustard seed
½ cup fresh coriander leaves
2 bay leaves
pinch of asafoetida

Vegetable and Dahl Dishes

1. Soak tamarind in ½ cup water.
2. Bring 5 cups water to a boil in a large saucepan. Add split peas, turmeric, and ½ teaspoon salt. Boil a few minutes. Continue to cook over medium-low heat until most of the liquid evaporates.
3. Mash dahl thoroughly. Add 5 cups water and bring to a boil. Turn to medium-low heat. Add tomatoes and simmer.
4. Meanwhile, separately roast cumin seed, whole red peppers, peppercorns, and fenugreek seed. Cool. Then grind together with roasted ground coriander and shredded coconut. Add to simmering dahl.
5. Heat 2 tablespoons butter in a skillet. Sauté the eggplant lightly 2 to 3 minutes. Add potatoes and cook 2 minutes. Add potatoes and eggplant to dahl and stir a few times.
6. Heat 2 tablespoons butter in skillet. Add onions and sauté until translucent.
7. Add onions and butter to dahl. Add sugar and salt to taste. Simmer 15 to 20 minutes, or until the vegetables are done.
8. Strain the tamarind juice and discard pulp. Add tamarind juice or lemon juice to dahl and simmer 5 minutes.
9. Heat remaining 2 tablespoons butter in skillet. Add mustard seed and coriander leaves. When mustard seeds stop crackling, add bay leaves and asafoetida. Add this to the dahl and serve. Yield: 5 to 8 servings.

Moong Dahl

This is the most popular dahl in North India. It is eaten by people of all classes. A whole moong bean is cylindrical and green, but when the green skin is removed and the bean is halved, the split bean is rectangular and yellow. This spicy recipe can be prepared easily and quickly.

1 cup split moong dahl, soaked 1 hour in 2 cups water
4 cups water
½ teaspoon turmeric

3 tablespoons butter
2 green chilies, chopped
1 small onion, sliced
1 teaspoon chopped fresh ginger
7 cloves garlic, chopped
2 tablespoons chopped fresh coriander leaves
1 teaspoon garam masala (see index)
¼ teaspoon red pepper (optional)
salt to taste

1. Clean and wash the dahl. Soak in 2 cups water 1 hour. Then drain.
2. Bring 4 cups water to boil in a large saucepan. Add turmeric and dahl. Boil 2 minutes. Continue to cook over medium-low heat until done, about 20 to 30 minutes.
3. Meanwhile, heat butter in a skillet. Add chilies, onions, ginger, garlic, and coriander leaves. Sauté until onions are translucent. Add garam masala and red pepper. Cook 1 minute.
4. Add this mixture to the dahl. Add salt to taste. Serve with plain boiled rice and Chapatis (see index). Yield: 4 to 6 servings.

Whole Urad Dahl

The urad bean is small, black, and cylindrical. It is rectangular and off-white when hulled and split. This dish requires a long cooking time, which allows one to go about other business. This is a specialty of Punjab cooks, who let the urad dahl simmer in tandoori ovens over 24 hours. Eliminate the 3 whole dry red peppers if you prefer a mild flavor.

1 cup whole urad dahl, soaked 1 hour in 2 cups water
4 cups water
½ teaspoon turmeric
3 tablespoons butter
2 green chilies, chopped (optional)
1 teaspoon chopped fresh ginger
3 whole dry red peppers (optional)

2 tablespoons chopped fresh coriander leaves
7 cloves garlic, chopped
1 teaspoon garam masala (see index)
salt to taste

Proceed as in the preceding Moong Dahl recipe. Red peppers are fried along with the other fried ingredients. Yield: 4 to 6 servings.

Sukhi Urad Dahl

This dry version is highlighted by shredded coconut, cashew nuts, and raisins.

1 cup urad dahl, soaked 1 hour in 2 cups water
7 cups water
1 teaspoon salt
½ teaspoon turmeric
4 tablespoons butter
1 large onion, thinly sliced
½ teaspoon cumin seeds
2 tablespoons fresh shredded coconut
1 tablespoon roughly chopped unsalted cashew nuts
1 tablespoon golden raisins
2 green chilies, chopped (optional)
1 tablespoon lemon juice
2 tablespoons chopped fresh coriander leaves

1. Clean and wash the dahl. Soak in 2 cups water 1 hour. Then drain.
2. Bring 7 cups water to boil in a large pot. Add salt, turmeric, and dahl. Cook over medium heat until tender. Lower heat and cook until all the liquid has evaporated. Remove from heat.
3. Heat 2 tablespoons butter in a skillet. Add onions and sauté lightly. Add onions to dahl.
4. Heat remaining 2 tablespoons butter in same skillet. Add cumin seed, coconut, cashew nuts, raisins, and chilies. Sauté until golden.

5. Add to dahl mixture and cook over low heat 2 minutes. Add lemon juice and sprinkle with coriander leaves. Serve with rice and Chapatis (see index). Yield: 4 to 6 servings.

Yellow Split-Pea Dahl

Yellow split peas are cooked with tomatoes in this spicy dish.

1¼ cups yellow split peas
8½ cups water
2 medium onions, sliced
½ teaspoon turmeric
1 teaspoon garam masala (see index)
3 medium tomatoes, quartered
2 tablespoons chopped fresh coriander leaves
salt to taste
3 tablespoons butter
1 teaspoon chopped fresh ginger
½ teaspoon mustard seed
½ teaspoon cumin seed
2 green chilies (optional)
4 cloves garlic, chopped
pinch of ground asafoetida
1 tablespoon lemon juice

1. Clean and wash the dahl.
2. Bring 6 cups of the water to boil in a large pot. Add half of the sliced onions, the split peas, and the turmeric. Cook, uncovered, over medium heat until most of the liquid has evaporated.
3. Mash the peas thoroughly. Add garam masala, tomatoes, 1 tablespoon of the chopped coriander leaves, and remaining 2½ cups water. Cook over low heat 15 minutes. Add salt to taste.
4. Heat 2 tablespoons of the butter in a skillet. Sauté remaining onions lightly. Add onions to dahl mixture and stir.

5. Heat remaining 1 tablespoon butter in same skillet. When butter becomes quite hot, add ginger, mustard seed, cumin seed, chilies, and garlic. When garlic is translucent, add asafoetida.
6. Immediately pour entire mixture into the dahl. Add lemon juice and sprinkle with remaining 1 tablespoon coriander leaves. Yield: 4 to 6 servings.

Masoor Dahl

Masoor Dahl is a tiny, round, shiny salmon-colored lentil. It turns yellow when cooked. This dahl dish can be prepared in about 30 minutes.

1 cup masoor (lentils)
8 cups water
¼ teaspoon turmeric
3 tablespoons butter
1 large onion, sliced
1 teaspoon sugar
½ teaspoon cumin seed
1 teaspoon chopped fresh ginger
4 cloves garlic, chopped
2 green chilies, chopped (optional)
salt to taste
1 tablespoon lemon juice

1. Clean and wash the lentils.
2. Bring 6 cups water to a boil in a large pot. Add lentils and turmeric. Cook, uncovered, over medium-low heat until lentils are tender and almost all the liquid has evaporated.
3. Mash lentils lightly. Add remaining 2 cups water. Bring to a boil and simmer over low heat 10 minutes.
4. Meanwhile, heat 2 tablespoons butter in a skillet. Add onions and sauté until translucent. Add onions and sugar to lentils and stir.

5. Heat remaining 1 tablespoon butter in skillet. Add cumin seed, ginger, garlic, and chilies. Cook until garlic is golden.
6. Add to lentil mixture along with salt to taste and lemon juice. Stir a few times. If dahl is too thick, add ½ cup water and cook over low heat for a few more minutes. Serve with rice and Chapatis (see index). Yield: 4 to 6 servings.

Kadhi

Kadhi is a rich chick-pea flour and yogurt curry served warm with rice and Chapatis. If made with a little water, Kadhi could be served as a soup.

½ cup chick-pea flour
3 cups yogurt, well-beaten
½ teaspoon turmeric
¼ teaspoon sugar
1-inch stick cinnamon
4 cloves
3 green chilies, seeds removed and chilies sliced lengthwise
1 teaspoon chopped fresh ginger
3 cups water
1 tablespoon vegetable oil
1 teaspoon mustard seed
½ teaspoon cumin seed
½ cup chopped fresh coriander leaves
salt to taste

1. Break up any lumps in chick-pea flour. Combine it with yogurt, turmeric, sugar, cinnamon, cloves, green chilies, ginger, and 3 cups water in a saucepan. Bring to a boil. Then simmer over medium heat 15 minutes.
2. Heat vegetable oil in a skillet. Add mustard seed. When seeds start crackling, add cumin seed and ¼ cup chopped coriander leaves. Cook 1 minute.
3. Pour the mustard-cumin seed mixture into the yogurt. Add salt to taste and sprinkle with remaining ¼ cup coriander leaves. Yield: 4 to 6 servings.

Pakora Kadhi

In this version, the kadhi serves as a sauce for the fried chick-pea flour pakoras.

1 cup chick-pea flour
1 cup onions, chopped
2 tablespoons fresh coriander leaves
½ teaspoon ground coriander
½ teaspoon garam masala (see index)
½ teaspoon salt
½ teaspoon baking soda
1 teaspoon vegetable oil
vegetable oil for deep frying
Kadhi (see previous recipe)

1. In a mixing bowl, combine chick-pea flour, onions, coriander leaves, ground coriander, garam masala, salt, baking soda, and 1 teaspoon oil. Add enough water to make a thick batter.
2. Heat vegetable oil for deep frying.
3. Drop batter into oil by the spoonful. Batter will form a small ball as it fries. Fry several at a time, until golden. Place on paper towels to dry.
4. Prepare the kadhi as described in the previous recipe.
5. Add the pakoras to the kadhi and soak for 1 hour. Serve with rice and Chapatis (see index). Yield: 4 to 6 servings.

Dahi Vada

These fried lentil balls in yogurt are eaten as a tea-time snack, mainly in the North.

½ cup urad dahl (lentils)
2 cups water
2 green chilies, chopped
4 tablespoons chopped coriander leaves
1½ teaspoon cumin seed
1 teaspoon chopped fresh ginger
1 teaspoon freshly grated coconut

1½ teaspoon salt
pinch of baking soda
2 cups yogurt, well-beaten
½ cup buttermilk
pinch of red pepper
1 teaspoon freshly ground black pepper
vegetable oil for deep frying

1. Clean and soak urad dahl in 2 cups water 3 to 4 hours. Drain in a colander.
2. Grind dahl, green chilies, 2 tablespoons of the coriander leaves, ½ teaspoon of the cumin seed, ginger, coconut, and ½ teaspoon salt to a very smooth paste, adding a few tablespoons of water.
3. Place the paste in a bowl. Add baking soda and mix well. Set aside, covered, 1 hour.
4. Meanwhile, combine well-beaten yogurt with buttermilk. Add red pepper, remaining 1 teaspoon salt, remaining 1 teaspoon ground cumin seed, and black pepper. Set aside and keep chilled.
5. Heat vegetable oil for deep frying.
6. Mix the seasoned dahl well. Drop a tablespoon at a time into the hot oil. Fry 8 to 10 at a time until golden. Drain on paper towels.
7. Soak the vadas in seasoned yogurt 2 hours. Sprinkle with remaining coriander leaves and serve. Yield: 5 to 6 servings.

9

Rice Dishes

When Indians shop for rice in food markets, they carefully examine handfuls of several varieties before making a selection. They pass them under their noses to sniff the bouquet, and they scrutinize each variety for color, shape, and texture.

That is hardly the way one goes about buying rice in American food stores, where rice is sold in packages labeled "quick-cooking," "instant," "pre-cooked," or "mixed with herbs and spices." Before the rice even reaches the grocer's shelves, it is often scraped, polished, and stripped of the vitamins and minerals contained in the bran and skin covering.

Most Americans would not recognize the rice sold in Indian markets, because it still has its thin red skin, which is rich in vitamins A and B_1. Many Indians would rather starve than eat American rice contributions, which Indians have been known to dump into the ocean.

There are some good rices grown in the United States, especially in Arkansas and in the Carolinas. These varieties are the best selections for the rice preparations in this book. The rice should be the long-grain uncooked variety; however, parboiled rice is acceptable. The parboiling process relocates nutrients from the outer layers to the center of the grain. It then undergoes a final steaming process to seal in the vitamins and nutrients.

Because different types and ages of rice vary in cooking times, it might be necessary to test the rice and adjust the cooking time accordingly. Indians eat rice with their hands, so each cooked grain must be separate. It should not be gummy like Chinese rice, which is eaten with chopsticks. An Indian chef is concerned with the appearance of the rice as well as the flavor.

It is understandable that Indians are true epicures of rice, since more than a thousand varieties have grown in the subcontinent for about 5000 years. *Patna, basmati, pulao,* and *rangoon* are a few of the more prominent strains. Patna is used by upper-class Indians as "table rice." Basmati, grown in eastern Punjab at the foothills of the Himalayas, is the rice the wealthy dine on at weddings and other special occasions. It can be identified immediately by its aroma and nutty flavor. Basmati can be found in American specialty food stores.

Rice is the staple diet for the majority of Indians, particularly in the South. Statisticians believe an average Indian eats about ½ to ⅔ of a pound of rice per day. An American, on the other hand, consumes about six pounds of rice a year.

Indians do not think of rice as a filler, like pasta or potatoes. They often use it to soak up savory curries. Even the poorest Indian can make an exciting meal by combining a variety of curry sauces with rice.

In India, rice is important not only as a sustainer of life. İt also plays a very important role in the Hindu wedding ceremony as one of the foods offered to the gods and goddesses. The groom ties a handful of rice in his bride's sari during one part of the ritual. At the end, bride and groom spinkle each other with red-colored rice as a symbol of prosperity and fruitful union. This custom has traveled to the Western nations.

Bhat

Since no butter is used in this plain boiled rice, it is somewhat sticky. Serve bhat with meat or vegetable curries and dahl dishes.

2 cups rice
4 cups water
salt to taste

1. Bring 4 cups water to a boil in a saucepan. Add rice and stir a few times, to prevent it from sticking to the bottom. Add salt to taste. Bring water to a boil again and boil 3 minutes.
2. Lower heat and cook, covered, until all the liquid is absorbed. Yield: 4 to 6 servings.

Kheer Bhat

This South Indian rice dish is sugary and rich with grated coconut and cashew nuts. Serve it as a dessert or with a main dish such as baked ham or roast loin of pork.

2 tablespoons butter
¼ cup chopped cashew nuts
2 tablespoons raisins
¼ cup butter
3 cups rice, long-grain
5 cups water
pinch of saffron
⅔ cup butter
2 cups freshly grated coconut
2 cups sugar
pinch of nutmeg

½ teaspoon ground cardamom
1 tablespoon rose water

1. Heat 2 tablespoons butter in a skillet. Cook cashew nuts and raisins a few minutes. Remove from heat and set aside.
2. Heat ¼ cup butter in a large saucepan. Add the rice and cook until light gold.
3. Add 5 cups water and saffron to rice. Bring to a boil; then cook over medium-low heat until most of the liquid dries up and rice is tender.
4. Add remaining ⅔ cup butter, coconut, sugar, nuts and raisins. Mix well.
5. Add nutmeg and cardamom. Mix and cook a few minutes. Sprinkle with rose water and serve. Yield: 6 servings.

Khichadi

Khichadi (porridge or "a bit of a mess") is prepared from inexpensive, short-grain brown rice and dahls. It can be made with masoor dahl, moong dahl, gram, or chana dahl. *Geeli* (soft khichadi) is fed to invalids and infants.

1 cup split peas or moong dahl
5 cups water
1 cup rice, short-grain
½ teaspoon turmeric
salt to taste
¼ cup butter
2 large onions, thinly sliced
1 teaspoon mustard seed
1 teaspoon cumin seed
2 tablespoons chopped fresh ginger
10 cloves garlic, chopped
4 whole red peppers
pinch of ground asafoetida

2 tablespoons fresh lemon juice
1 tablespoon garam masala (see index)
½ cup chopped fresh coriander leaves

1. Bring 5 cups water to a boil in a large saucepan. Add split peas or moong dahl and stir a few times. Bring the water to a boil again and boil 15 minutes.
2. Add rice, turmeric, and salt to taste. Mix. Bring water to a boil again, and boil a few minutes. Lower heat and cook, covered, until the rice and split peas are quite soft.
3. Meanwhile, heat butter in a skillet. Add onions and sauté until golden.
4. Add onions to the rice and pea mixture, along with most of the butter. Leave 1½ to 2 tablespoons of the butter in the skillet.
5. The last step in making khichadi is called *baghar*. Begin by reheating the remaining butter in skillet over high heat. Add mustard seeds. When they begin to pop, add cumin seeds, ginger, garlic, and whole red pepper. Cook a few minutes.
6. Add asafoetida and pour all the contents of skillet into the rice and pea mixture, keeping your face turned away from the pan. Cover immediately.
7. When the sizzling sound subsides, remove the cover. Add lemon juice and garam masala. Mix well. Sprinkle with coriander leaves. Serve with yogurt, papads and hot pickles. Yield: 4 to 6 servings.

Punjabi Khichadi

The Punjabis use expensive, nutty-flavored basmati for their khichadi. They simmer it in aromatic whole cardamom, cloves, bay leaves, and cinnamon.

¾ cup moong dahl
1½ cups basmati, or any long-grain rice
4 tablespoons butter
5 cloves

3 whole cardamom pods
1-inch stick cinnamon
2 bay leaves
5 black peppercorns
2 medium onions, chopped
3 green chilies, chopped
5 cups hot water
salt to taste
3 tablespoons raisins
3 tablespoons chopped cashew nuts
2 medium onions, sliced
1 cup chopped fresh coriander leaves
lemon wedges

1. Clean and soak the dahl and rice separately, 30 minutes. Drain each separately in a colander.
2. Heat 2 tablespoons of the butter in a saucepan. Add cloves, cardamom, cinnamon, bay leaves, and peppercorns. Cook 2 to 3 minutes.
3. Add 2 chopped onions and sauté until translucent.
4. Add green chilies, rice, and dahl. Cook 5 minutes.
5. Pour in 5 cups hot water and salt to taste. Bring to a boil and boil on medium heat until dahl and rice are done, about 25 minutes. Stir a few times. Cook until most of the liquid dries up and the grains are separate.
6. Heat 1 tablespoon butter in a skillet and cook raisins and cashew nuts a few minutes. Set aside for garnish.
7. Heat remaining 1 tablespoon butter in skillet and sauté 2 sliced onions until translucent.
8. Add coriander leaves and cook 1 minute. Add this to the cooked dahl and rice mixture. Serve garnished with fried cashew nuts and raisins and lemon wedges. Khichadi is eaten with pickle, yogurt, papads, and lots of ghee (clarified butter) poured over it. Yield: 6 servings.

Lime Rice

Limes are among the acidic fruits grown in South India. This lime rice is crunchy with cashew nuts and hot with 4 green chilies.

1½ cups rice
4 cups water
1 tablespoon salt
5 tablespoons butter
1 tablespoon mustard seed
½ cup chopped cashew nuts
4 green chilies (optional)
½ cup freshly shredded coconut
¼ teaspoon turmeric
½ cup chopped fresh coriander leaves
juice of 4 large limes

1. Boil rice in 4 cups water and 1 tablespoon salt 7 to 10 minutes. Drain and set aside.
2. Heat butter in a large pan. Add mustard seeds and cook until they start popping. Add cashew nuts, chilies, coconut, turmeric, coriander leaves and rice. Cook a few minutes.
3. Add lime juice and mix well. Cook over low heat, covered, 10 to 15 minutes, or until rice is done. Yield: 4 to 6 servings.

Lemon Rice

Lemon juice lends a tang to this South Indian rice dish.

1½ cups rice
5 cups water
1 tablespoon salt

4 tablespoons butter
1 teaspoon mustard seed
20 cashew nuts, halved
2 tablespoons peanuts, chopped
1 teaspoon chopped fresh ginger
2 tablespoons blanched almonds
1 cup chopped fresh coriander leaves
4 green chilies, chopped (optional)
2 tablespoons shredded coconut
¼ teaspoon turmeric
juice of 4 large lemons

1. Boil rice in 5 cups water and 1 tablespoon salt 7 to 10 minutes. Drain and set the rice aside in a large skillet.
2. Heat butter in a skillet. Add mustard seed, cashew nuts, peanuts, ginger, almonds, coriander leaves, chilies, and coconut. Cook 2 minutes, or until nuts are light gold. Add turmeric and stir a few times.
3. Add this mixture to the cooked rice. Also add the lemon juice and mix well. Add salt to taste, if desired. Cook 2 to 3 minutes over low heat and serve. Yield: 4 to 6 servings.

Rice Pongal

Pongal (January 13-15) is the time when Indians thank the gods for the sun and water that produced the surplus harvest. The rice, millet and cotton will now be marketed. This rice pongal is one of the many grain dishes eaten during the lavish festivals in Tamil Nadu, Andhra Pradesh, and Mysore.

4 tablespoons butter
2 bay leaves
1 cup freshly shredded coconut
15 golden raisins
10 cashew nuts
½ teaspoon cumin seed
3½ cups water
1 teaspoon ground cardamom

½ teaspoon turmeric
1½ cups rice
salt to taste

1. Heat 2 tablespoons of the butter in a skillet. Add bay leaves, coconut, raisins, cashew nuts, and cumin seed. Cook 3 minutes.
2. Pour in 3½ cups water and bring to a boil.
3. Add cardamom, turmeric, remaining 2 tablespoons butter, rice, and salt to taste. Mix and cook over low heat until rice is done. Yield: 4 to 6 servings.

Coconut Rice

Milk from the coconut gives this softly spiced rice dish its characteristic taste.

1½ cups rice, soaked 30 minutes in 1½ cups water
1½ cups freshly shredded coconut, soaked 30 minutes in 2 cups water
3 tablespoons butter
1 medium onion, chopped
salt to taste
1 teaspoon ground cardamom

1. Drain the rice and set aside. Reserve the water.
2. Blend the coconut, using the water in which it was soaked. Strain and reserve the coconut milk.
3. Heat butter in a skillet. Add onions and sauté until golden.
4. Add rice and fry a few minutes.
5. Add coconut milk and water in which the rice was soaked. Bring to a boil. Add salt to taste and cardamom. Lower heat and cook until rice is done. Yield: 4 to 6 servings.

Biryani

Biryanis, the royalty of rice dishes, were introduced to North India by the Moguls. They are prepared by arranging half-cooked rice in layers with meat, poultry, fish, or vegetables in a casserole. Butter and Mogul saffron are sprinkled on top, and the lid is sealed. They are garnished with sautéed raisins, nuts, quartered eggs, onion rings, rose water, and sometimes gold leaf—the feast of rajahs. This vegetable version includes tomatoes, peas, carrots, and mushrooms.

4 cups water
8 black peppercorns
9 whole cardamom pods
1-inch stick cinnamon
8 cloves
1½ cups parboiled rice
2 tablespoons salt
5 tablespoons butter
2 onions, thinly sliced
2 tablespoons golden raisins
2 tablespoons slivered almonds
2 onions, chopped
5 cloves garlic, chopped
1 tablespoon chopped fresh ginger
1 teaspoon poppy seed
½ teaspoon cumin seed
1 teaspoon garam masala (see index)
2 green chilies, chopped (optional)
1-inch stick cinnamon
2 tomatoes, chopped
½ cup green peas
½ cup chopped carrots
½ cup chopped mushrooms
salt to taste
¼ teaspoon string saffron, soaked in 4 tablespoons warm milk for 10 minutes
silver leaf paper (optional)
1 medium cucumber, peeled and sliced
raisins for garnish
almonds for garnish

Rice Dishes

1. Preheat oven to 350° F. Bring 4 cups water to a boil in a large saucepan. Add peppercorns, 3 of the cardamom pods, 1-inch stick cinnamon, 4 of the cloves, and parboiled rice. Bring to boil again. Add 2 tablespoons salt. Boil the rice 5 to 7 minutes, until three-quarters done. Drain the water from the rice, using a colander.
2. Heat 2 tablespoons of the butter in a large skillet. Add 2 thinly sliced onions and sauté until golden. Remove from skillet with a slotted spoon and set aside.
3. Reheat the butter and add 2 tablespoons raisins and slivered almonds. Brown the almonds, lightly. Remove both from skillet and set aside.
4. Heat 1 tablespoon butter in skillet. Add 2 chopped onions. Sauté until golden.
5. Add garlic, ginger, poppy seed, cumin seed, garam masala, green chilies, 4 cloves, remaining 6 cardamom pods, and cinnamon. Fry 2 to 3 minutes.
6. Add tomatoes, peas, carrots, mushrooms, and salt to taste. Cook, covered, over low heat until the vegetables are almost done.
7. In a large baking dish, arrange the vegetables, rice, and fried onions in alternating layers, using only half of each per layer.
8. Sprinkle the saffron-soaked milk on top, along with remaining 2 tablespoons butter.
9. Cover tightly with aluminum foil and bake 20 to 30 minutes. Before serving, garnish with raisins, almonds, cucumber, and silver leaf paper (available at Indian specialty shops). Serve with a yogurt raita (see index). Yield: 4 to 6 servings.

Lamb or Beef Biryani

On February 26, Moslems observe *Id*—the month of fasting is over. Platters are heaped with this rich, aromatic meat biryani.

5 tablespoons butter
5 cloves garlic, chopped

1 teaspoon chopped ginger
1 large onion, sliced
1½ pounds lamb or beef, cubed
¼ teaspoon ground cloves
¼ teaspoon ground cardamom
⅛ teaspoon red pepper (optional)
¼ teaspoon cinnamon
½ teaspoon salt
7 cups water
5 whole cardamom pods
1-inch stick cinnamon
2 bay leaves
5 cloves
10 black peppercorns
3 tablespoons salt
1 cup rice, long-grain
15 to 20 golden raisins
¼ cup slivered almonds
1 large onion, chopped
¼ cup cream
¼ teaspoon saffron
4 hard-cooked eggs, shelled and quartered
2 medium tomatoes, sliced
1 teaspoon garam masala (see index)
1 tablespoon lemon juice
½ cup yogurt, beaten
2 tablespoons chopped coriander leaves

1. Heat 2 tablespoons of the butter in a skillet. Add garlic, ginger, and 1 sliced onion. Sauté until onions are translucent.
2. Add meat and brown.
3. Add ground cloves, ground cardamom, red pepper, ground cinnamon, and ½ teaspoon salt. Stir a few times.
4. Pour in 2 cups warm water. Bring to a boil. Turn heat to low and cook, covered, until meat is tender. Preheat oven to 350° F.

5. Meanwhile, bring 5 cups water to a boil in a saucepan. Add whole cardamom, stick cinnamon, bay leaves, whole cloves, peppercorns, 3 tablespoons salt, and rice. Stir a few times so that rice does not stick to bottom. Boil until rice is almost done. Use a colander to drain rice.
6. Heat remaining 3 tablespoons butter in skillet. Sauté raisins and almonds lightly. Remove from skillet with slotted spoon and set aside.
7. Add 1 chopped onion to same skillet and sauté until golden. Remove and set aside.
8. Warm the cream and add saffron. Mix well and set aside.
9. Spread half of the rice in a layer on bottom of a large ovenproof dish. Over the rice, spread meat, eggs, tomatoes, fried onions, raisins, and almonds in alternating layers, using only half of each per layer. Sprinkle with half of the garam masala, lemon juice, yogurt, saffron-cream and coriander leaves. Repeat with other half. Pour any leftover butter on top.
10. Cover with aluminum foil. Bake 10 to 15 minutes. Serve with a yogurt-potato-onion raita. Yield: 4 to 6 servings.

Hyderabadi Biryani

Many professional biryani chefs are from Hyderabad in the South Indian state of Andhra Pradesh. This dish is on the spicy side.

3 cups basmati rice, or any long-grain rice
12 cups water
2 1-inch sticks cinnamon
8 whole cardamom pods
8 cloves
1 tablespoon chopped fresh ginger
5 cloves garlic
4 green chilies (optional)

2 pounds lamb, cubed
2 cups yogurt
2 teaspoons salt
¾ cup butter
½ teaspoon turmeric
4 large onions, sliced

1. Clean and soak rice in 6 cups of the water 30 minutes. Strain in a colander and set aside.
2. Grind 1 of the cinnamon sticks, 4 of the cardamom pods, 4 of the cloves, ginger, garlic, and chilies to a paste. Set aside.
3. Pat meat dry and place in a mixing bowl. Pour well-beaten yogurt and 1 teaspoon of the salt over meat. Rub well over meat.
4. Add ground paste to meat. Mix and rub the paste over meat. Marinate 1 hour.
5. Heat ¼ cup butter in skillet. Add remaining cinnamon stick, 4 cardamom pods, and 4 cloves. Cook 1 minute.
6. Add rice and cook 3 minutes. Pour in remaining 6 cups hot water, turmeric, and 1 teaspoon salt. Bring to a boil. Simmer over medium-low heat, covered, 25 minutes.
7. Heat ¼ cup butter in a skillet. Add the meat and marinade. Brown the meat well over high heat. Simmer, covered, over medium-low heat until meat is almost cooked.
8. Pour meat over the rice and mix. Cook, covered, over very low heat, until the rice has become quite soft and most of the liquid dries up, about 20 minutes. Stir gently a few times.
9. Sauté onions in remaining ¼ cup butter until golden. Garnish with onions before serving. Yield: 6 servings.

Kheema Biryani

This is a rich meat biryani that is spicy but not hot.

5 cloves garlic
1 tablespoon chopped ginger

Rice Dishes 177

1 tablespoon blanched almonds
1 cup chopped fresh coriander leaves
5 cups water
5 cloves
5 whole cardamom pods
2 bay leaves
1 teaspoon salt
2 cups rice, long-grain
½ cup butter
½ teaspoon cumin seed
1 medium onion, chopped
½ teaspoon turmeric
1 teaspoon ground coriander
1 teaspoon ground cumin
1 pound lean ground lamb or beef
½ teaspoon ground cardamom
salt to taste
2 medium onions, sliced
¼ teaspoon saffron, soaked in ¼ cup warm milk

1. Grind garlic, ginger, almonds, and ½ cup of the coriander leaves to a paste. Set aside.
2. Bring 5 cups water to a boil. Add cloves, whole cardamom, bay leaves, and 1 teaspoon salt. Add rice and boil 7 minutes. Strain in a colander and set aside. Preheat oven to 350° F.
3. Heat ¼ cup of the butter in a saucepan. Add cumin seed and 1 chopped onion. Sauté lightly, 2 to 3 minutes.
4. Add the ground paste and cook until the butter separates.
5. Add turmeric, ground coriander, and ground cumin. Cook 1 to 2 minutes.
6. Add ground meat and ground cardamom. Cook over medium heat until meat is browned. Keep stirring frequently to break up any lumps.
7. Add salt to taste. Mix and cook over moderate heat 15 minutes, or until meat is almost done.
8. Fry 2 sliced onions in remaining ¼ cup butter until crisp and golden.

9. In a shallow ovenproof dish with a tightly fitting lid, spread meat, onions, and rice in alternating layers, using half of each per layer. Sprinkle saffron milk over the top and seal the lid.
10. Bake 20 minutes. Garnish with remaining ½ cup coriander leaves. Yield: 4 to 6 servings.

Chicken Biryani

Tender chicken is marinated in 10 heavenly herbs and spices and baked in fluffy, aromatic rice.

4 pounds chicken legs and breasts
5 cloves garlic
2 onions, chopped
½ teaspoon cumin seed
1 tablespoon chopped fresh ginger
3 tablespoons fresh coriander leaves
seeds of 5 cardamom pods
1 teaspoon garam masala (see index)
2 teaspoons salt
1 tablespoon lemon juice
2 green chilies (optional)
7 tablespoons butter
2 bay leaves
1-inch stick cinnamon
5 cups water
¼ teaspoon turmeric
5 whole cardamom pods
5 cloves
10 black peppercorns
1 teaspoon sugar
2 cups rice, long-grain
2 tablespoons raisins
2 tablespoons slivered almonds

Rice Dishes 179

2 onions, sliced
½ cup melted butter
¼ teaspoon saffron, soaked in ½ cup cream

1. Skin chicken and pat dry. Fork the meat lightly and set aside.
2. Blend garlic, half of the chopped onion, cumin seed, ginger, 1 tablespoon of the coriander leaves, cardamom seeds, garam masala, 1 teaspoon salt, lemon juice, and chilies to a paste. Marinate chicken in ground paste 2 to 3 hours.
3. Heat 2 tablespoons of the butter in a skillet. Cook bay leaves and cinnamon lightly.
4. Add remaining half of the chopped onion and sauté until translucent.
5. Add chicken and marinade to onions and cook over medium-high heat 5 minutes.
6. Turn heat to medium-low and cook until chicken is almost done, about 25 minutes. Remove chicken.
7. Remove bones from chicken and cut it into small pieces. Place chicken pieces back in sauce and set aside. Preheat oven to 350° F.
8. Boil 5 cups water in a saucepan. Add turmeric, whole cardamom, cloves, peppercorns, sugar, 1 teaspoon salt, and rice. Boil 10 minutes. Drain in a colander.
9. Heat 3 tablespoons butter in skillet. Sauté raisins and almonds lightly. Remove from butter and set aside.
10. Add 2 more tablespoons butter to the skillet and sauté 2 sliced onions until crisp and golden. Set aside.
11. In a shallow dish with a tightly fitting lid, spread chicken, rice, and onions in alternating layers, using half of each per layer. Pour any remaining sauce and melted butter over the top.
12. Seal the lid and place the dish in preheated oven. Bake 15 minutes.
13. Pour saffron-cream over the top and decorate with fried raisins, almonds, and remaining 2 tablespoons coriander leaves. Serve with a raita. Yield: 4 to 6 servings.

Sada Pulao

The fragrant pulaos that originated in Persia were introduced to India by the romantic Mogul kings. Their recipes were passed from one generation to another until they were blended into the rich Indian cuisine. The rice is first fried, then buttered and steamed. The choice of spices and other items varies regionally. Sada Pulao is a basic recipe for these grain dishes.

4 tablespoons butter
1 onion, thinly sliced
1 onion, finely chopped
½ teaspoon cumin seed
5 whole cardamom pods
1-inch stick cinnamon
5 cloves
10 black peppercorns
1 cup rice
3 cups water
salt to taste

1. Heat 2 tablespoons of the butter in a skillet. Add 1 thinly sliced onion and sauté until golden. Remove onions from butter and set aside for garnish.
2. Heat remaining 2 tablespoons butter in skillet. Add chopped onion and sauté until golden.
3. Add cumin seed, cardamom, cinnamon, cloves and peppercorns. Cook 2 to 3 minutes. Add 1 cup rice and fry 2 minutes.
4. Add 3 cups water and salt to taste. Mix. Bring to a boil. rice is cooking, stir occasionally, very gently. Garnish with fried onions. Serve with curry, vegetables, or dahls. Yield: 4 to 6 servings.

Matar Pulao

Green peas mingle with fragrant masalas in this light vegetarian pulao.

2 cups rice
4 cups water

Rice Dishes

4 tablespoons butter
2 large onions, thinly sliced
1 tablespoon blanched almonds
1 tablespoon golden raisins
1 tablespoon chopped cashew nuts
1 teaspoon cumin seed
1 tablespoon finely chopped fresh ginger
5 whole cardamom pods
8 cloves
1-inch stick cinnamon
10 black peppercorns
3 green chilies (optional)
1½ cups green peas, fresh or thawed
¼ teaspoon red pepper (optional)
salt to taste
1 teaspoon garam masala (see index)
1 large tomato, sliced
2 tablespoons chopped fresh coriander leaves

1. Soak rice in 4 cups water 30 minutes. Drain rice and set aside. Reserve the water.
2. Heat 2 tablespoons of the butter in a large saucepan. Add 1 thinly sliced onion and sauté until crisp and golden. Remove and set aside for garnish.
3. Add to the same saucepan almonds, raisins, and cashew nuts. Cook until the nuts are light brown. Remove and set aside for garnish.
4. Heat remaining 2 tablespoons butter in same saucepan. Add remaining thinly sliced onion and sauté until golden.
5. Add cumin seed, ginger, cardamom, cloves, cinnamon, peppercorns, and green chilies. Cook 1 minute.
6. Add peas. Cook 2 to 3 minutes.
7. Add well-drained rice, red pepper, and salt to taste. Cook 2 to 3 minutes. Add garam masala and stir a few times.
8. Pour in the water in which the rice was soaked and bring to a boil. Mix. Lower heat and cook, covered, until rice is done and each grain separates.

9. Transfer the rice and peas to a large baking pan. Garnish with fried onions, nuts, and raisins. Cover with foil and keep warm.
10. Just before serving, decorate with sliced tomatoes and sprinkle with coriander leaves. Serve with any meat curry and/or yogurt-onion-potato rice. Yield: 4 to 6 servings.

Gobhi Pulao

This cauliflower pulao is thick and spicy.

1 cup freshly grated coconut
3 green chilies (optional)
6 cloves garlic
4 cloves
1-inch stick cinnamon
5 whole cardamom pods
4 tablespoons butter
1 large onion, chopped
1 small cauliflower, separated into flowerets
1 cup rice, long-grain
3 cups water
salt to taste
1 teaspoon garam masala (see index)
2 tablespoons lemon juice

1. Grind coconut, chilies, garlic, cloves, cinnamon, and cardamom to a paste. Set aside.
2. Heat butter in a skillet and sauté onions until translucent.
3. Add ground paste and cook 5 to 6 minutes, or until the oil separates.
4. Add cauliflower and cook 7 minutes over low heat.
5. Add rice and cook 2 minutes.
6. Add 3 cups water, salt to taste, and garam masala. Bring to a boil. Simmer over medium-low heat until the rice and cauliflower are done.
7. Sprinkle with lemon juice and serve. Yield: 4 to 6 servings.

Badi Mirch Pulao

Badi are the big Kashmiri sweet peppers. This is one of the prized recipes for their preparation.

4 large sweet peppers
4 tablespoons butter
3 cloves
5 black peppercorns
1-inch stick cinnamon
3 whole cardamom pods
½ teaspoon cumin seed
2 cups rice, long-grain
1 teaspoon sugar
salt to taste
1 teaspoon ground coriander
1 teaspoon ground cumin
5 cups water

1. Clean the sweet peppers. Remove seeds and slice them lengthwise into thin strips.
2. Heat butter in a skillet and cook cloves, peppercorns, cinnamon, and cardamom 2 minutes.
3. Add ½ teaspoon cumin seed and cook 1 minute.
4. Add sliced sweet peppers and cook 10 minutes.
5. Add rice and cook 2 minutes.
6. Add sugar, salt to taste, ground coriander and ground cumin. Cook 1 minute.
7. Pour in 5 cups water. Bring to a boil. Cook over medium-low heat until rice is tender. Yield: 6 servings.

Lamb or Beef Pulao

This is a truly rich meat pulao.

¾ cup rice
3 tablespoons butter
½ teaspoon cumin seed
2 bay leaves

6 black peppercorns
4 cloves
4 whole cardamom pods
1-inch stick cinnamon
4 cloves garlic
1 teaspoon chopped fresh ginger
3 green chilies, chopped (optional)
2 large onions, sliced
1 teaspoon ground coriander
1½ pounds lamb or beef, cubed
2 cups water
1 teaspoon sugar
1 teaspoon salt
1 tablespoon lemon juice
2 tablespoons chopped fresh coriander leaves
3 tablespoons vegetable oil
¼ cup chopped cashew nuts
15 to 20 golden raisins

1. Soak the rice in cold water 30 minutes. Drain and set aside.
2. Heat butter in a saucepan. Add cumin seed, bay leaves, peppercorns, cloves, cardamom, and cinnamon. Cook 1 minute.
3. Add garlic, ginger, chilies and 1 large sliced onion. Sauté until onions are translucent.
4. Add ground coriander and cook ½ minute.
5. Add the meat and brown.
6. Add ½ cup warm water. Stir a few times. Turn heat to low and cook, covered, 20 minutes.
7. Add rice, remaining 1½ cups water, sugar, and salt. Bring to a boil. Lower heat and cook, covered, until rice and meat are done and all the liquid evaporates. Cook, uncovered, a few minutes.
8. Add lemon juice and coriander leaves.
9. Heat vegetable oil in a skillet. Sauté the remaining sliced onion until golden. Use a slotted spoon to remove onions from oil.

Rice Dishes 185

10. In the same oil, sauté the cashew nuts and raisins lightly. Garnish the pulao with nuts, raisins, and onions. Yield: 4 to 6 servings.

Shrimp Pulao

This mellow shrimp and coconut milk pulao is served on festive occasions in coastal towns.

1 cup rice, soaked 30 minutes in 2 cups cold water
1 cup freshly shredded coconut
2½ cups water
2 medium onions, chopped
5 cloves garlic
1-inch stick cinnamon
1 teaspoon ground coriander
½ teaspoon cumin seed
1 tablespoon chopped fresh ginger
3 tablespoons butter
1½ pounds shrimp, shelled
⅛ teaspoon red pepper
½ teaspoon turmeric
1½ teaspoons salt
1 tablespoon lemon juice

1. Drain rice and set aside.
2. In an electric blender, grind coconut with 1 cup water. Pour into a pan. Add 1½ cups lukewarm water and set aside.
3. Wash the blender. Using a little water, blend 1 chopped onion, garlic, cinnamon, coriander, cumin seed, and ginger to a paste. Set aside.
4. Strain coconut and reserve the milk.
5. Heat butter in a skillet. Sauté remaining chopped onions until translucent.
6. Add shrimp and cook lightly, 2 minutes. Add red pepper and turmeric. Cook 1 minute.
7. Add ground paste and cook 5 minutes.

8. Add rice and cook 3 minutes.
9. Add salt and coconut milk. Bring to a boil. Turn heat to low and cook, semi-covered, until rice and shrimp are done. Add lemon juice and serve. Yield: 4 to 6 servings.

Kerala Prawn Pulao

The chefs of Kerala prepare this lovely pink and white giant shrimp coconut curry, which is hot and spicy.

2 cups long-grain rice
2 dry red chilies
5 cloves garlic
1 tablespoon chopped fresh ginger
4 green chilies
1 tablespoon blanched almonds
5 whole cardamom pods
¼ cup butter
2 large onions, sliced
4 medium tomatoes, chopped
½ teaspoon turmeric
¼ teaspoon red pepper
2 cups uncooked shrimp, shelled and deveined
2 cups freshly shredded coconut, soaked 30 minutes in 3 cups water
3 cups warm water
2 sprigs mint
salt to taste
½ cup chopped fresh coriander leaves

1. Clean and soak the rice in water 30 minutes. Drain in colander and set aside.
2. Grind red chilies, garlic, ginger, green chilies, almonds, and cardamom to a paste. Set aside.
3. Heat butter in a skillet. Sauté onions until translucent.
4. Add ground paste and sauté until butter separates, about 5 minutes.
5. Add chopped tomatoes, turmeric, and red pepper. Cook over medium heat until a thick sauce is obtained, 5 to 7 minutes.

6. Add shrimp and cook 5 to 7 minutes.
7. Blend coconut and 3 cups water in an electric blender.
8. Place in a large jar and add 3 cups warm water. After 5 minutes, strain and reserve coconut milk.
9. Add coconut milk to shrimp and bring to a boil.
10. Add rice, mint, and salt to taste. Simmer, covered, over medium-low heat until rice and shrimp are done, about 30 minutes. Stir gently during cooking period. Sprinkle with coriander leaves and serve. Yield: 6 servings.

Anda Pulao

This softly spiced egg pulao does not take long to prepare and makes an unusual brunch entrée.

2 cups rice, soaked in 4 cups cold water
2 tablespoons butter
4 whole cardamom pods
2 bay leaves
1 teaspoon chopped fresh ginger
1 onion, sliced
⅛ teaspoon red pepper (optional)
4 cups water
½ teaspoon sugar
1 teaspoon salt
6 hard-cooked eggs, shelled

1. Drain rice and set aside.
2. Heat butter in a skillet. Add cardamom, bay leaves, ginger, and onions. Sauté until onions are translucent.
3. Add drained rice. Cook 1 to 2 minutes.
4. Add red pepper, 4 cups water, sugar, and salt. Stir and bring to a boil. Turn heat to low and cook, covered, until rice is done.
5. Quarter the eggs and gently stir them into the rice. Yield: 4 to 6 servings.

Yakhni Pulao

Rice is cooked in a fragrant stock made from chicken, beef, or lamb, for a hearty pulao.

1 cup rice
2 pounds lamb, beef, or chicken cut into small pieces
3 cups water
2 teaspoons salt
1 onion, chopped
8 whole cardamom pods
8 black peppercorns
8 cloves
5 tablespoons butter
1 onion, sliced
2 tablespoons slivered almonds
5 cloves garlic, chopped
1 teaspoon chopped fresh ginger
½ teaspoon cumin seed
½ teaspoon turmeric
⅛ teaspoon red pepper (optional)
1 teaspoon garam masala (see index)
5 fresh mint leaves
2 tablespoons chopped fresh coriander leaves

1. Soak rice in cold water 30 minutes. Drain and set aside.
2. Place meat in a saucepan with 3 cups water. Add 1 teaspoon salt, 1 chopped onion, 4 of the cardamom pods, 4 of the peppercorns, and 4 of the cloves. Bring to a boil. Turn heat to low and simmer until meat is half cooked. Remove the meat from the stock and reserve stock.
3. Heat 2 tablespoons butter in a skillet. Sauté sliced onion and almonds lightly. Remove from the oil and set aside for garnish.
4. Add remaining 3 tablespoons butter to skillet and heat. Add remaining 4 cardamom pods, 4 cloves, 4 peppercorns, and garlic, ginger, and cumin seed. Cook 1 to 2 minutes.
5. Add meat and brown it. Remove the meat and set aside.

6. Add turmeric, red pepper, and garam masala to skillet spices. Cook for 1 minute.
7. Add rice and cook 3 to 5 minutes.
8. Add stock, remaining 1 teaspoon salt, and mint leaves. Bring to a boil. Turn heat to medium-low and cook 15 minutes.
9. Add meat and stir gently a few times. Cook, covered, until meat and rice are done. Garnish with fried onions and almonds. Sprinkle with coriander leaves. Serve with yogurt raita. Yield: 4 to 6 servings.

Saffron Rice

The Indians use a lot of saffron in their foods. Saffron colors this sweetly scented rice the yellow of monks' robes.

1½ cups rice
2 tablespoons milk
¼ teaspoon string saffron, crushed
3 tablespoons butter
5 whole cardamom pods
½ teaspoon cumin seed
20 golden raisins
15 cashew nuts
2 cups milk
1 tablespoon sugar
salt to taste

1. Soak the rice in 2 cups water 30 minutes. Drain the rice and reserve the water.
2. Warm 2 tablespoons milk and soak saffron in it.
3. Heat butter in a skillet. Add cardamom, cumin seed, raisins, and cashew nuts. Brown lightly.
4. Add well-drained rice and cook 2 to 3 minutes.
5. Add 2 cups milk, sugar, milk-soaked saffron, water from rice, and salt to taste. Bring to a boil. Lower heat and cook, covered, until all the liquid is absorbed and rice is cooked. Yield: 4 to 6 servings.

Tahari

This dish is popular in Bombay, Central, and North India. Vegetables, spices, and herbs are mixed with rice and lentils.

1 cup rice
½ cup split yellow peas or lentils
½ cup butter
5 whole cardamom pods
1-inch stick cinnamon
3 bay leaves
6 cloves
2 large onions, chopped
1 cup green peas, fresh or thawed
1 cup chopped carrots
1 cauliflower, separated into flowerets
1 medium potato, peeled and cubed
¼ teaspoon nutmeg
¼ teaspoon mace
¼ teaspoon red pepper (optional)
½ teaspoon turmeric
1 tablespoon sugar
1 tablespoon garam masala (see index)
3 medium tomatoes, quartered
6 cups hot water
salt to taste
1 teaspoon mustard seed
½ teaspoon cumin seed
1 tablespoon chopped fresh ginger
2 tablespoons freshly grated coconut
½ cup chopped fresh coriander leaves

1. Clean and soak rice and split peas separately in cold water 30 minutes. Use twice as much water as amounts of rice and split peas. Drain in a colander and set aside.
2. Heat ¼ cup butter in a skillet. Cook cardamom, cinnamon, bay leaves, and cloves 2 minutes.
3. Add onions and sauté 3 minutes. Add green peas, carrots, cauliflower and potatoes. Cook 2 minutes.
4. Add rice and split peas. Cook 3 minutes.

5. Add nutmeg, mace, red pepper, turmeric, sugar and garam masala. Stir a few minutes. Add tomatoes and cook 5 minutes.
6. Pour in 6 cups hot water and salt to taste. Bring to a boil. Cook over medium heat 30 minutes, or until vegetables, rice, and split peas are done. Stir a few times during cooking period to make sure the mixture is not sticking to bottom of skillet.
7. Heat remaining ¼ cup butter in a skillet. Add mustard seed. When seeds stop popping, add cumin seed, ginger, and coconut. Cook 2 minutes.
8. Add coriander leaves and cook 1 minute. Pour the ingredients into the cooked rice-split pea mixture and serve. Yield: 6 servings.

Mitha Chawal

Another sweet (*mitha*) rice (*chawal*) mixed with lots of chewy raisins and crunchy, heavenly scented almonds. The final touch is pistachio nuts and cardamom seeds.

2 cups rice, long-grain
5 cups water
2 cups sugar
¼ teaspoon saffron, soaked in ½ cup milk
½ cup raisins
½ cup slivered almonds
1 tablespoon chopped cashew nuts
2 tablespoons unsalted butter
seeds from 10 cardamom pods, crushed
2 tablespoons chopped pistachio nuts
silver leaf paper (optional)
1 tablespoon rose water

1. Soak rice in 5 cups water 30 minutes.
2. Boil rice in same water over medium heat until most of the liquid dries up.

3. Add sugar, saffron-milk, raisins, almonds, cashew nuts, and butter to rice. Cook over low heat until all the sugar is dissolved and rice grains are separate and very soft.
4. Decorate with cardamom seeds, pistachio nuts, and silver leaf paper (available at Indian specialty stores). Serve hot or warm. Just before serving, add rose water. Yield: 6 servings.

10

Breads

The finest breads in India are baked from wheat sun-dried on the northern plains in the states of Punjab and Haryana, the major suppliers of grain. Wheat is second to rice as a staple food, and bread is one of the mainstays of a meal in northern and western India. If the monsoon clouds that hang heavily over the wheat fields fail to yield rain, it can mean famine for a large part of the subcontinent.

Dahls, whole wheat, millet, and rice are just a few of the many grains that go into the making of Indian breads. The flours vary with the regions and religions. The usually disk-shaped bread can be flat or puffy, thick or thin, depending upon the expertise of the chef, as well as preference. The breads are almost exclusively unleavened. The few exceptions that use leavening agents, such as yeast, are the result of the British influence.

One would have to search long and hard in Indian markets to find cellophane-wrapped breads pumped with preservatives. Indian women prepare and serve piping-hot breads with almost every meal in North and West India. They are used to sop up rich curries and to dip in chutneys and raitas.

Many Indian women grind the flours, which are mostly unrefined, by hand at home. The *paraat*, a large brass platter, is used for kneading the dough, which is often the consistency of thick batter. The cooking methods include deep frying the breads in a wok-shaped *karhai*, cooking on a *tawa* (a curved cast iron griddle), and baking in the fierce heat of the ancient clay tandoori oven.

Indian women take pride in personally preparing the household breads. When an Indian woman is described as wheat-complexioned, she is considered exotically lovely.

The following recipes have been adapted for Western flours and cooking utensils. Most of the breads can be kept overnight in aluminum foil and reheated later. Do not become discouraged if at first you experience difficulty with the breads. As with all types of bread, getting to know the medium through practice can make all the difference in the final product.

Chapati

This unleavened tortilla-like bread is most popular in North India. It is baked on a griddle and can range from the size of a saucer to a dinner plate. When baked paper-thin and puffy in the saucer version, it is called *phulka* ("blown up"). Since it requires the use of fine wheat, it is usually served in the homes of the wealthy.

1 cup white flour
1 cup whole wheat flour
½ teaspoon salt
1 cup water
3 tablespoons melted butter

1. Sift together the flours and salt, using enough water to make a soft dough. Knead well, 5 to 10 minutes. Cover with a warm, damp cloth and set aside 1 hour.
2. Knead lightly again. Shape into 12 small balls. Flatten each into 6½-inch rounds on a floured board.

3. Heat griddle or skillet and place the chapatis on it. When cooking them, wait until the first bubbles rise on the bread; then turn them over. After a minute, press the edges and rotate the bread. Chapatis should be brown but not hard.
4. For puffy chapatis, place them in a 350° F. oven a few minutes, after they have been cooked. Or you can lift them from the griddle with tongs and place directly over a medium-low flame, turning the chapatis a few times. Brush with melted butter before serving. Yield: 12 chapatis.

Poori

Another favorite in the North and the West is *poori*, a deep-fried puff of whole wheat bread, similar to chapati but with a little oil added to the dough. It is very much in demand at festive occasions and served with whole Bengal dried peas.

1 cup white flour
1 cup whole wheat flour
1 teaspoon salt
⅓ teaspoon cumin seed
¼ teaspoon red pepper (optional)
1 tablespoon melted butter or vegetable oil
¾ cup warm water
vegetable oil for deep frying

1. Place the flours in a bowl and mix well.
2. Add salt, cumin seed, red pepper, and butter or vegetable oil. Rub the flour mixture between the palms to break up any lumps. Mix well, adding ¾ cup warm water.
3. Knead the flour mixture into a not-too-soft dough. Cover with a warm damp cloth and set aside 1 hour.
4. Knead the dough again for a few minutes. Divide it into 12 equal parts and shape into balls. Flatten balls into 6½-inch rounds. After flattening, keep pooris covered unless fried immediately.

5. Heat vegetable oil in a wok or saucepan. Fry the pooris until light gold on both sides. They should be crisp and puffy. Yield: 12 pooris.

Luchi

Light and crisp *luchi* is the Bengal version of poori. Very little water is used in making the dough.

2 cups white flour
1 teaspoon salt
2 tablespoons butter
vegetable oil for deep frying

1. Sift together the flour and salt. Rub in the butter. Add just enough water to form a stiff dough. Knead until soft and smooth.
2. Divide dough into 10 balls. Using a little flour, flatten each into a thin round.
3. Heat vegetable oil and fry the luchis quickly until golden on each side. Yield: 10 luchis.

Paratha

This is a very rich, crisp bread with many flaky layers, sheer as sari silk. The secret is in the repeated brushing of the dough with butter, the folding, and the rerolling. Paratha is eaten plain or stuffed with spiced vegetables.

2 cups whole wheat flour, or 1 cup white flour and 1 cup whole wheat flour
½ teaspoon salt
2 tablespoons butter
melted butter

1. Sift together the flour and salt. Work in the butter. Add just enough water to form a supple and elastic dough. Knead well, at least 15 minutes. Cover with a warm, damp cloth and set aside 1 hour.

2. Knead well again. Shape into 10 balls. Flatten each into a 6- to 7-inch round. Brush lightly with melted butter. Fold in half and brush again. Fold each into a triangle. Press into thin triangles.
3. Heat a griddle or skillet and lightly brush with melted butter. Fry the parathas on both sides, generously brushing with butter, until pale gold, crisp, and flaky. Yield: 10 parathas.

Radish-Stuffed Paratha

These parathas are spicy and a little on the hot side.

Paratha dough (see preceding recipe)
1 cup grated radishes
1 small onion, grated
1 teaspoon chopped green chili
1 teaspoon chopped ginger
1 teaspoon salt
1 tablespoon lemon juice
2 tablespoons butter
melted butter

1. Prepare paratha dough and set aside.
2. Combine radishes, onions, chili, ginger, salt, and lemon juice.
3. Heat butter in a skillet. Cook the radish mixture over low heat 5 minutes.
4. Spread some of the filling on one paratha and cover it with another paratha. Seal the edges with a little milk.
5. Grease a heated griddle or skillet. Brush the paratha with melted butter. Fry on each side until crisp and brown. Yield: 5 servings.

Nan

The people of Punjab are among the few Indians who bake leavened breads. Nan is a flat, oval-shaped bread baked in a tandoori oven. It is an exotic accompaniment to tandoori chicken and Mogul meat dishes.

½ cup yogurt

½ cup milk
½ teaspoon baking soda
1 teaspoon sugar
4 tablespoons butter
2 eggs, lightly beaten
3/10 ounce packaged dry yeast
3 cups white flour
½ teaspoon salt
½ teaspoon poppy seed

1. Warm yogurt and stir in the milk, until thoroughly mixed. Remove from heat.
2. Add baking soda, sugar, 2 tablespoons of the butter, eggs, and yeast.
3. Sift together the flour and salt. Make a well in the flour and gradually add the yogurt mixture.
4. Knead the flour 15 to 20 minutes, until smooth and elastic. Brush the dough with some of the remaining butter. Cover with a warm, damp cloth and set aside in a warm place 3 hours, until dough has risen to twice its size.
5. Dust hands with flour. Knead the dough again for a few minutes and divide into 8 balls. Roll each ball into a 10-inch pancake. Pull each pancake gently to give it an oval shape. Cover with damp cloth 20 minutes.
6. Heat a griddle until very hot. Mix the remaining 2 tablespoons butter with poppy seed. Brush one side of each nan with the mixture and the other side with warm water.
7. Place the warm-water side on the griddle for ½ minute. Remove from the griddle and place nan under broiler for about 2 minutes. Serve with curries and tandoori dishes. Yield: 8 nans.

Bhatura

Bhatura is a deep-fried version of nan, favored at breakfast and tea in the North.

2 cups white flour
½ teaspoon salt

½ teaspoon baking soda
½ cup yogurt (plain or natural)
1 teaspoon sugar
vegetable oil for frying

1. Mix the flour, salt, and baking soda. Then sift into a bowl.
2. Warm yogurt slightly and add to the flour. Work in well. Then add sugar and a few sprinkles of warm water.
3. Knead until dough no longer sticks to the hands or board. Continue kneading until smooth. Rub hands with butter and knead until satiny. Cover with a warm, damp cloth and set aside in a warm place 4 hours.
4. Punch down the dough. Shape into small balls. Flatten each ball into a 4-inch round, about ⅛-inch thick. Keep covered.
5. Heat vegetable oil in a skillet until smoking hot. Drop bhaturas, one at a time, into the oil. Turn a few times. Remove when puffy and brown on both sides. Bhaturas can be eaten with any meat or vegetable dish. Yield: 8 to 10 bhaturas.

Bhakhri

Turmeric gives this fried bread its warm golden color. *Bhakhri* is like a thick chapati and is much enjoyed by the people of Gujarat.

2 cups whole wheat flour
¼ teaspoon turmeric
½ teaspoon chili powder
1 teaspoon salt
4 tablespoons butter

1. Mix flour with turmeric, chili powder, and salt. Work in the butter with hands, adding cold water a little at a time to form a smooth dough. Knead well. Cover with a damp, warm cloth and set aside 1 hour.

2. Knead the dough well again. Divide into 8 to 10 portions. Roll into balls and flatten into 4-inch rounds.
3. Heat a griddle or skillet and brush it with butter. Fry bhakhris on each side until brown and crisp. Yield: 8 to 10 bhakhris.

Kulcha

Kulcha is a flour- and potato-based fried bread. If the oil is too hot, the bread will turn red.

1 cup flour
½ teaspoon salt
2 potatoes, boiled and mashed
vegetable oil for frying

1. Sift together flour and salt.
2. Very gradually mix the flour with the potatoes. Do not add any water. However, moisten hands with water and knead the dough.
3. Shape into 8 balls. Flatten each into a 3-inch round. Cover and set aside 1 hour.
4. Heat vegetable oil below the smoking point. Fry kulchas until crisp and golden. Yield: 8 kulchas.

Khamiri Poori

Deep-fried Khamiri Poori is another northern bread made with white flour and leavened with yeast.

2 cups all-purpose flour
3/10 ounce packaged dry yeast
1 cup warm milk
2 tablespoons yogurt, beaten
1 teaspoon sugar
2 tablespoons butter
½ teaspoon salt

½ teaspoon baking soda
vegetable oil for deep frying

1. Sift flour into a bowl.
2. Dissolve yeast in warm milk. Add yogurt, sugar, butter, salt, and baking soda.
3. Add to the flour as much of the warm milk-yeast mixture as is necessary to make a soft, pliable dough. Cover and set aside in a warm place 3 hours.
4. Divide dough into 12 portions. Shape each portion into a ball; then roll it into a 6-inch round.
5. Heat vegetable oil and deep fry poori until golden. Serve with any meat curry. Yield: 12 pooris.

Shir Mal

Mogul bakers prepare this bread with tender loving care. It is eaten with richly seasoned korma meats and kheer.

3 cups all-purpose flour
¾ teaspoon salt
1 teaspoon baking powder
½ teaspoon baking soda
4 tablespoons butter
½ cup warm milk
1 teaspoon sugar
1 egg, beaten
¼ teaspoon saffron, soaked in ½ cup warm water

1. Sift flour into a mixing bowl. Add salt, baking powder, and baking soda and mix well.
2. Combine 3 tablespoons of the butter, milk, sugar, and egg. Add to the flour mixture.
3. Knead well into a pliable dough. Add a little more milk if needed.
4. Shape into a round ball. Brush with butter and set aside in a warm place 2 to 3 hours.

5. Knead the dough and divide into 12 balls, adding a little flour to prevent sticking. Roll each ball into an 8-inch round.
6. Heat a skillet. Wet one side of the bread with water. Brush skillet with saffron water. Place rounds, water-brushed side down, in the skillet. Cook until bottom side is dotted brown, about 2 minutes.
7. Place bread under grill with saffron side toward source of heat. Cook 1 to 2 minutes. Yield: 12 shir mals.

Puran Poli

This is a Gujarati paratha stuffed with sweet dahls. It is washed down with tea and served to guests on special occasions.

½ cup yellow split peas, chana dahl or tuar dahl
¾ cup water
1 cup all-purpose flour
1 cup whole wheat flour
pinch of baking powder
½ teaspoon salt
2½ cups water
½ cup brown sugar
seeds from 5 cardamom pods, crushed
3 tablespoons butter

1. Clean and soak dahl in 1 cup water 30 minutes.
2. Mix the two flours, baking powder, and salt. Add water gradually. Knead to a smooth, medium-soft dough. Keep covered.
3. Bring 2½ cups water to a boil. Drain and add dahl and cook over medium heat until dahl is cooked and most is absorbed.
4. Remove dahl from heat. Mash lightly. Add brown sugar and crushed cardamom seeds and cook over low heat until sugar is completely dissolved and the mixture is almost dry, about 8 to 10 minutes.
5. Knead the dough well. Divide into 10 portions and shape each into a ball. Flatten a little and make a big dent in the center of each.

6. Fill dent with a portion of dahl mixture. Gather the edges together and seal them completely so stuffing is entirely enclosed. Use a little flour, if necessary, to roll the rounds as thin as possible without the stuffing coming out.
7. Heat a skillet. Place one of the rounds on it and brush the top with melted butter. Turn after 1 to 2 minutes. Brush with butter. Fry, turning a few times until golden on both sides. Yield: 4 to 5 servings.

Tandoori Roti

This bread is a favorite in Punjabi restaurants. One side of the roti is cooked in a skillet and the other side is broiled.

2 cups all-purpose flour
1 cup whole wheat flour
1 teaspoon salt
¼ teaspoon sugar
pinch of baking soda
1 egg, beaten well
1 cup warm water

1. Mix flours together in a bowl. Add salt, sugar, baking soda, and well-beaten egg. Add about 1 cup warm water to prepare a medium-soft dough.
2. Knead dough well. Cover with a damp cloth and set aside 1 hour.
3. Knead dough again. Divide into 12 portions. Shape each into a ball. Roll each ball into an 8-inch round with a rolling pin.
4. Heat a skillet. Brush a little water on one side of each roti. Place with wet side down on the skillet, for about 2 minutes.
5. Brush the top side with water and place rotis under broiler, brushed side toward source of heat, for 2 minutes or until brown dots appear. Serve with any meat or vegetable curry. Yield: 4 to 6 servings.

Dosa

This dosa is a crisp and feather-light South Indian dahl-rice bread, shaped like a pancake. Dosas are eaten with coconut chutney and sambar. They taste best when served immediately.

1 cup urad dahl
2 cups rice, long-grain
½ cup water
2 teaspoons salt
½ teaspoon chopped fresh ginger
2 tablespoons fresh coriander leaves
¼ cup vegetable oil

1. Clean dahl and rice of any foreign particles. Soak dahl in 1½ cups cold water and rice in 3 cups cold water overnight. Drain each in colander.
2. Blend rice into a smooth paste, adding about ½ cup water. Blend the dahl in the same way. Mix rice and dahl pastes in a bowl.
3. Add salt, ginger, and coriander leaves to rice-dahl mixture. Mix well. Cover with a damp cloth and set aside in warm place 4 to 5 hours.
4. Beat the rice-dahl mixture well. It should be a little thinner than a pancake batter.
5. Heat a skillet. When hot, pour ½ teaspoon oil on it and spread it over entire skillet.
6. Pour a ladleful of batter into skillet, spreading it like a pancake, but much thinner. When top side is dry, scrape it from skillet and cook on other side for ½ minute. Total cooking time for one dosa is about 2 to 3 minutes. Yield: about 12 dosas.

Kachori

Kachori is a deep-fried bread stuffed with an exciting hot and spicy dahl filling.

½ cup all-purpose flour
1½ cups whole wheat flour

pinch of baking soda
1 teaspoon salt
½ cup urad dahl or split yellow peas, soaked 30 minutes in 1 cup water
2 cups water
½ teaspoon turmeric
2 tablespoons butter
½ teaspoon cumin seed
2 green chilies, chopped
1 teaspoon chopped fresh ginger
1 small onion, chopped
1 tablespoon fresh coriander leaves
vegetable oil for deep frying

1. Mix flours, baking soda, and ½ teaspoon of the salt. Add enough water to prepare a medium-soft dough. Keep covered until needed.
2. Drain dahl.
3. Bring dahl to boil in 2 cups water. Add turmeric and remaining ½ teaspoon salt. Cook over medium heat until most of the liquid dries up. Mash dahl lightly and set aside.
4. Heat butter in a skillet. Add cumin seed, green chilies, ginger, and onions. Cook 2 to 3 minutes. Add coriander leaves. Add entire mixture to dahl and stir well. This is the filling.
5. Divide dough into 10 balls; flatten balls a little. Make a dent in the middle of each and fill it with dahl mixture. Enclose the stuffing completely by bringing the edges together and sealing them. Roll gently as thin as possible without stuffing coming out.
6. Heat oil for deep frying. Fry kachoris until golden. Serve with vegetable curries and chutneys. Yield: 10 kachoris.

11

Chutneys and Pickles

There is such a myriad of taste-teasing Indian chutneys and pickles that an entire book could be devoted to their recipes. Very few Indian meals and snacks, no matter how humble, are served unaccompanied by some kind of appetite-stimulating chutney or pickle.

Indian condiments are used much like such American condiments as mustard, catsup, and pickle relish—to enhance the flavor of food—but Indian condiments have far more variety and sophistication. Unlike American condiments, Indian chutneys and pickles are hot and pungent. Here, we buy them from a grocery store. But in India, women prepare chutneys and pickles daily in their kitchens. The treasured family recipes are carefully guarded and passed down from mother to daughter.

Chutneys are made from such ingredients as mangos, papayas, dates, raisins, coconut, tomatoes, onions, coriander, mint, garlic, yogurt, tamarind, vinegar, lemon juice, salt, and sugar. They can taste sweet or salty, sour or hot. Their textures can vary from smooth and pasty to chopped or nugget-like. They need not be prepared and eaten on the same day; they can be stored in airtight jars in the refrigerator several days.

In India, where there is limited refrigeration, pickling is a way of preserving many fruits, vegetables, meats, and fish. The hot and sour or sweet and sour Indian pickles are usually prepared with oil, water, lemon juice, or vinegar. Oil pickle can take several weeks to a month to mature and will keep for years. Water pickle, however, is good for only 2 to 3 weeks. Indian women store water pickles in half-baked clay jars, which give the pickle an earthy taste.

One could spend years savoring Indian chutneys and pickles and never taste all the infinite varieties. In this section are just a few of the many taste-tantalizers to help lure the appetite. They are excellent not only with meals but also with appetizers. Experiment and create your own mouth-watering concoctions.

Lemon Pickle

Lemons are a basic ingredient for many Indian pickles. This spicy lemon pickle goes well with any meal.

18 whole fresh lemons
8 tablespoons mustard oil or peanut oil
pinch of asafoetida
1 teaspoon ground turmeric
1 teaspoon ground mustard seed
1 teaspoon red pepper
3 tablespoons salt
½ teaspoon fennel seed
2 ounces sliced fresh ginger

1. Wash and dry the lemons. Cut each into 4 pieces.
2. Heat 1 tablespoon of the mustard or peanut oil in a skillet. Remove skillet from heat and add asafoetida, turmeric, mustard seed, and red pepper. Return to low heat and cook 30 seconds.
3. Add salt to skillet and mix spices well. Set aside to cool. Then rub the paste over the lemons.
4. Place lemons in jars and leave them 2 weeks. Shake the jars a few times each week. If possible, place the open jar in sunlight for 1 hour or so every other day.

5. After 2 weeks, heat 1 tablespoon mustard or peanut oil in a skillet. Cook fennel seed and ginger 1 minute. Set aside to cool.
   6. Add this and remaining 6 tablespoons oil to the lemons. If the skins are still not tender, leave them in the jars for another week. This pickle keeps several months.

Lemon-Vinegar Pickle

Whole lemons are pickled in spiced lime juice and vinegar for a pungent flavor.

10 whole limes
18 whole fresh lemons, with thin skins
4 ounces sliced ginger
1½ cups white vinegar
4 tablespoons salt
1 tablespoon garam masala (see index)

   1. Extract the juice from limes and set aside.
   2. Wash and wipe the lemons dry. Place them in a big mixing bowl.
   3. Mix ginger, vinegar, salt, garam masala, and lime juice.
   4. Pour lime mixture over the lemons. Mix and stir until entirely coated.
   5. Pour contents into jars and cover them with towels, tied around the jar necks. Do not cover with tightly fitting lids. Set the jars in the sun a few hours every other day. It takes about 1 month for this pickle to be ready.

Sweet Lemon Pickle

A lemon pickle that is brown-sugar sweet and mellow.

18 whole lemons
2 tablespoons salt
1 tablespoon red pepper

1 cup brown sugar
¼ teaspoon turmeric
1 tablespoon raisins

1. Cut lemons into 4 pieces each.
2. Mix all other ingredients and pour over the lemon pieces.
3. Store in jars 2 to 3 weeks. Every other day, stir the lemons and set in the sun 1 hour.

Lemon-Mango Pickle

This recipe make a very attractive, rich-tasting pickle.

1 pound green mangos
8 whole lemons
10 green chilies
1 teaspoon cumin seed
1 teaspoon fennel seed
½ teaspoon fenugreek seed
½ teaspoon caraway seed
1 cup mustard oil or peanut oil
½ teaspoon turmeric
1 teaspoon red pepper
4 ounces sliced fresh ginger
½ cup button onions
5 tablespoons salt

1. Wash and dry mangos, lemons, and chilies.
2. Slice mangos, quarter lemons, and cut chilies in two.
3. Using a mortar and pestle, crush cumin, fennel, fenugreek, and caraway seeds together.
4. Heat oil until quite hot. Remove it from heat and add turmeric and red pepper. Stir until oil picks up turmeric and pepper color.
5. Add crushed spices to turmeric and red pepper. Add lemons, ginger, mangos, onions, chilies, and salt. Mix well and place in a jar until ready, about 2 to 3 weeks.

Chukandar Achar

These Indian-style pickled beet roots are flavored with garam masala.

2 pounds beet roots
2 cups vinegar
20 black peppercorns, crushed
1 tablespoon garam masala (see index)
1 teaspoon red pepper
2 tablespoons salt
2 cups vinegar

1. Wash beets and boil them in water 40 to 45 minutes.
2. Wipe dry; then peel and slice the beet roots.
3. Place beets in saucepan and pour in vinegar and all other ingredients. Bring to a boil; then simmer over medium heat 20 minutes. Cool.
4. Place beets in a jar and stir well. Beets are ready to be served.

Gobhi Achar

That versatile vegetable, cauliflower, makes a deliciously hot and spicy Indian pickle.

1 large cauliflower, separated into flowerets
1 tablespoon salt
½ teaspoon turmeric
1 teaspoon ground mustard seed
1 teaspoon red pepper
1 tablespoon garam masala (see index)
3 ounces sliced ginger
1 teaspoon freshly ground black pepper
1 tablespoon salt

1. Preheat oven to 450° F.
2. If flowerets are too big, cut them in half. Place flowerets in baking dish and sprinkle with 1 tablespoon salt. Bake 5 minutes, or until completely done.

3. Mix all other ingredients together.
4. Place flowerets in a jar and pour in the spice mixture. Mix well. Place the jar, with lid off, in the sun for 1 week.

Pyaz Achar

A sweet-sour button onion pickle, Pyaz Achar is flavored with ginger.

2 pounds button onions
1 tablespoon salt
1½ cups vinegar
1 cup brown sugar
3 ounces sliced fresh ginger
1 tablespoon salt
1 tablespoon crushed black peppercorns
1 teaspoon red pepper

1. Peel onions. Wash and wipe dry.
2. Place onions on a plate and sprinkle them with 1 tablespoon salt. Cover and set aside overnight.
3. Combine all other ingredients in a saucepan. Boil 1 minute; then add onions and boil another 6 to 7 minutes. Set aside to cool.
4. Store in a jar. This pickle will be ready in 8 to 10 days.

Gajar Achar

This carrot pickle is pungent with asafoetida.

1½ pounds carrots
5 tablespoons mustard oil or vegetable oil
¼ teaspoon ground asafoetida
1 teaspoon turmeric
1 teaspoon red pepper
1 tablespoon ground mustard seed
¼ cup vinegar
1 tablespoon garam masala (see index)

1. Scrape, wash, and cut the carrots into thin rounds.
2. Heat mustard or vegetable oil in a skillet. Remove from heat and add asafoetida and turmeric. Stir a few times.
3. Add carrots and all other ingredients. Simmer over low heat 2 to 3 minutes. Cool, then store in a jar.

Papita Achar

Tropical papaya fruit is pickled to a hot, exotic delight.

2 pounds green papaya
2 tablespoons salt
¼ cup mustard oil or peanut oil
1 teaspoon turmeric
1 teaspoon fennel seed
2 tablespoons crushed mustard seed
1 teaspoon red pepper
2 ounces finely chopped ginger

1. Skin and slice papaya into small pieces.
2. Boil in water 3 to 4 minutes. Drain.
3. Sprinkle papaya pieces with 1 tablespoon salt and spread them in the sun to dry.
4. Heat mustard or peanut oil in a skillet. Add turmeric, fennel seed, mustard seed, red pepper, and ginger. Cook 1 to 2 minutes.
5. Add papaya and remaining 1 tablespoon salt. Set aside to cool.
6. Store papaya pickle in a jar. It should be tender and ready to eat in a few days.

Orange and Lemon Skin Pickle

Hot (8 to 10 red chilies), sweet, and sour! Adjust the number of chilies to suit your palate.

skins of 4 oranges
skins of 4 lemons

skins of 4 limes
1½ cups vinegar
2 cups brown sugar
8 to 10 whole dry red chilies
2 tablespoons raisins
2 ounces sliced ginger
2 tablespoons crushed peppercorns
1 teaspoon cumin seed
1½ tablespoons salt
½ teaspoon turmeric

1. Slice orange, lemon, and lime skins. Dry them in the sun a few days.
2. Combine vinegar and brown sugar. Boil 5 minutes.
3. Add all other ingredients and fruit skins to vinegar and sugar. Simmer 5 minutes; then cool.
4. Store the pickle in a jar 10 to 15 days before serving.

Chili Pickle

These pickled chilies are stuffed with ground onion, garlic, ginger, and rich spices.

25 medium to large green chilies
8 tablespoons vegetable oil
6 cloves garlic, chopped
1 tablespoon chopped fresh ginger
½ cup chopped onion
¼ teaspoon ground asafoetida
½ teaspoon turmeric
½ teaspoon red pepper
1 tablespoon ground cumin seed
1 tablespoon ground coriander
1 teaspoon garam masala (see index)
½ teaspoon salt
1 tablespoon dry mango powder or 2 tablespoons lemon juice

1. Wash and clean chilies. Leave stems intact. Make a deep lengthwise slit in each chili.

2. Heat 3 tablespoons of the vegetable oil in a skillet. Add garlic, ginger, and onions. Cook until light golden. Add asafoetida, turmeric, and red pepper. Cook 1 minute. Then cool.
3. Grind cooked spices to a paste, adding some lemon juice if necessary.
4. Dry roast cumin seed and ground coriander separately for 1 to 2 minutes. They are completely roasted when you can smell their aroma.
5. Place the ground paste in a mixing bowl. Add garam masala, salt, roasted ingredients, and dry mango powder or lemon juice. Mix well.
6. Fill chilies with the paste. It might be necessary to wrap a piece of string around each chili so stuffing does not fall out. Reserve extra stuffing.
7. Heat remaining 5 tablespoons vegetable oil in skillet. Place stuffed chilies in skillet in a single layer. Pour any left-over stuffing over them. Cover and cook over medium-low heat 30 minutes. Turn the chilies a few times, to make sure they do not burn. Store them in a bottle or jar.

Onion Chutney

Onions, coriander leaves, and hot green chilies mingle in this chutney. It is especially good with appetizers.

1 large onion, chopped
1 cup chopped fresh coriander leaves
4 green chilies
1 tablespoon chopped fresh ginger
1 tablespoon chopped fresh mint or dry mint
½ teaspoon sugar
3 tablespoons lemon juice
salt to taste

1. Grind all ingredients in an electric blender until smooth. Do not use any water.
2. Bottle and keep refrigerated. Yield: 15 to 20 servings.

Dhania Chutney

Coriander leaves (*dhania*) form the base of this chutney. Italian parsley leaves can be used as a substitute.

3 cups chopped fresh coriander leaves
5 green chilies
1 teaspoon ground coriander
1 teaspoon ground cumin
3 tablespoons lemon juice
1 clove garlic, chopped
salt to taste

1. Blend all ingredients in a blender. Add a few tablespoons water to make a smooth paste.
2. Bottle and refrigerate. Yield: 15 servings.

Podina Chutney

Use three cups of chopped mint leaves (*podina*) instead of coriander leaves and proceed as in the preceding recipe for Dhania Chutney. This chutney is ideal with lamb and pork dishes.

Dahi Chutney

Mint and coriander leaves, yogurt, and 8 green chilies are blended for a fiery chutney.

1 tablespoon ground cumin
8 green chilies
1 cup chopped fresh mint leaves
2 cups yogurt, beaten
1 teaspoon sugar
2 tablespoons ground dry mango powder
2 tablespoons lemon juice
1 cup chopped fresh coriander leaves
salt to taste

1. Dry roast cumin lightly for about 1 minute. Set aside to cool.
2. Blend chilies, mint leaves, and ½ cup yogurt.
3. Beat remaining yogurt well in a bowl. Add contents of the blender and all other ingredients. Mix well.
4. Bottle and keep refrigerated. Yield: 20 servings.

Nariyal Chutney

This coastal coconut chutney is quite thick. Add a little water and blend until thinner, if you prefer.

2 cups fresh shredded coconut or 2 cups shredded, unsweetened packaged coconut
1 cup chopped fresh coriander leaves
3 tablespoons lemon juice
1 tablespoon chopped fresh ginger
salt to taste

1. Blend all ingredients together.
2. Bottle and refrigerate. Yield: 20 servings.

Spicy Coconut Chutney

South Indians smother their idlis and dosas with this chutney and wash it all down with thick coffee.

2 cups shredded fresh coconut
6 green chilies
½ teaspoon pepper
½ teaspoon sugar
3 tablespoons lemon juice
1 tablespoon chopped fresh ginger
1 cup chopped coriander leaves
salt to taste
1 teaspoon mustard seed

1. Dry roast coconut until light gold. Set aside to cool.
2. Blend together coconut and all other ingredients except mustard seed. Place blended mixture in a bowl.
3. Dry roast mustard seeds until they stop crackling. Add to chutney.
4. Bottle and refrigerate the chutney. Yield: 15 servings.

Kismis Chutney

Raisins (*kismis*) have a sweet and sour flavor in this spicy chutney.

2 cups seedless raisins, black or brown
2 cups water
2 tablespoons lemon juice
4 green chilies, chopped
5 cloves garlic, chopped
¼ cup sugar
1 tablespoon chopped fresh ginger
1 teaspoon red pepper
1 tablespoon vinegar
½ teaspoon cumin seed
salt to taste

1. Soak raisins in 2 cups water, until soft and full. Drain.
2. Blend all ingredients together, adding a little water if necessary.
3. Bottle and refrigerate the chutney. Yield: 15 servings.

Green Tomato Chutney

This chutney has both an exciting sweet-sour taste and a varied texture.

½ cup sugar
2 cups vinegar
2 pounds small green tomatoes, chopped
1 cup raisins

¼ cup chopped fresh ginger
5 green chilies, chopped
2 large onions, chopped
2 tart apples, chopped
salt to taste

1. Dissolve sugar in vinegar in a saucepan. Simmer the mixture over medium heat 30 to 40 minutes.
2. Add remaining ingredients. Cook over low heat until vegetables are tender. If too thick, add more vinegar.
3. Cool, then bottle the chutney. Yield: 15 to 20 servings.

Tomato Chutney

Tomato pulp is simmered with chopped apples, vinegar, garlic, and coriander leaves for this thick chutney.

5 medium tomatoes
2 tart apples
1 teaspoon sugar
1 tablespoon chopped fresh ginger
½ teaspoon red pepper
4 cloves garlic, chopped
2 cups vinegar
1 cup chopped fresh coriander leaves
salt to taste

1. Scald tomatoes in boiling water. Remove skins.
2. Place tomatoes in a saucepan and convert them into a pulp, using a fork.
3. Peel and slice the apples.
4. Add apples and all other ingredients to tomatoes. Simmer over medium-low heat until chutney is thick. Yield: 10 to 15 servings.

Khajoor Chutney

This thick and sugary date chutney is spiced with lots of garlic.

2 cups sugar

2 cups vinegar
2 pounds pitted dates, finely chopped
7 cloves garlic, chopped
¼ cup chopped fresh ginger
1 teaspoon cumin seed
¼ teaspoon red pepper
salt to taste

1. Dissolve sugar in vinegar in a saucepan.
2. Add all ingredients. Simmer over medium-low heat until a thick chutney is obtained and dates are soft. Bottle and refrigerate. Yield: 15 to 20 servings.

Spicy Date Chutney

There is no sugar in this date chutney, which is flavored with green chilies, lots of cumin, and red pepper.

2 pounds pitted dates
4 cups water
1 tablespoon chopped fresh ginger
1 tablespoon ground coriander
1 tablespoon ground cumin
1 teaspoon red pepper
3 green chilies
3 tablespoons lemon juice
1 teaspoon salt

1. Soak dates in 4 cups water 1 to 2 hours. Drain and reserve the water.
2. Blend all ingredients in an electric blender, using as much water as necessary to make a thick chutney.
3. Bottle and refrigerate. Yield: 20 servings.

Imli Chutney

This puckery South Indian tamarind (*imli*) delight is especially good with samosas and pakoras.

1½ cups tamarind
1 teaspoon cumin seeds
1 tablespoon chopped fresh ginger
½ teaspoon red pepper
salt to taste

1. Soak tamarind in 3 cups water 2 hours.
2. Extract the juice and discard the residue.
3. Using 1 tablespoon of the juice, blend together cumin and ginger in an electric blender.
4. Combine all ingredients in a bowl.
5. Bottle and refrigerate. Yield: 10 to 15 servings.

Peanut Chutney

This crunchy Indian peanut butter has a yogurt base.

1½ cups chopped peanuts
1 tablespoon chopped fresh ginger
½ teaspoon red pepper
½ cup chopped fresh coriander leaves
1 cup yogurt
2 green chilies
2 tablespoons lemon juice
1 teaspoon sugar
salt to taste

1. Lightly blend all ingredients in an electric blender until small chunks of peanuts can still be seen.
2. Bottle and refrigerate. Yield: 15 to 20 servings.

Mango Chutney

This is one of the most popular Indian chutneys.

4 medium green mangos
¼ cup sugar
¼ cup raisins
1 tablespoon chopped fresh ginger
½ teaspoon red pepper
1 tablespoon blanched almonds
1 cup vinegar
1 teaspoon ground coriander
salt to taste

1. Cut mangos into thick slices and discard the stones.
2. Dissolve sugar and raisins in a saucepan.
3. Add all other ingredients to sugar and raisins. Simmer over medium-low heat until mangos become soft.
4. Cool, then bottle tightly. Yield: 10 to 15 servings.

12

Desserts

India's lavish super-sugary sweets (*mithais*) are reserved for occasions that are festive and happy. The often silver-coated, nut-studded confectioner's dreams play a prominent role in religious observations and other holidays. Mohammed, the Mogul prophet, loves sweets above all other foods, and they are offered to him at the many temples throughout India. Hindus believe the mind is affected by the types of foods one eats: eating sweets gives one pleasant thoughts.

While it is customary for Americans to bring meals to a sweet closing with pies, cakes, and puddings, sweets are seldom served as desserts with Indian meals. Chilled fresh fruit, or paan leaves wrapped with spices and betel nuts inside are the usual ending to a meal.

Indian women spend many hours preparing sweets during October and November, the last months of the Hindu year. It is truly a labor of love, because their ingredients are costly and the cooking is time consuming. The most luscious sweets are made from *khoya* (dry whole milk), which is prepared by a lengthy process of boiling and stirring the milk to a powder, and *chenna* (Indian semi-soft cream cheese), made by a boiling and curdling process that takes hours. Both these milk bases are mixed with spices, coconut, nuts, and rose water, and most assume a solid form. There are also flour-dough dumplings or stuffed pastries that are soaked in pure sugar syrups and sprinkled with nuts. Many pudding-type sweets are made from yogurt, sour cream, and vegetable bases. The state of Bengal is world famous for its sweets, especially the chenna-based ones.

Chenna and dry whole milk-based sweets are usually purchased from professional sweet makers (*mithaiwalas*). They have a special position in every Indian community, and people often stand and watch them in their shops for long periods of time.

At special meals, sweets are served along with vegetables, rice, and other dishes during the meal, rather than afterward. Everyday sweets are also eaten at tea time or with other savories. You can serve Indian sweets as desserts or as tea and coffee snacks. The amount of sugar called for in each recipe has been reduced to satisfy the Western sweet tooth.

Shrikhand

This saffron-yellow sour cream dish is kissed with sugar, cardamom, and almonds. It is eaten with pooris in the western state of Gujarat and in Central India on festive occasions.

¼ teaspoon saffron
1 tablespoon cream or milk, lukewarm
6 cups sour cream
2 cups sugar
½ teaspoon ground cardamom
4 tablespoons slivered almonds
4 tablespoons chopped pistachio nuts
pinch of paprika

1. Crush the saffron and soak it in lukewarm cream or milk 10 minutes.
2. Beat the sour cream and pour it into a piece of cheesecloth. Squeeze out all the liquid into a mixing bowl and beat again.

3. Add sugar, cardamom, saffron-cream, and almonds to sour cream. Mix well.
4. Pour into 4 to 6 dessert bowls. Sprinkle with pistachio nuts and paprika. Serve immediately or refrigerate. Yield: 4 to 6 servings.

Kushli

This pastry, stuffed with coconut and cream of wheat, is one of many sweets sold outside Indian temples as offerings to be placed at the altars of the gods.

1 cup all-purpose flour
pinch of salt
pinch of baking soda
6 tablespoons butter
½ cup water
½ cup freshly shredded coconut
2 tablespoons blanched almonds
1 cup cream of wheat
1 cup sugar
seeds from 10 cardamom pods, crushed
2 tablespoons raisins
vegetable oil for deep frying

1. Sift together flour, salt, and baking soda. Rub in 2 tablespoons butter. Prepare a stiff dough with some water, about ½ cup. Set aside.
2. To prepare the pastry filling, heat remaining butter in a skillet. Add coconut, almonds, and cream of wheat. Cook until mixture is golden.
3. Add sugar, cardamom seeds, and raisins. Cook until sugar is completely dissolved, about 5 to 7 minutes.
4. Divide dough into 12 equal portions. Roll each portion into a 4-inch round. Place some filling on half of the round, leaving ¼ inch border around the edge. Fold the other half over the mixture and seal edges completely.
5. Heat vegetable oil for deep frying. Fry the pastries until golden. Yield: 12 Kushli.

Balu Sahi

These are eggless Indian doughnuts that are deep-fried. Balu Sahis are glazed with sugar and pistachio nuts.

2 cups all-purpose flour
1 teaspoon baking soda
4 tablespoons unsalted butter
2 tablespoons yogurt
2 cups sugar
2 cups water
vegetable oil for deep frying
1 tablespoon rose water
3 tablespoons chopped unsalted pistachio nuts

1. Sift together flour and baking soda into a bowl. Add butter and rub it into the flour. Add yogurt and enough warm water to form a stiff dough. Cover and set aside 30 minutes.
2. To make the syrup, dissolve sugar in 2 cups water. Boil 7 to 8 minutes. Let it sit over very low heat.
3. Divide dough into 16 portions. Shape each portion into a ball; then flatten slightly. Make a deep dent in the center of each one.
4. Heat vegetable oil for deep frying. Fry doughnuts until golden.
5. Place doughnuts in warm syrup. Add rose water and soak 3 to 4 hours.
6. Remove doughnuts from syrup and arrange them in the shape of a cone on a small plate. Mix pistachio nuts and ¼ cup of the syrup and pour it over the doughnuts. Keep unrefrigerated until served. They will stay fresh several days. Yield: 16 doughnuts.

Sandesh

This Indian cheese fudge is cut into diamonds and studded with almonds and pistachio nuts. *Sandesh* means "good news," and one legend is that princesses used to stuff them with love letters.

3 quarts milk
juice of 3 lemons
2 cups sugar
seeds from 10 cardamom pods, crushed
1 tablespoon unsalted pistachio nuts
1 tablespoon slivered almonds

1. Bring milk to a boil in a large saucepan. Add lemon juice. Within a few minutes, the milk should curdle and solid lumps (*chenna*) will form. Boil 1 to 2 minutes longer.
2. Remove milk from heat. Pour into a colander and drain off all the liquid.
3. Tie chenna in a cheesecloth bag and hang it over the sink for 3 to 4 hours to drain off most of the liquid.
4. Place the chenna in a skillet and knead it well to obtain a smooth, dough-like appearance, about 5 minutes.
5. Mix in sugar and cardamom. Cook over medium heat 7 to 8 minutes or until all the sugar has dissolved and the mixture is quite thick. Stir continuously.
6. Grease a large platter. Pour the mixture in the center and spread evenly all over the platter. It should be about ¼ inch thick. When cool, cut into cubes or diamonds and decorate with pistachio nuts and almonds. Yield: 25 to 30 pieces.

Gulab Jamun

These spongy, deep-fried balls are served in syrup laced with rose (*gulab*) water. The rich balls are made from dry whole milk, cream, and flour.

1 cup dry whole milk
½ cup self-rising flour (Bisquick)
seeds of 10 cardamom pods, crushed
5 tablespoons unsalted butter
7 ounces evaporated milk or cream
2 cups sugar
2½ cups water
vegetable oil for deep frying
2 tablespoons rose water

1. Mix together dry whole milk, flour, and cardamom seeds. Add butter and rub gently 4 to 5 minutes.
2. Gradually pour evaporated milk or cream into the mixture and blend well. It should form into a sticky lump. If too sticky, cover it for a few minutes and it will harden a bit.
3. Shape the milk-flour substance into 20 balls. Cover and set aside.
4. To prepare the syrup, dissolve sugar in 2½ cups water. Boil 8 to 10 minutes; then simmer gently over very low heat.
5. Heat vegetable oil on low flame for deep frying. Fry balls until golden, turning frequently. Since the gulab jamun swell during frying, fry them in several batches. Drain balls on paper towels.
6. Add fried gulab jamun to warm syrup. Add rose water. Soak them overnight or at least 4 to 5 hours. Gulab jamun are served hot, but they also taste good at room temperature. Refrigerate until needed and warm them before serving. Yield: 20 gulab jamun.

Gulab Jamun Barkhera

These are oversized gulab jamun from the small town of Barkhera in Central India. People passing through Barkhera should never miss an opportunity to taste these delicious sweets, stuffed with raisins and blanched almonds.

1 tablespoon ground almonds
6 tablespoons butter
1 tablespoon cream of wheat or semolina
½ cup chenna or panir (see Rasgulla recipe)
1½ cups dry whole milk
½ cup self-rising flour (Bisquick)
seeds from 15 cardamom pods, crushed
1 cup evaporated milk
½ cup raisins
½ cup blanched almonds
2½ cups sugar
5½ cups water
vegetable oil for deep frying

1. Fry almonds and cream of wheat separately in 1 tablespoon butter each, for 1 minute over medium-low heat. Set aside.
2. Fry chenna or panir in remaining 4 tablespoons butter 2 to 3 minutes over medium-low heat.
3. In a large bowl, mix dry whole milk, flour, cardamom seeds, and all fried ingredients along with butter in which they were fried. Rub butter in well. Pour in evaporated milk and mix well. Cover for a minute if too sticky.
4. Divide the flour-milk substance into 12 to 15 portions. Shape them into balls. Break each ball in two and stuff with a few raisins and blanched almonds.
5. To make the syrup, dissolve sugar in 5½ cups water. Boil 10 minutes. Simmer over very low heat until the gulab jamun are added to it.

6. Heat vegetable oil for deep frying and fry the gulab jamun until golden.
7. Soak in syrup 5 to 6 hours or overnight. Serve warm. Yield: 12 to 15 gulab jamun.

Rasgulla

This prized Bengal sweet is usually taken with tea. It is also eaten throughout India during holiday celebrations such as Diwali, the Festival of Lights. Soft chenna balls the size of walnuts float in syrup.

10 cups milk
1½ cups whipping cream
juice of 3 lemons
2½ cups sugar
7 cups water
2 tablespoons rose water

1. Mix milk and cream in a saucepan. Bring to a boil. Add lemon juice and stir until milk curdles.
2. Drain the liquid in a colander and tie the solid lumps (*chenna, or panir*) in a cheesecloth bag. Hang over the sink overnight to drain.
3. Using a rolling pin, pound and roll the chenna several times, until it becomes creamy and smooth.
4. Divide into 15 to 18 portions and shape each into a ball. Cover and set aside.
5. Dissolve sugar in 7 cups water in a large saucepan. Boil 2 minutes.
6. Lower heat to medium-low and drop chenna balls gently into syrup. Cover and cook 35 minutes. There is no need to remove the lid during this period.
7. Sprinkle chenna balls with rose water and cool. Soak 3 to 4 hours. Serve at room temperature. Some people prefer them cold, but they become hard if refrigerated. They are usually decorated with pistachio nuts and silver leaf paper. Yield: 15 to 18 rasgullas.

Ras Malai

Prepare chenna balls as in the preceding Rasgulla recipe; then flatten them into patties. Continue exactly as in making Rasgulla. Then proceed as follows to prepare the rich almond cream in which they are served. This cream is often served by itself as a pudding by the people of Punjab.

1 tablespoon unsalted butter
¼ cup ground almonds
7 cups whipping cream
¾ to 1 cup sugar
pinch of nutmeg
2 tablespoons rose water
4 tablespoons finely chopped unsalted pistachio nuts

1. Heat butter in a saucepan and cook ground almonds 1 to 2 minutes until golden.
2. Add whipping cream. Bring to a boil and cook over medium heat until liquid is reduced to 3 cups.
3. Add sugar and nutmeg. Stir.
4. Take the rasgullas out of their syrup and place them in the cream. Simmer over low heat 5 minutes. Sprinkle with rose water and pistachio nuts. Yield: 15 to 18 ras malai.

Chum-Chum

These soft, heart-shaped cheese patties float in colorful syrup.

chenna (see Rasgulla recipe)
½ tablespoon cream of wheat
2½ cups sugar
7 cups water
1 drop food coloring, your choice
2 tablespoons rose water
1 tablespoon chopped pistachio nuts

1. Tie chenna in a cheesecloth bag and hang overnight.
2. Using a rolling pin, pound and roll chenna until smooth and creamy.
3. Place in a mixing bowl. Add cream of wheat and mix well.
4. Divide chenna into 12 portions and shape them like hearts, about 2 inches long. Cover and set aside.
5. Dissolve sugar in 7 cups water in a large saucepan. Boil 3 to 4 minutes. Add food color and reduce heat to medium-low.
6. Add chum-chum hearts to syrup and cook, covered, 30 to 35 minutes. Add 1 tablespoon cold water every 15 minutes.
7. Add rose water and cool. Serve at room temperature or chilled. (Chum-chum hardens when chilled.) Sprinkle the individual servings with pistachio nuts. Yield: 12 chum-chum hearts.

Kheer

This is a glorious Indian rice pudding, served by Hindus on religious occasions and as an everyday sweet.

¼ cup rice, long-grain
3 cups milk
3 cups whipping cream
¾ to 1 cup sugar
pinch of salt
3 tablespoons raisins
4 tablespoons blanched almonds
a few drops of rose water
seeds from 10 cardamom pods, crushed
2 tablespoons unsalted pistachio nuts

1. Wash rice in cold water. Drain and set aside.
2. Combine milk and half-and-half in a saucepan. Bring to a boil.
3. Add rice and cook over medium heat until rice is tender.

4. Add sugar and salt to rice. Stir and continue to cook over medium-low heat until mixture thickens to pouring consistency, about 10 minutes.
5. Add raisins and almonds. Mix well. Add rose water and stir a few times.
6. Pour into individual dessert bowls and sprinkle each with crushed cardamom seeds and pistachio nuts. Serve at room temperature or cold. Yield: 6 servings.

Suji Halva

Halva is a sweet pudding made from cream of wheat, eggs, fruits, vegetables, nuts, or flour combined with milk, sugar, and butter. It is made for weddings and certain religious services, where it is offered to the gods and then eaten by the followers as *prasad* ("God's leftovers"). This is a cream of wheat (*suji*) version.

½ **cup sugar**
¾ **cup water**
1 tablespoon milk
¼ **teaspoon saffron, soaked in ½ teaspoon warm water**
4 tablespoons unsalted butter
½ **cup cream of wheat**
2 tablespoons raisins
2 tablespoons blanched almonds
seeds from 6 cardamom pods, crushed

1. Dissolve sugar in ¾ cup water in a saucepan. Boil 5 minutes.
2. Add 1 tablespoon milk to boiling syrup to clean it. Remove the scum from the syrup.
3. Add saffron soaked in water and simmer 1 minute. Keep warm over low heat.
4. Heat butter in a skillet and cook cream of wheat until butter separates from it.
5. Pour syrup into cream of wheat, stirring constantly.

6. Add raisins, almonds, and cardamom seeds. Cook until the mixture forms a thick lump and butter separates, about 5 minutes. Serve hot or at room temperature. Yield: 4 to 6 servings.

Gajar Halva

One taste of this sweet and it is difficult to believe it has a carrot base.

1½ pounds carrots, scraped and grated
1 cup water
¾ cup sugar
3 cups milk
¼ cup unsalted butter
seeds of 10 cardamom pods, crushed
3 tablespoons blanched almonds
4 tablespoons raisins
3 tablespoons chopped unsalted pistachio nuts

1. Cook grated carrots in 1 cup water over medium heat until most of the liquid dries up. Mash the carrots lightly.
2. Add sugar and milk. Bring to a boil. Simmer over medium-low heat until mixture thickens, about 10 minutes.
3. Add butter, cardamom seeds, almonds, and raisins. Reduce heat and cook until butter separates from the mixture.
4. Place the halva in individual dessert bowls and decorate with pistachio nuts. Yield: 6 servings.

Moong Halva

This lentil-based halva is just one of the many kinds that are covered with white lace and sent to friends on the celebration of Id.

1 cup moong dahl
¼ cup unsalted butter

2 cups milk
1 tablespoon ground almonds
seeds of 10 cardamom pods, crushed
pinch of crushed saffron
1 cup sugar
2 tablespoons chopped unsalted pistachio nuts

1. Wash and soak dahl in cold water overnight, then drain it.
2. Grind dahl in an electric blender, in several batches. Use some water during the grinding.
3. Heat butter in a skillet. Cook ground dahl until golden.
4. Gradually pour in milk, stirring constantly.
5. Add almonds, cardamom seeds, saffron, and sugar. Cook over medium-low heat until butter separates. Sprinkle with pistachio nuts. Yield: 6 servings.

Besan Halva

Cardamom-flavored chick-pea flour halva is a solid version cut into squares.

2 cups sugar
1½ cups water
pinch of crushed saffron
1 cup unsalted butter
2 cups chick-pea flour
seeds of 10 cardamom pods, crushed
2 tablespoons slivered almonds
2 tablespoons chopped unsalted pistachio nuts

1. Dissolve sugar in 1½ cups water. Add saffron and boil 5 minutes.
2. Heat butter in a skillet. Cook chick-pea flour until golden, stirring constantly.
3. Add saffron-syrup and continue cooking over medium heat until butter separates. Add cardamom seeds and mix.

4. Pour mixture into a greased tray and spread into a ¼-inch thick layer. When cool, cut into 1½-inch squares. Decorate with almonds and pistachio nuts. Yield: about 20 pieces.

Jalebi

This is an unusual sweet from the North. Saffron-colored flour spirals are deep-fried, then soaked in rose water syrup. Indian chefs use a coconut shell with one hole in it instead of a funnel to form the spirals.

1½ cups all-purpose flour
pinch of crushed saffron
2 tablespoons yogurt
1 cup warm water
2 cups sugar
2 cups water
1 tablespoon rose water
vegetable oil for deep frying

1. Sift flour into a mixing bowl. Add saffron and yogurt. Gradually pour in 1 cup warm water. Keep mixing until a smooth batter is obtained. Cover and set aside in a warm place overnight.
2. Dissolve sugar in 2 cups water. Boil 5 minutes. Simmer over medium-low heat 5 minutes. Add rose water and set aside.
3. Heat vegetable oil for deep frying.
4. Beat batter well, making sure it is free from lumps. Fill a funnel with a small opening (a little smaller than the thickness of a pencil) or a plastic catsup bottle with a nozzle. With a rapid motion, squeeze the batter in a spiral into the hot oil. Fry 4 to 5 at one time until golden.
5. Soak the jalebis in the syrup 4 to 5 minutes. Remove from syrup and serve immediately. Yield: 20 pieces.

Bundi

Bundi is Indian for "rain drops," an appropriate name for these tiny chick-pea flour balls in syrup.

1 cup chick-pea flour or yellow split-pea flour
1 tablespoon rice flour
½ teaspoon baking soda
1 cup warm water
few drops of yellow food coloring
1 tablespoon unsalted butter
2 cups sugar
2 cups water
few drops of rose water
2 tablespoons slivered almonds
seeds from 10 cardamom pods, crushed
vegetable oil for deep frying
2 tablespoons chopped unsalted pistachio nuts

1. Mix together chick-pea flour or split-pea flour, rice flour, and baking soda with 1 cup warm water. Mix to a thick batter. Add yellow food coloring and butter. Mix. Cover and set aside.
2. To prepare the syrup, dissolve sugar in 2 cups water. Boil 5 minutes. Add rose water, almonds, and cardamom seeds. Keep warm over very low heat.
3. Heat vegetable oil for deep frying.
4. Beat the batter well. Pour a small quantity through a slotted spoon, spreading the mixture over the spoon rapidly with fingers. Fry tiny balls until golden. Remove them from oil and drain on paper towels. Drop them into the syrup. Decorate with pistachio nuts and let soak for a few hours. Serve warm. Yield: 8 servings.

Bundi Laddoo

Ganesh the elephant god is an epicure of fine food. Bundi laddoo is his favorite food. The men and children sculpt a mud Ganesh and offer bundi laddoo as a sacrifice. In this recipe, use 1½ cups chick-pea flour or yellow split-pea flour. Follow all the steps of the preceding Bundi recipe. When the bundi and syrup mixture becomes a little cold, lump the tiny balls together into 15 balls and dust them with sugar.

Besan Laddoo

In this South Indian version, the laddoo are made with chick-pea flour, coconut, and pistachio nuts.

3 cups sugar
4 cups water
few drops of rose water
2 cups unsalted butter
3 cups chick-pea flour
seeds from 15 cardamom pods, crushed
1 cup freshly grated coconut
½ cup chopped unsalted pistachio nuts
white poppy seeds

1. Dissolve sugar in 4 cups water. Boil 7 minutes. Simmer over medium heat 7 minutes. Add rose water.
2. Heat butter in a skillet. Cook chick-pea flour until golden, stirring constantly.
3. Gradually add syrup and keep cooking on low heat until butter separates.
4. Add cardamom seeds, coconut, and pistachio nuts. Remove from heat to cool.
5. When cool enough to handle, make 20 balls. Roll balls in poppy seeds.

Ginger Burfi

Burfi is a fudge-like Indian sweet usually made from a dry whole milk and sugar base. Other ingredients are added to give it varying flavors. In this recipe, ginger plays the stellar role.

½ pound fresh ginger, chopped
1 tablespoon water
½ pound unsalted butter
½ pound cream of wheat
¾ pound sugar
½ teaspoon ground cardamom

1. Grind the ginger in 1 tablespoon of water. Extract the juice and set aside.
2. Heat butter in a skillet and cook cream of wheat over low heat until golden.
3. Add ginger juice, sugar, and cardamom to cream of wheat. Cook over low heat until sugar is completely dissolved and the mixture is quite thick.
4. Pour the burfi into a greased platter. When cold, cut it into squares or diamond-shaped pieces. Yield: enough for 6 people.

Panir Burfi

Bengal is famous for its *panir*, an Indian soft cheese.

¼ cup unsalted butter
1 tablespoon ground almonds
2 cups panir, made from 3 quarts milk (see Rasgulla recipe)
1 cup sugar
seeds from 8 cardamom pods, crushed
1 cup dry whole milk
2 tablespoons whipping cream
1 tablespoon rose water
2 tablespoons chopped unsalted pistachio nuts

1. Heat butter in a skillet. Add almonds and cook 2 minutes. Then add panir and cook over low heat 5 minutes, stirring continuously.
2. Add sugar, cardamom seeds, dry whole milk and half-and-half. Cook over medium-low heat until the mixture is quite thick and does not stick to bottom of pan, about 15 minutes.
3. Add rose water and mix. Pour into a greased platter in a ¼-inch thick layer. Decorate with pistachio nuts. When cold, cut into squares or desired shapes. Yield: 20 pieces.

Alu Burfi

One never knows what an Indian chef will create next with a potato.

1 pound potatoes
1½ cups dry whole milk
3 tablespoons unsalted butter
2 pounds sugar
2 cups water
1 tablespoon rose water
seeds from 6 cardamom pods, crushed
2 tablespoons slivered almonds

1. Boil potatoes in their jackets. Peel and mash them completely.
2. Gradually add dry whole milk to mashed potatoes and mix well.
3. Heat butter in a skillet. Cook potatoes until golden, about 4 to 5 minutes. Remove from heat.
4. Dissolve sugar in 2 cups water in a saucepan. Boil over medium heat 10 minutes.
5. Add rose water, cardamom seeds, and potatoes, stirring continuously. Cook a few minutes more or until the mixture is quite thick.
6. Pour into a greased platter. Decorate with slivered almonds. When cold, cut into desired shapes. Yield: 25 pieces.

Peda

These milk cookies are a very popular North Indian sweet. When a new baby is born, the parents offer pedas to friends.

4 tablespoons unsalted butter
1 teaspoon ground almonds
1 cup panir or ricotta cheese (see Rasgulla recipe)
1 cup sugar
pinch of saffron, soaked in 1 tablespoon warm cream
2 cups dry whole milk
seeds from 8 cardamom pods, crushed
¼ cup unsalted pistachio nuts

1. Heat butter in a skillet. Add ground almonds and cook 1 minute.
2. Add panir and cook 5 minutes over medium-low heat.
3. Add sugar and saffron mixture. When sugar is completely dissolved, add dry whole milk and cardamom seeds, stirring vigorously. Cook over medium-low heat until the mixture is thick and does not stick to bottom of pan. It should come out in a solid lump. Let it cool a little.
4. Divide into 25 equal portions. Shape into balls, then flatten a little. Make a dent in the center of each and place a pistachio nut in the dent. Yield: 25 cookies.

Appam

These sweet balls stuffed with nutty-flavored cream of wheat are a favored South Indian sweet.

5 tablespoons butter
2 tablespoons chopped cashew nuts
1 cup cream of wheat
2 cups milk
1 cup sugar
seeds from 5 cardamom pods, crushed
1 cup all-purpose flour
vegetable oil for deep frying

1. Heat 1 tablespoon butter in a skillet. Sauté cashew nuts. Remove from butter and grind coarsely. Set aside.
2. Add 2 tablespoons butter to the skillet and cook cream of wheat until golden.
3. Add milk, sugar, cashew nuts, and cardamom seeds. Cook over medium-low heat until the mixture is thick and does not stick to bottom of pan. Remove from heat.
4. Mix flour and remaining 2 tablespoons butter in a bowl. Rub butter well into the flour, adding a little water to prepare a stiff dough. Divide into 12 balls. Divide the cream of wheat into 12 portions.
5. Flatten the dough balls and make a dent in the center of each. Fill dents with cream of wheat mixture. Enclose the stuffing completely. Seal edges well. Roll the balls lightly with a rolling pin.
6. Heat vegetable oil for deep frying. Deep fry balls until golden. Serve them warm.

Payasam

Something a little unusual—a South Indian vegetable dessert.

1 medium cauliflower, cut into small pieces
2 cups shredded cabbage
1 cup green peas
1 cup chopped carrots
1 medium potato, peeled and cubed
2 quarts milk
3 cups sugar
½ teaspoon saffron, soaked in 2 tablespoons warm milk
¼ cup blanched almonds
1 tablespoon unsalted butter
¼ cup chopped cashew nuts
2 tablespoons raisins
seeds from 10 cardamom pods, crushed

1. Boil vegetables in water to cover in a large saucepan 45 minutes, over medium heat. Drain and discard the water.

2. Place vegetables back in pan and add milk, sugar, saffron, and almonds. Bring to a boil. Reduce heat to medium-low and cook 45 minutes, or until the mixture becomes quite thick.
3. Sauté cashew nuts and raisins lightly in butter. Add fried ingredients and cardamom seeds to vegetables. Yield: 6 to 8 servings.

13

Beverages

The tropical heat throughout most of India makes it necessary for one to drink deeply from tall glasses of ice cold beverages to soothe the parched throat and cool the body.

City and village snack vendors with their refreshing frothy fruit drinks made from coconut, mango, guava, and pineapple are popular all over the subcontinent. But these exotic tropical fruit coolers are not the only icy liquids Indians take to quench their thirst.

There are many milk-based coolers made from sweet and creamy buffalo milk and buttermilk. They are usually blended with crushed ice, spices, and nuts and sometimes delicately colored. Indian-style milkshakes are made from whipped and seasoned yogurt.

Beverages are also drunk for their medicinal properties. Water, taken many times during the day and at meals, is the most popular and important beverage. For centuries, tea has been prescribed as a relief for sore throats and colds, and has been recognized as a stimulant. It is second to water as an essential drink in India. This is especially true in the North, where the majority of tea grows in the lush Himalayan foothills—the aromatic Darjeeling strains are among the most famous in the world.

When a visitor asks for a tea bag, Indians are quick to inform him "Indian tea does not grow in bags." Only loose leaves are used to prepare the brews, which are often spiced with cinnamon, cloves, and cardamom. The Chinese introduced India to tea centuries ago, but it was the British who, in the early 1900s, taught them to drink it "neat" with milk and sugar. Iced tea has been catching on rapidly in the big cities like New Delhi and Bombay. North Indians drink tea upon rising, again with breakfast, at midmorning, late in the afternoon with savories, after the last meal of the day, and sometimes at night before retiring.

Coffee takes the place of tea in South India, where some of the richest coffee beans in the world are grown in the hills of the Western Ghats. Indian coffee is brewed thick and creamy like Italian cappucino. It is quickly mixed back and forth between two tumblers until it is wickedly thick and frothy.

Try to use loose tea when preparing the tea-based beverages. Store the tea in opaque airtight containers away from strongly scented herbs and spices. These teas are especially good with Indian meals, rather than wine or heavy drinks. The thick and icy-cold beverages make a delicate and refreshing dessert with any Indian meal or buffet, but they are delicious any time.

Lassi

Yogurt is whipped with cardamom and sugar to create an Indian milk shake. It is served plain, salted, or sweetened.

5 cups yogurt
seeds from 5 cardamom pods, crushed
6 tablespoons sugar
1 tablespoon rose water
⅛ teaspoon nutmeg

1. Combine 3 cups yogurt, cardamom, and sugar in an electric blender and blend well.
2. Beat remaining yogurt well in a bowl. Add to contents of blender and mix well.
3. Add rose water to yogurt and mix well. Serve in individual glasses and sprinkle with nutmeg. Yield: 4 to 6 servings.

Sherbat

This is an ancient Indian thirst quencher, made from fruit juices and other flavorings such as nuts, sandalwood and rose petals. It is a popular summer drink in small towns and villages.

1 cup sugar
1 cup crushed ice
4 cups water
juice of 2 fresh lemons
2 tablespoons rose water
few drops of food coloring, if desired

1. In a saucepan, combine sugar, crushed ice, 4 cups water, lemon juice, rose water, and food coloring.
2. When sugar is completely dissolved, strain and serve the sherbat in frosty glasses. Yield: 4 servings.

Amm Rus

The mango is the king of Indian fruits. When unripe, it is used in chutneys and pickles; when ripe, it is eaten fresh or used for rich and cooling mango juice (*amm rus*). Sometimes a layer of extracted juice is spread over cloth and set in the sun several days to dry. A few of the layers are stacked together and sold to be used in making chutneys or eaten as is.

6 ripe mangoes
1 cup milk

1 tablespoon sugar
¼ teaspoon freshly ground black pepper

1. Peel mangoes and scrape all edible parts from seeds.
2. Chop the fruit and grind in an electric blender.
3. Place ground mango in a bowl and add milk and sugar. Mix well. Pour in glasses and sprinkle with black pepper. Yield: 4 servings.

Thandai

This is a rich almond and milk cooler served at festive occasions and during marriage ceremonies.

½ cup blanched almonds
10 black peppercorns
5 cloves
½ cup chopped unsalted pistachio nuts
¼ cup fennel seed
½ cup seedless raisins
2 cups water
seeds from 8 cardamom pods
pinch of saffron
1¼ cups sugar
2 cups milk
3 cups water
1 cup crushed ice
3 tablespoons rose water
2 tablespoons chopped fresh mint leaves

1. Soak almonds, peppercorns, cloves, pistachio nuts, fennel seeds, raisins, and cardamom seeds in 2 cups water 30 minutes. Strain and discard water.
2. In an electric blender, grind strained ingredients with saffron to a smooth paste, adding as much water as necessary.
3. In a large bowl, combine sugar, milk, 3 cups water, crushed ice, and blender contents. Mix well.

4. When sugar is completely dissolved, strain the mixture into another bowl and discard the residue. Add rose water and sprinkle with mint. Serve in frosted glasses. Yield: 4 to 6 servings.

Garam Doodh

This milk-based beverage is a drink to good health among Indians. The soft, saffron-yellow drink is flavored with almonds and pistachio nuts. A glass of this hot milk taken before retiring can mean a night of pleasant slumber.

6 cups milk
⅛ teaspoon crushed saffron
6 tablespoons sugar
2 tablespoons slivered almonds
2 tablespoons chopped unsalted pistachio nuts
seeds from 5 cardamom pods, crushed

1. Bring milk to boil in a saucepan.
2. Add saffron, sugar, almonds, pistachio nuts and cardamom seeds to milk. Boil 5 minutes. Serve hot. Yield: 4 to 6 servings.

Masala Chai

This tea is considered very good for relieving cold symptoms. *Chai masala* (ground tea spices) is available in Indian grocery stores, or you can use one of the garam masala recipes in this book.

3 cups water
3 cups milk
5 to 6 tablespoons sugar
5 whole cardamom pods
1 small piece fresh ginger, crushed
1-inch stick cinnamon, broken into small pieces

¼ teaspoon chai masala
6 tablespoons loose tea

1. Combine water and milk in a saucepan and bring to boil.
2. Add sugar, cardamom, ginger, cinnamon, chai masala, and tea to boiling liquid in saucepan. Stir a few times and boil over medium heat 3 to 4 minutes. Make sure it does not boil over.
3. Strain tea through cheesecloth into another pan.
4. Place tea over heat and bring to a boil. Serve in cups immediately. Yield: 4 to 6 servings.

Masala Coffee

This is a favorite in South India, where it is poured back and forth between two gleaming containers until it becomes thick and creamy.

3 cups milk
3 cups water
1-inch stick cinnamon
5 whole cardamom pods
6 tablespoons sugar
6 tablespoons coffee, regular grind

Proceed as in preceding recipe for Masala Chai. Yield: 4 to 6 servings.

14

Indian Food and Supply Stores in the United States and Canada

United States

Midwest

India Grocers
5002 North Sheridan Road
Chicago IL 60640
312/334-3351

International Food & Emporium
3436-38 North Halsted
Chicago IL 60657
312/248-8024

India Spice Co.
437 South Boulevard
Oak Park IL 60302

Indian Groceries and Spices
2527 West National Ave.
Milwaukee WI

International House of Foods
440 West Gorham St.
Madison WI 53703

India Foods and Boutique
3729 Cass
Detroit MI 48201

India Grocers
3546 Cass
Detroit MI 48201
313/831-5480

West

Bezjian Grocery
4725 Santa Monica Boulevard
Los Angeles CA 90029

California Direct Import Co.
2651 Mission St.
San Francisco CA 94110

Haig's Delicacies
441 Clement St.
San Francisco CA 94118

Bazaar of India
1331 University Ave.
Berkeley CA 94702

Porter's Foods Unlimited
270 West 8th Ave.
Eugene ORE 97401

House of Rice
4112 University Way N.E.
Seattle WA 98105

Specialty Spice Shop
Pike Place Market
Seattle WA 98101

America Tea, Coffee and Spice Co.
1511 Champa St.
Denver COLO 80202

East

Foods of India
120 Lexington Ave.
New York NY 10016

India Foods and Condiments
811 Lexington Ave.
New York NY 10016

Java Indian Condiment Company
440 Hudson St.
New York NY 10014

K. Kalustyan, Orient Export Trading Corporation
123 Lexington Ave.
New York NY 10016

Kalpana Indian Groceries
42-75 Main St.
Flushing NY 10014

House of Spices
76-17 Broadway
Jackson Heights NY 11373

Maya Indian Spice Center
89-20 163rd St.
Jamaica NY 11432

Sahadi Importing Co.
187 Atlantic Ave.
Brooklyn NY 11201

Kumar Brothers
Bloomfield Ave.
Hoboken NJ 07030

Cambridge Coffee, Tea and Spice House
1765 Massachusetts Ave.
Cambridge MA 02138

Vinod Shah
3 Prescott St.
North Woburn MA 01801

India Health Foods
1169 State St.
Bridgeport CT 06605

Spices and Foods Unlimited Inc.
2018 A. Florida Ave., N.W.
Washington D.C. 20009

Bombay Emporium
3343 Forbes Ave.
Pittsburgh PA 75213

House of India
5840 Foxwood Ave.
Pittsburgh PA 15217

India Food Mart
808 South 47th St.
Philadelphia PA 19143

India Super Bazaar
4101 Walnut St.
Philadelphia PA 19104

India Super Bazaar
4707 Miller Ave.
Bethesda MD 20014

India Sub-Continental Stores
908 Philadelphia Ave.
Silver Spring MD 20910

South

Raj Enterprises
881 Peachtree St.
Atlanta GA 30309

Central Grocery
923 Decatur St.
New Orleans LA 70116

Indian Food Center
15-43 McCausland Ave.
St. Louis MO 63117

Quality Imported Foods
717 North Sixth St.
St. Louis MO 63101

Antone's
2606 Sheridan
Tulsa OK 74129

Giant Foods of America
100 Oaks Shopping Center
Nashville TN 37204

Jung's Oriental Foods & Gifts
2519 North Fitzhugh
Dallas TX 75204

Yoga and Health Center
6039 Berkshire Lane
Dallas TX 75222

Antone's Import Co.
4232 Harry Hines Blvd.
Dallas TX 75219

Antone's Import Co.
1639 South Boss Rd.
Houston, TX 77027

Antone's Import Co.
8111 South Main St.
Houston TX 77027

Canada

S. Enkin Inc.
1201 St. Lawrence
Montreal 129 Quebec

T. Eaton's Co.
190 Younge St.
Toronto 205 Ontario

Top Banana, Limited
62 William St.
Ottawa 2 Ontario

The Government of India Tourist offices may be of help to you in locating Indian food stores in your area.

Government of India Tourist Offices:

30 Rockefeller Plaza
North Mezzanine
New York NY 10020

201 North Michigan Ave.
Chicago IL 60601

685 Market St.
San Francisco CA 94105

Index

A

Alu Burfi, 240
Alu Dum, 147-48
Alu Raita, 46-47
Alu Vada, 18-19
Amm Rus, 247-48
Anchoor. *See* Mango
Anda Pulao, 187
Anglo-Indian Beef Liver, 70-71
Aniseed, 5, 7
Appam, 241-42
Appetizers, 15-35
   Bombay Duck, 29
   Dahi Anda, 35
   Dahi Vada, 161-62
   Jhinga Khasta, 115-16
   Kababs, 30-32
   Koftas, 32-34
   Murukus, 26-27
   Oopma, 25
   Pakoras, 21-24
   Papads, 29
   Rava Dosas, 27-29
   Samosas, 19-21
   Vadas, 16-19
Asafoetida, 7

B

Badi Mirch Pulao, 183
Baigan Pakora, 21-22
Baigan Raita, 48-49
Baigan Subji, 138-39
Baked Fish Kerala Style, 128
Balu Sahi, 226
Banana
   Banana Pachadi, 49
   Kela Raita, 47
Batta, 6
Beef
   Cubed
      Beef Biryani, 173-75
      Beef Kabab, 31-32
      Beef Pulao, 183-85
      Beef Vindaloo, 71-72
      Moslem Beef Curry, 68-69
   ground
      Hoosaini Kababs, 79-80
      Kheema Samosa, 20-21
      Nargisi Kofta, 54-56
      Shami Kababs, 82-83
      Sheekh Kabab, 78
      Sukha Kofta, 33-34
   liver

Anglo-Indian Beef Liver, 70-71
Beef Liver Curry, 69-70
Beets
  Chukandar Achar, 211
Bengal Lancers Garam Masala, 11
Besan Halva, 235-36
Besan Ladoo, 238
Beverages, 2, 245-50
  Amm Rus, 247-48
  Garam Doodh, 249
  Lassi, 246
  Masala Chai, 249-50
  Masala Coffee, 250
  Sherbat, 247
  Thandai, 248-49
Bhakhri, 199-200
Bhara Mirch Subji, 140-41
Bhari Baigan, 137-38
Bhat, 165
  Kheer Bhat, 165-66
Bhatura, 198-99
Bhindi Subji, 150
Bhoona Raan, 62
Bhuna Batak, 101
Bhuna Kekada, 129
Biryani, 172-73
  Chicken, 178-79
  Hyderabadi, 175-76
  Kheema, 176-78
  Lamb or Beef, 173-75
Bombay Duck, 29
Boti Kabab, 81
Breads, 2, 193-205
  Bhakhri, 199-200
  Bhatura, 198-99
  Chapati, 194-95
  Dosa, 204
  Kachori, 204-5
  Kulcha, 200
  Luchi, 196
  Nan, 197-98
  Parathas, 196-97, 202-3
  Pooris, 195-96, 200-201
  Puran Poli, 202-3
  Shir Mal, 201-2
  Tandoori Roti, 203
Broiled Lobster, 132-33
Buffet menus, 2-3
Bundi, 237

Bundi Laddoo, 238
Burfi
  Alu, 240
  Ginger, 239
  Panir, 239-40
Butter, clarified, 2, 13

C

Cabbage
  Sukha Bundhgobi, 151
Cabbage, red
  Carrot Salad, 44-45
  Kachumbar, 45
Caraway, 7
Cardamom, 5, 6, 8
Carrot
  Carrot Salad, 44-45
  Gajar Achar, 212-13
  Gajjar Halva, 234
Cashews
  Kajoo Vada, 17
Cauliflower
  Gobhi Achar, 211-12
  Gobhi Gosht, 59
  Gobhi Masalam, 145-46
  Gobhi Matar, 144-45
  Gobhi Pulao, 182
  Sukha Gobhi, 146-47
Cayenne, 9
Chana Masala, 153-54
Chapati, 194-95
Cheese
  chenna or panir, 230
  Matar Panir, 142-44
  Panir Pakora, 22-23
Chenna, 223, 224, 227, 230
Chicken, 85-99
  Chicken Biryani, 178-79
  Chicken Korma, 88-89
  Chicken Molee, 92
  Chicken Vindaloo, 92-93
  Chili Chicken, 87-88
  Country Captain, 91
  Malabari Chicken, 93-94
  Malai Chicken, 94-96
  Mulligatawny Soup, 38
  Murg Musallam, 89-91
  Pakora, 23-24

Index 259

Parsee Chicken Curry, 97-98
Sour Chicken Curry, 98-99
Tandoori Chicken, 86-87
Tika Kabab, 30-31
Yakhni Pulao, 188-89
livers
    Chicken Liver Curry, 97
Chick-peas
    Chana Masal, 153-54
    Kabuli Chana, 152-53
Chili Chicken, 87-88
Chili Pickle, 214-15
Chili powder, 9
Chilies, green, 10
Chinese parsley, 8
Chukandar Achar, 211
Chum-Chum, 231-32
Chutney, 9, 207, 215-22
    Dahi, 216-17
    Dhania, 216
    Green Tomato, 218-19
    Imli, 221
    Khajoor, 219-20
    Kismis, 218
    Mango, 22
    Nariyal, 217
    Onion, 215
    Peanut, 221
    Podina, 216
    Spicy Coconut, 217-18
    Spicy Date, 220
    Tomato, 219
Cilantro, 8
Cinnamon, 5, 8
Cloves, 8
Coconut, 13
    Coconut Muruku, 26-27
    Coconut Rice, 171
    Dahl Rasam, 40-41
    Nariyal Chutney, 217
    Spicy Coconut Chutney, 217-18
Coconut milk, 13, 27
Cod
    Fish Curry, 124-25
    Fish Kofta, 126-28
    Fish Molee, 121-22
    Fish with Tomato Sauce, 122-23
    Machi Khasta, 125-26
    Machi Palak, 124

Tandoori Fish, 117-18
Coffee, 246
    Masala Coffee, 250
Coriander, 8-9
Country Captain, 91
Crab
    Bhuna Kekada, 129
    Crab Curry, 129-30
    Crab Kofta, 130-31
Cream of wheat
    Appam, 241-42
    Oopma, 25
    Suji Halva, 233-34
Cucumber
    Raita, 46
    Salad, 44
Cumin, 6, 9
Curry, 7, 52
    beef
        Beef Liver Curry, 69-70
        Beef Vindaloo, 71-72
        Hoosaini Kababs, 79-80
        Moslem Beef Curry, 68-69
    chicken
        Chicken Korma, 88-89
        Chicken Liver Curry, 97
        Country Captain, 91
        Fowl Curry, 96
        Murg Musallam, 89-91
        Parsee Chicken Curry, 97-98
        Sour Chicken Curry, 98-99
    crab, 129-30
    duck
        Duck Curry, 100-101
        Duck Korma, 99-100
    egg
        Madras Egg Curry, 103-4
        Matar Anda Curry, 105-6
        Omelette Pakaki Curry, 106-7
    fish
        Dahi Machi, 120-21
        Fish Curry, 124-25
        Fish Curry Bengal Lancers, 118-19
        Fish with Tomato Sauce, 122-23
        Malabari Machi, 119-20
        Tandoori Fish, 117-18
    lamb
        Dahl Gosht, 61

Gobhi Gosht, 59
Hoosaini Kababs, 79-80
Kashmir Gosht, 60
Kheema Curry, 65-66
Kofta Curry, 51-52
Lamb Vindaloo, 72-73
Madras Kheema Curry, 66-67
Madras Lamb Curry, 67
lobster, 131-32
pheasant or partridge, 103
pork
  Goanese Pork Curry, 76-77
  Pork Korma, 77
powder, 6-7
rabbit, 83-84
sauce, 88
shrimp
  Curry Madras, 110-11
  Shrimp Curry Bengal Lancers, 113
  Shrimp Masala, 111-12
  Shrimp Molee, 114
  Shrimp Vindaloo, 112
soup
  Curry Soup, 88
  Khadhi, 160
vegetable, 135-36. *See also under names of vegetables*

D

Dahi Anda, 35
Dahi Chutney, 216
Dahi Machi, 120-21
Dahi Vada, 161-62
Dahl, 2, 136-37
  bread
    Puran Poli, 202-3
  dahl-based dishes
    Chana Masala, 153-54
    Dahl Palak, 151-52
    Kabuli Chana, 152-53
    Masoor Dahl, 159-60
    Moong Dahl, 155-56
    Sambar, 154-55
    Sukhi Urad Dahl, 156-57
    Whole Urad Dahl, 156-57
    Yellow Split-pea Dahl, 158-59
Dahl Gosht, 61
Dates

Khajoor Chutney, 219-20
Spicy Date Chutney, 220
Desserts, 223-43
  Appam, 241-42
  Balu Saki, 226
  Bundi, 237-38
  Burfi, 239-40
  Chum-Chum, 231-32
  Gulab Jamun, 228-30
  Halva, 233-36
  Jalebi, 236
  Kheer, 232-33
  Kushli, 225
  Laddoo, 238
  Payasam, 242-43
  Peda, 241
  Rasgulla, 230
  Ras Malai, 231
  Sandesh, 227
  Shrikhand, 224-25
Dhania Chutney, 216
Dhan Sak, 64
Dosa, 204
Duck, 99-102
  Bhuna Batak, 101
  Duck Curry, 100-101
  Duck Korma, 99-100
  Duck Vindaloo, 102

E

Eggplant, 9
  Baigan Pakora, 21-22
  Baigan Raita, 48-49
  Baigan Subji, 138-39
  Bhara Baigan, 137-38
  Eggplant Kottu, 139-40
  stuffed, Madras Kharma Curry, 66-67
Eggs, 85, 103-7
  Anda Pulao, 187
  Dahi Anda, 35
  Madras Egg Curry, 103-4
  Matar Anda Curry, 105-6
  Nargisi Kofta, 54-56
  Omelette Pakaki Curry, 106-7
  Tandoori Eggs, 104-5

F

Fennel, 9

Fenugreek, 9
Fish, 109-33. *See also* Shellfish
    Baked Fish Kerala Style, 128
    Dahi Machi, 120-21
    Fish Curry, 124-25
    Fish Curry Bengal Lancers, 118-19
    Fish Kofta, 126-28
    Fish Molee, 121-22
    Fish with Tomato Sauce, 122-23
    Machi Khasta, 125-26
    Machi Palak, 124
    Malabari Machi, 119-20
    Tamatar Machi, 123-24
    Tandoori Fish, 117-18
    appetizers
        Bombay Duck, 29
        Machchi Kabab, 30
        Pakora, 24-25
Flounder
    Fish Molee, 121-22
    Malabari Machi, 119-20
    Tandoori Fish, 117-18
Foogaths, 148
Fowl Curry, 96

G

Gajar Achar, 212-13
Gajar Halva, 234
Galab Jamun, 228
    Galab Jamun Barkhera, 229-30
Garam Doodh, 249
Garam Masalas, 11-12
Ghee, 2, 13
Ginger, 9-10
    Ginger Burfi, 239
Goanese Pork Curry, 76-77
Goanese Sheekh Kababs, 78-79
Goat meat, 51
Gobhi Achar, 211-12
Gobhi Gosht, 59
Gobhi Masalam, 145-46
Gobhi Matar, 144-45
Gobhi Pulao, 182
Gosht
    Dahl Gosht, 61
    Gobhi Gosht, 59
    Kashmir Gosht, 60

Green Tomato Chutney, 218-19

H

Haddock
    Tamatar Machi, 123-24
Halibut
    Dahi Machi, 120-21
    Fish Curry, 124-25
    Fish Molee, 121-22
    Fish with Tomato Sauce, 122-23
    Machi Palak, 124
    Tandoori Fish, 117-18
Halva
    Besan Halva, 235-36
    Gajjar Halva, 234
    Moong Halva, 234-35
    Suji Halva, 233-34
Hara Dhania. *See* Coriander
Herbs, 5-13
    roasting seeds, 8
Hindu beef taboo, 51-52
Holiday menus, 2
Hoosaini Kababs, 79-80
Hors d'oeuvres. *See* Appetizers
Hyderabadi Biryani, 175-76

I

Imli Chutney, 221
Indian dining, 1-3
Irani Kababs, 80-81

J

Jalebi, 236
Jhinga Khasta, 115-16

K

Kababs, 30-32, 78-83
    Boti Kabab, 81
    Goanese Sheekh Kababs, 78-79
    Hoosaini Kababs, 79-80
    Irani Kababs, 80-81
    Kathi Kabab, 83
    Shami Kabab, 82-83
    Sheekh Kabab, 78
    appetizers
        Beef Kabab, 31-32
        Chicken Tika Kabab, 30-31

Machchi Kabab, 30
Kabuli Chana, 152-53
Kachori, 204-5
Kachumbar, 45
Kadhi, 160
  Pakora Kadhi, 161
Kajoo Vada, 17
Karhai, 194
Kashmere Lamb or Pork Chops, 74-75
Kashmir Gosht, 60
Kashmiri Mirch Subji, 141
Kathi Kabab, 83
Katoris, 1, 137
Kela Raita, 47
Kerala Prawn Pulao, 186-87
Khajoor Chutney, 219-20
Khamiri Poori, 200-201
Khasta
  Jhunga, 115-16
  Machi, 125-26
Kheema Biryani, 176-78
Kheema Curry, 65-66
  Madras Kheema Curry, 66-67
Kheema Samosa, 20-21
Kheer, 232-33
  Kheer Bhat, 165-66
Khichadi, 166-67
  Punjab Khichadi, 167-68
Khoya Matar, 142
Kismis Chutney, 218
Kofta
  Crab, 130-31
  Curry, 51-52
  Fish, 126-28
  Lobster, 33
  Nargisi, 54-56
  Shrimp, 32
  Sukha, 33-34
Korma
  Chicken, 88-89
  Duck, 99-100
  Pork, 77
Kulcha, 200
Kushli, 225

L

Laddoo, 238
Lamb

chops, 34
  Kashmere Lamb Chops, 74-75
  Madras Lamb Chops, 75-76
cubed
  Boti Kabab, 81
  Dahl Gosht, 61
  Dhan Sak, 64
  Goanese Sheekh Kababs, 78-79
  Gobhi Gosht, 59
  Hyderabadi Biryani, 175-76
  Kashmir Gosht, 60
  Kathi Kabab, 83
  Lamb Biryani, 173-75
  Lamb Do Pyaza, 58
  Lamb Pulao, 183-85
  Lamb Vindaloo, 72-73
  Lamb with Spinach, 63
  Madras Lamb Curry, 67
  Rogan Josh, 56-57
  Yakhni Pulao, 188-89
ground
  Hoosaini Kababs, 79-80
  Irani Kababs, 80-81
  Kheema Biryani, 176-78
  Kheema Curry, 65-66
  Kheema Samosa, 20-21
  Kofta Curry, 51-52
  Madras Kheema Curry, 66-67
  Nargisi Kofta, 54-56
  Shami Kabab, 82-83
  Sheekh Kabab, 78
leg of, Bhoona Raan, 62
sliced, Lamb Molee, 73-74
Lassi, 246
Lemon
  pickle, 208-9
    Lemon-Mango Pickle, 210
    Lemon-Vinegar Pickle, 209
    Orange and Lemon Skin Pickle, 213-14
    Sweet Lemon Pickle, 209-10
  Rice, 169-70
  Sherbat, 247
Lentils, 136-37. *See also* Dahl
  Dahi Vada, 161-62
  Dahl Gosht, 61
  Masoor Dahl, 159-60
  Masoor Dahl Soup, 43-44
Lime

Index   263

pickle
   Lemon-Vinegar Pickle, 209-10
   Orange and Lemon Skin Pickle, 213-14
   Rice, 169
Liver
   Anglo-Indian Beef Liver, 70-71
   Beef Liver Curry, 69-70
   Chicken Liver Curry, 97
Lobster
   Broiled Lobster, 132-33
   Lobster Curry, 131-32
   Lobster Kofta, 33
Luchi, 196

M

Mace, 10
Machi Khasta, 125-26
Machi Palak, 124
Madras Egg Curry, 103-4
Madras Garam Masala, 11-12
Madras Kheema Curry, 66-67
Madras Lamb Curry, 67
Madras Shrimp Curry, 110-11
Malabari Chicken, 93-94
Malabari Machi, 119-20
Malai Chicken, 94-96
Malai Jhinga, 114-15
Mango, 10
   Amm Rus, 247-48
   Lemon-Mango Pickle, 210
   Mango Chutney, 222
Masala, 6
   garam masala, 11-12
Masala Chai, 249-50
Masala Coffee, 250
Masoor Dahl, 159-60
Masoor Dahl Soup, 43-44
Matar Anda Curry, 105-6
Matar Panir, 142-44
Matar Pulao, 180-82
Meatballs. *See also* Kofta
   Kofta Curry, 51-52
   Sukha Kofta, 33-34
Menus, buffet, 2-3
Mint
   Dahi Chutney, 216-17
   Podina Chutney, 216
Mitha Chaval, 191-92

Molee
   Chicken, 92
   Fish, 121-22
   Lamb, 73-74
   Shrimp, 114
Moong Dahl, 155-56
   Kichadi, 166-67
   Punjab Kichadi, 167-68
Moong Halva, 234-35
Moslem Beef Curry, 68-69
Mulligatawny Soup
   Chicken, 38
   Pepper Water, 38-39
Murg Musallam, 89-91
Muruku, 26
   Coconut, 26-27
Mustard seeds, 10
Mutton, 51

N

Nan, 197-98
Nargisi Kofta, 54-56
Nariyal Chutney, 217
Nutmeg, 10

O

Okra
   Bhindi Subji, 150
   Sukhi Bhindi, 149-50
Omelette Pakaki Curry, 106-7
Onions
   Lamb Do Pyaza, 58
   Onion Chutney, 47-48
   Onion Raita, 47-48
   Pyaz Achar, 212
Oopma, 25
Orange and Lemon Skin Pickle, 213-14

P

Pachadi
   Banana, 49
   Tomato-Onion, 49-50
Pakoras, 21-24
   Baigan, 21-22
   Chicken, 23-24
   Fish, 24
   Kadhi, 161

Panir, 22-23
  vegetable suggestions, 22
Palak Raita, 48
Palak Tomatar, 148
Panir, 22, 230
  Matar Panir, 142-44
  Panir Burfi, 239-40
  Panir Pakora, 22-23
Papads, 29
Papaya, 213
Papita Achar, 213
Paprika, 9
Paraat, 194
Paratha, 196-97
  Radish-Stuffed, 197
Parsee Chicken Curry, 97-98
Partridge, Indian Style, 103
Pastries. *See* Appetizers; Desserts
Payasam, 242-43
Peanut Chutney, 221
Peas
  Khoya Matar, 142
  Matar Panir, 142-44
  Matar Pulao, 180-82
Peas, split
  Dahl Palak, 151-52
  Dahl Rasam, 40-41
  Kachori, 204-5
  Khichadi, 166-67
  Puran Poli, 202-3
  Tomato Rasam, 42
  Yellow Split-pea Dahl, 158-59
Peda, 241
Peppers, dry red, 6, 9
Peppers, green sweet, 10
  Badi Mirch Pulao, 183
  Kashmiri Mirch Subji, 141
  stuffed
    Bhara Mirch Subji, 140-41
    Madras Kheema Curry, 66-67
Pepper Water, 38-39
Perch
  Fish Kofta, 126-28
  Machi Khasta, 125-26
Pheasant, Indian Style, 103
Pickles, 7, 208-15
  Chili, 214-15
  Chukandar Achar, 211
  Gajar Acher, 212-13

Gobhi Achar, 211-12
Lemon, 208
Lemon-Mango, 210
Lemon-Vinegar, 209
Orange and Lemon Skin, 213-14
Papita Achar, 213
Pyaz Achar, 212
Sweet Lemon, 209-10
Podina Chutney, 216
Pomfret, 109
Poori, 195-96
  Khamiri Poori, 200-201
Poppy seed, 10
Pork
  chops, 34
    Kashmere Pork Chops, 74-75
    Madras Pork Chops, 75-76
  cubed
    Goanese Pork Curry, 76-77
    Goanese Sheekh Kababs, 78-79
    Pork Korma, 77
  cutlets, 74
  ground
    Shami Kabab, 82-83
Potatoes
  Alu Burfi, 240
  Alu Dum, 147-48
  Alu Raita, 46-47
  Alu Vada, 18-19
  herbs for, 9
  Kulcha, 200
  Masala Rava Dosa, 28-29
  Samosa, 19-20
  Sukha Bundhgobi, 151
Poultry, 85-103. *See also kinds of poultry*
Prawns, 109
Pulao
  Anda, 187
  Badi Mirch, 183
  Gobhi, 182
  Kerala Prawn, 186-87
  Lamb or Beef, 183-85
  Matar, 180-82
  Sada, 180
  Shrimp, 185-86
  Yakhni, 188-89
Punjab Khichadi, 167-68
Puran Poli, 202-3

Index   265

Pyaza, 58
Pyaz Achar, 212

R

Rabbit Curry, 83-84
Radish
   Carrot and Red Cabbage Salad, 44-45
   Radish-Stuffed Paratha, 197
Raisins
   Kismis Chutney, 218
Raita
   Alu, 46-47
   Baigan, 48-49
   Cucumber, 46
   Kela, 47
   Onion, 47-48
   Palak, 48
Rasam, 39-42
   Dahl Rasam, 40-41
   Rasam Masala, 12
   Shrimp Rasam, 41
   Tomato Rasam, 42
Rasgulla, 230
Ras Malai, 231
Rava Dosa, 27-28
   Masala Rava Dosa, 28-29
Rice, 163-92
   Bhat, 165-66
   Biryani, 172-79
   Coconut, 171
   Khichadi, 166-68
   Lemon, 169-70
   Lime, 169
   Mitha Chawal, 191-92
   Pongal, 170-71
   Pulao, 180-89
   Saffron, 189
   Tahari, 190-91
Rogan Josh, 56-57

S

Sada Pulao, 180
Saffron, 6, 10
   Rice, 189
Salads, 37, 44-50
   Alu Raita, 46-47
   Baigan Raita, 48-49

   Banana Pachadi, 49
   Carrot, 44-45
   Cucumber, 44
   Cucumber Raita, 46
   Kachumbar, 45
   Kela Raita, 47
   Onion Raita, 47
   Palak Raita, 48
   Tomato-Onion Pachadi, 49-50
Sambar, 154-55
Sambar Masala, 12
Samosas, 19-21
   Kheema, 20-21
Sandesh, 227
Seafood, 109-33. *See also* Fish; Shellfish
Seminola
   Oopma, 25
Service dishes, 1
Shami Batter, 82-83
Shami Kabab, 82-83
Sheekh Kabab, 78
   Goanese, 78-79
Shellfish. *See* Crab; Lobster; Shrimp
Sherbat, 247
Shir Mal, 201-2
Shrikhand, 224-25
Shrimp
   Jhinga Khasta, 115-16
   Kerala Prawn Pulao, 186-87
   Malai Jhinga, 114-15
   Shrimp Curry Bengal Lancers, 113
   Shrimp Curry Madras, 110-11
   Shrimp Kofta, 32
   Shrimp Masala, 111-12
   Shrimp Molee, 114
   Shrimp Pulao, 185-86
   Shrimp Rasam, 41
   Shrimp Vindaloo, 112
   Tandoori Shrimp, 116-17
Sil, 6
Sole
   Malabari Machi, 119-20
Soups, 37-44
   Chicken Mulligatawny, 38
   Curry, 42-43
   Dahl Rasam, 40-41
   Kadhi, 160

Masoor Dahl, 43-44
Pepper Water, 38-39
Rasam, 39-40
Shrimp Rasam, 40-41
Tomato Rasam, 42
Sour Chicken Curry, 98-99
Sour Cream
   Shrikhand, 224-25
Spices, 5-13
Spicy Coconut Chutney, 217-18
Spicy Date Chutney, 220
Spinach
   Dahl Palak, 151-52
   Lamb with Spinach, 63
   Palak Raita, 48
   Palak Tomatar, 148
Suji Halva, 233-34
Sukha Bundhgobi, 151
Sukha Gobhi, 146-47
Sukha Kofta, 33-34
Sukhi Bhindi, 149-50
Sukhi Urad Dahl, 157-58
Sweet Lemon Pickle, 209-10

T

Tahari, 190-91
Tamarind, 13
   Imli Chutney, 221
Tamatar Machi, 123-24
Tandoori
   Chicken, 86-87
   Eggs, 104-5
   Fish, 117-18
   Roti, 203
   Shrimp, 116-17
   Tandoori cooking, 52-53
Tawa, 194
Tea, 245-46
   Masala Chai, 249-50
Thali, 1, 137
Thandai, 248-49
Tomato
   Bhindi Subji, 150
   Green Tomato Chutney, 218-19
   Kachumbar, 45
   Tomato Chutney, 219
   Tomato-Cream Sauce, 95-96

Tomato Foogath, 148-49
Tomato-Onion Pachadi, 49-50
Tomato Rasam, 42
Trout
   Baked Fish Kerala Style, 128
Turbot
   Machi Palak, 124
Turmeric, 5, 6, 10-11

U

Urad dahl, 16
   Dahi Vada, 161-62
   Dosa, 204
   Kachori, 204-5
   Rava Dosa, 27-28
   Sukhi Urad Dahl, 157-58
   Vada, 16-17
   Whole Urad Dahl, 156-57

V

Vadas, 16-19
   Alu, 18-19
   Kajoo, 17
   Urad dahl, 16-17
Vegetables, 135-62. *See also names of vegetables*
   curries, 135-36
Vindaloo
   Beef, 71-72
   Chicken, 92-93
   Duck, 102
   Lamb, 72-73
   sauce, 78-79
   Shrimp, 112

W

Whole Urad Dahl, 156-57

Y

Yakhni Pulao, 188-89
Yellow Split-Pea Dahl, 158-59
Yogurt
   Lassi, 246-47
   Pachadis, 49-50
   Raitas, 46-49